Access to Knowledge in the Developing World

Access to Knowledge in the Developing World

The Role of International Copyright Law

VANDANA MAHALWAR

OXFORD
UNIVERSITY PRESS

OXFORD
UNIVERSITY PRESS

Great Clarendon Street, Oxford, OX2 6DP,
United Kingdom

Oxford University Press is a department of the University of Oxford. It furthers the University's objective of excellence in research, scholarship, and education by publishing worldwide. Oxford is a registered trade mark of Oxford University Press in the UK and in certain other countries.

Published in the United States of America by Oxford University Press
198 Madison Avenue, New York, NY 10016, United States of America.

British Library Cataloguing in Publication Data
Data available

Library of Congress Control Number: 2025949924

ISBN 9780198986751

DOI: 10.1093/9780198986782.001.0001

Printed in India by Replika Press Pvt. Ltd.

The manufacturer's authorized representative in the EU for product safety is Oxford University Press España S.A. of Parque Empresarial San Fernando de Henares, Avenida de Castilla, 2 – 28830 Madrid (www.oup.es/en or product.safety@oup.com). OUP España S.A. also acts as importer into Spain of products made by the manufacturer.

For Sumeet and Arudra

Preface

The relationship between copyright and the encouragement of education and learning has been more critical in developing countries. In developing nations, the impact of high prices of copyrighted knowledge goods is more deteriorating than in developed countries. The top-down approach of the international copyright regime seems to have fallen short in addressing the interests and special needs of the developing countries. By contrast, the bottom-up approach emphasizes the needs of the developing world for accessible, affordable, and available print learning resources. There exist many ways to estimate the social costs, benefits, and costs of copyright protection. However, the primary focus of this book is on the development dilemma that the high levels of copyright protection have posed for the developing world.

The Statute of Anne, 1710, the world's first copyright statute, aimed to strike a balance between incentives and access to copyrighted works, with the goal of fostering learning. But the current copyright regime seems to fail in walking along the utilitarian lines drawn in the Statute of Anne by advancing the social utility considerations of public interests. Copyright maximalism seeks absolute control over the dissemination of copyrighted works and is opposed to any limitations, exceptions, or fair uses of these works. The copyright regime assumes a market serving copyrighted works to an undifferentiated world of consumers, leaving the global inequalities unnoticed. It comes as no surprise that the copyright maximalist approach contributes to promoting socio-economic disparities worldwide, and by advancing 'selective mobility' of knowledge by letting only those who can afford to pay high prices have access to copyrighted works. Developing countries are starkly affected by the high prices of knowledge goods compared to developed economies. This construction of copyright results in uneven benefits and scarcity of learning materials in developing states, which further exacerbates the disturbing issues of social justice. In this vein, the issue of access to knowledge stands at the forefront of the copyright-related disputes. In contrast with the principles of access to knowledge, the international copyright system not only diminishes the global public goals of access but also weakens its own ability to sustain and reward creativity in the long term.

This book builds on the role of copyright in building capacity for economic growth and development. As a doctrinal matter, the relationship between access, development, and copyright law is used to reconceptualize the international copyright regime. Approaching the existing international copyright framework from a critical angle relates to the question of 'access from above or below'. Structured in a distributive justice framework, the book provides insights into substantive inequalities, because of which the developing countries lack adequate access to books and other learning resources. It poses some questions: Do copyright users in developed countries have the same interests as those in developing countries? How best to address the radical inequalities in relation to access to knowledge globally? In doing so, the book critically evaluates the current copyright framework, taking into account the special needs of developing countries.

This book views the concept of A2K as a 'part' of the international human rights regime. It elucidates that the right to access print books need not be introduced as a 'new' human right. Instead, it can be viewed as an implicit specification of the human rights given in the UDHR.

This book is an outgrowth of the Fulbright Nehru Postdoctoral research work. This book has a long gestation of more than 5 years. Conducting this research in two countries was an exciting as well as a challenging endeavour. With much gratitude, I express that it has been an honour to be a Fulbright Visiting Scholar at Duke Law School. I am most grateful to USIEF for awarding me the Fulbright Fellowship and providing an opportunity to spend an academic year at Duke Law School. Enormous thanks are due to Professor Jerome Reichman for his knowledge, support, and generosity. I was privileged to have discussions with Professor Reichman, which allowed me to greatly benefit from both his deep knowledge and sound judgement. I am incredibly grateful to Professor M. P. Singh and Professor Ranbir Singh for their invaluable guidance and for being the epitome of inspiration in my pursuit of academic excellence.

While writing this acknowledgement, it reminds me of the time spent at Duke Law Library. I began the preliminary work on this book in the

J. Michael Goodson Law Library of Duke Law School, which provided a conducive environment for research. I benefited greatly from the enormous resources offered by the Goodson Library. Special thanks to Michael McArthur and Jennifer L. Behrens for helping by providing the useful materials required for my research.

My stay at Duke Law could not be fulfilling without the support of Jennifer Maher, Leslie Allen, and Nancy Hare Robbins. I am grateful to Professor Lea Shaver, Professor Jeremy De Beer, Dr Susan Isiko Straba, and Dr Andrew Rens, who provided me with the material for this research or directed me to it, and granted access to their personal collections. I have been lucky to count on the support of several colleagues, whom I unfortunately cannot list here. I owe a debt of gratitude to many people who encouraged me in writing this book and helped me refine my ideas. While in the US, I had the opportunity to present my work and discuss it with professors at the Boyd Law School in Las Vegas, Nevada, and the Miami Law School. As my research and writing unfolded, I had the opportunity to present a small part of my work at the IPIRA (IP and Innovation Researchers of Asia Network) Conference.

I am grateful to Oxford University Press, in particular to Dhiraj Pandey, for supporting the publication of this volume, and to Amrita Brahmo for her efficient and friendly approach to the entire publication process. The anonymous reviewers need to be thanked who provided incredibly useful and critical feedback on crucial sections of the manuscript. Dr Dharam Veer Singh, Head and University Librarian, DULS, Dr Sudarsan Dash, Senior Program Officer, USIEF, Dr Inumulu Jaya Bharti, Program Coordinator of Indian Fulbright Program, and Mr Siddharth Batra, Advocate-on-Record, Supreme Court of India, deserve a further mention for their support, because of which I could proceed on my Fulbright journey and commence the research work.

The biggest thanks of all go to my family. An effort spread over half a decade would not have been possible without the forbearance and understanding of my family. I am grateful to my parents, who have been instrumental in shaping my academic life, for their encouragement and belief in my abilities. My mother, Anjana Mahalwar, also my best friend, has been a very strong pillar and renewed my enthusiasm whenever I experienced a decline in it while writing this book. My father, K.P.S. Mahalwar, gave me the dream and made it happen. The sense of strength and courage that he gave me knows no limits. I owe my gratitude to my grandparents, who always offered blessings and encouragement. To my grandfather, Sh. Ved Sharan Mahalwar, the first-generation teacher in the family, who had a deeper connection with books than with social circles. His fondness for books had a profound and lasting influence on me. I am grateful to my brother Vishal Mahalwar for always being there for me whenever I needed. My motivation lies in the way he takes pride in my small achievements.

Amidst the journey of writing this book, my son arrived in our lives, and I got the child-rearing responsibilities along with my regular professional responsibilities. I am immensely grateful to my parents-in-law, Sheela Sahu and S. S. Sahu, who made this journey much easier. Without their support, this book would have taken another couple of years to come into being.

My most outstanding debt and gratitude are to my husband, Sumeet Sahu, whose caring nature knows no bounds, and to my dearest little son, Arudra Sahu, for his love, patience, and understanding. Without their love, energy, and understanding, this book could not have materialized.

Vandana Mahalwar
New Delhi
July 2025

Contents

Abbreviations

4A	Available, accessible, acceptable, and adaptable
A2K	Access to Knowledge
ALAI	*Association Littéraire et Artistique Internationale* / International Literary and Artistic Association
ASEAK	Association of Students for Equitable Access to Knowledge
BIRPI	*Bureaux Internationaux Réunis pour la Protection de la Propriété Intellectuelle*
CESCR	Committee on Economic, Social and Cultural Rights
CISAC	International Confederation of Societies of Authors and Composers
DSB	Dispute Settlement Body
DSU	Dispute Settlement Understanding
EBU	European Broadcasting Union
GFD	Group of Friends of the Development Agenda
GNI	Gross National Income
HDI	Human Development Index
IAMAI	Internet and Mobile Association of India
ICESCR	International Covenant on Economic, Social and Cultural Rights
ICTSD	International Centre for Trade and Sustainable Development
INTERGU	*Internationale Gesellschaft fur Urheberrecht*
IP	Intellectual Property
IPR	Intellectual Property Rights
IRRO	Indian Reprographic Rights Organisation
JPC	Joint Parliamentary Committee
MHRD	Ministry of Human Resource Development
NGO	Non-governmental organization
OA	Open Access
OHCHR	Office of the High Commissioner for Human Rights
RTE Act	Right to Education Act
SDG	Sustainable Development Goal
SPEAK	Society for Promoting Educational Access and Knowledge
TRIPS (Agreement)	Agreement on Trade-Related Aspects of Intellectual Property Rights
UCC	Universal Copyright Convention

UDHR	Universal Declaration of Human Rights
UN	United Nations
UNDP	United Nations Development Programme
UNESCO	United Nations Educational, Scientific and Cultural Organization
URTNA	Union of National Radio and Television Organizations of Africa
WCT	WIPO Copyright Treaty
WIPO	World Intellectual Property Organization
WTO	World Trade Organization

1

Access to Knowledge and Development

An Overview

1. Introduction

For centuries, copyright law has been a significant public policy tool for knowledge mobility. However, strong copyright laws have contributed to the commercialization of knowledge, which impedes the public's access to adequate and affordable knowledge. The Statute of Anne, 1710, the world's first copyright statute, intended to strive for a balance between incentives and access to copyrighted works, aiming to foster learning. However, the current copyright regime appears to deviate from the utilitarian principles outlined in the Statute of Anne, thereby failing to advance the social utility considerations of public interest. Copyright maximalism seeks absolute control over the dissemination of the copyrighted work and is against any limitations, exceptions, or fair uses of the copyrighted works. The copyright regime assumes a market, serving the copyrighted works to an undifferentiated world of consumers, leaving the global inequalities unnoticed. It is no surprise that the copyright maximalist approach contributes to promoting socio-economic disparities in the world and advancing 'selective mobility' of knowledge by letting only those who can afford to pay high prices have access to copyrighted works. Developing countries are starkly affected by the high prices of knowledge goods compared to developed economies. This structure of copyright results in an uneven distribution of benefits and scarcity of educational materials in developing states, which further exacerbates the disturbing issues of social justice. In this vein, the issue of access to knowledge stands at the forefront of copyright-related disputes. In contrast with the principles of access to knowledge, the international copyright system not only diminishes the global public goals of access but also weakens its ability to

Access to Knowledge in the Developing World. Vandana Mahalwar, Oxford University Press.
 DOI: 10.1093/9780198986782.003.0001

sustain and reward creativity for the long-term future. The developing countries' Access to Knowledge ('A2K') movement (emerged in 2004), grounded in the principles of distributive justice, seeks to provide access to educational works, including books, academic journals, and other learning materials.

Access to knowledge is a core component of 'development', but, unfortunately, there is no single exception for 'educational use' in the Berne Convention for the Protection of Literary and Artistic Works, 1886, and the Agreement on Trade-Related Aspects of Intellectual Property Rights (TRIPS), 1995. Instead, there are a few limitations and exceptions that support educational purposes, such as teaching, personal use, and quotation rights. The existing configuration of limitations and exceptions in international instruments, which are coextensive with furthering public welfare, has not been able to cater to the educational needs of developing countries. In the international copyright system, a set of minimum rights for the copyright owner is derived by consensus among member countries; however, limitations and exceptions remain a matter of national discretion.

The current global copyright regime does not generate a sufficient range of policy choices to advance the 'development' objectives of developing countries. The well-established premise that education is a fundamental determinant of development gives rise to many questions that have no clear answers: What is the precise meaning of 'educational use'? To what extent does 'fair use' hold educational use within its fold? The development interests need to establish the exact contours of 'educational use', followed by reconceptualization of limitations and exceptions for educational purposes.

The book builds on the role of copyright in building capacity for economic growth and development. As a doctrinal matter, the relationship between access, development, and copyright law is used to reconceptualize the international copyright regime. Structured in a distributive justice framework, this book provides insights into substantive inequalities because the developing countries lack adequate access to books and other learning resources. It further poses new questions that need to be addressed: Do copyright users in developed states have the same interests as those in developing states? What could be the best manner to address the radical inequalities in access to knowledge at the global level? In doing so, it critically evaluates the current copyright framework, considering the special needs of developing countries to access knowledge. It examines whether the legal framework adequately addresses the educational and research requirements of the developing world.

2. Defining Global Public Goods

The world is constantly in need of both public goods and private goods for survival and improvement. In a market for private goods, the buyer gets the ownership or use of goods or services, and the seller receives monetary consideration in exchange for that.[1] Payment of price plays a crucial role in a private market economy. Private goods are those assets that are excludable and rivalrous in nature; for instance, a cookie that others cannot enjoy once it is consumed. Private goods markets also depend upon goods that cannot be provided by themselves, such as education, national defence, peace, equity, environmental resources, law enforcement, and investments in new technical information.[2] These are public goods, characterized by two prominent qualities: non-rivalry in consumption and non-excludability in use.[3] Public goods face a vast supply problem because they are non-excludable and non-rival in consumption.

In other words, these two qualities of the goods give rise to the free-rider phenomenon, i.e., when the public uses goods without paying for them. In 'Tragedy of the Commons', Hardin describes the free-rider phenomenon with the help of pasture land where all herdsmen want their maximum cattle to graze from the common pasture land, and eventually a situation comes when the inherent logic of the commons remorselessly generates tragedy.[4] Hence, unlike private goods, these goods are still underproduced and require cooperation and collective action.

[1] Inge Kaul, Isabelle Grunberg, and Marc Stern (eds) *Global Public Goods: International Cooperation in the 21st Century* (OUP 1999) 4.

[2] Rebecca M. Bratspies, 'Global Public Goods: An Introduction' [2010] Proceedings of ASIL Annual Meeting 104, 148; Tyler Cowen, 'Law as a Public Good' [1992] 8 Econ & Phil 249, 267; see generally Keith E. Maskus and Jerome H. Reichman, 'The Globalization of Private Knowledge Goods and the Privatization of Global Public Goods' [2005] 7 J Int'l Econ L 279, 284.

[3] Paul A. Samuelson, 'The Pure Theory of Public Expenditure' [1954] 36 Rev Econ Stat 387, 389.

[4] Garrett Hardin, 'The Tragedy of the Commons' [1968] 162 Science 1244.

Unlike earlier times, when public goods were largely national or territorial in character, over the past few decades, they have no longer been restricted to being produced and consumed within a limited geographical area. With growing globalization, public goods have progressively become international in their effects and supply needs.[5] Global public goods benefit the public worldwide, without any territorial restrictions. In this chapter, the concern is to evaluate knowledge as a global public good and impediments to its creation and diffusion.

2.1. Knowledge Goods as Public Goods

Knowledge, being a public good, is central to human welfare and development. Knowledge, as any other public good, has two basic attributes: non-rivalrousness and non-excludability.[6] Non-rivalrousness implies that the consumption of a good by one person does not prevent others from consuming it because the marginal cost of using it is zero. When an individual benefits from a public good, others can also benefit by consuming it simultaneously at zero marginal cost. For example, a novel is non-rival; when a person reads it, others can also read the same novel.

Non-excludable property denotes that no one can be excluded from using the public good. Once the knowledge about a recipe is made public, it can be used by many people simultaneously. No one can be excluded from its consumption. Some form of knowledge is excludable such as trade secrets or confidential information.[7] These critical characteristics of knowledge goods make them accessible to multiple individuals simultaneously. Here, the intellectual property (IP) regime comes into play to determine how the gains of knowledge goods are to be shared.

Unlike the tangible walls during the English enclosure movement, the knowledge goods are 'enclosed' by legal intangible walls.[8] During the

[5] Inge Kaul (ed) *Providing Global Public Goods: Managing Globalization* (UNDP 2003).

[6] Joseph E. Stiglitz, 'Knowledge as a Global Public Good' in Inge Kaul, Isabelle Grunberg, and Marc Stern (eds) *Global Public Goods: International Cooperation in the 21st Century* (OUP 1999) 309.

[7] Joseph E. Stiglitz, 'Knowledge as a Global Public Good' in Inge Kaul, Isabelle Grunberg, and Marc Stern (eds) *Global Public Goods: International Cooperation in the 21st Century* (OUP 1999) 310.

[8] James Boyle, 'The Second Enclosure Movement and the Construction of the Public Domain' [2003] 66 Law & Contemp Probs 33, 34.

enclosure movement, which began in the fifteenth century, the common land in England was fenced off and converted into private property. The enclosed property, hence, belonged only to the private owner and was no longer available to be used by the public. Hardin named the pre-existing overexploitation of common resources as 'the tragedy of the commons'.[9] Boyle draws a fitting analogy between IP rights (IPR) and the enclosure movement, referring to the IP regime as the 'second enclosure movement', whereby intellectual commons that were previously part of the public domain are fenced off.[10] Like the first enclosure movement, in which walls and barriers were put up to delineate property, the second enclosure movement uses legal, immaterial walls to enclose the IP. This analogy also reveals how the enclosure of the commons has become central for knowledge capitalism. In addition to industrial capitalism, 'knowledge capitalism' has taken place in the economy, where the central element is the commercialization of knowledge goods. In 'knowledge capitalism', control of the transfer of knowledge goods is what remains at stake. Electronic transfers of the property and appropriation of the means of production bring the IP into the picture.

Strong IP protection may lead to some advantageous consequences, like better innovations and technology transfers, but its impacts are uneven across the globe. The growth prospects of developing countries are adversely affected by the globalized minimum IP standards. This leads to a departure from conventional goals of the IP framework to strike a balance between the private interests of IP rights holders and larger public interest concerns. The imbalance between commercial profitability and large public interests has affected public health, human rights, biodiversity, and plant genetic resources.

Information and knowledge are the building blocks for the production of any immaterial property, goods, or inventions, and, hence, are fundamental for the enhancement of development and human welfare. When economic growth is the outcome of the transmission and processing of knowledge, the role of IP becomes most substantial. The IP framework controls and regulates the use and dissemination of knowledge by

[9] Garrett Hardin, 'The Tragedy of the Commons' [1968] Science 1243.

[10] James Boyle, 'The Second Enclosure Movement and the Construction of the Public Domain' [2003] 66 Law & Contemp Probs 34.

creating 'immaterial legal walls to enclose the information and knowledge'. Adam Smith says that 'the easiest and most natural way in which the state can recompense' the creators of knowledge goods is by granting them a temporal monopoly in the form of copyright.[11] IP works like a tax on the knowledge goods, allowing producers to charge higher prices for their work. Knowledge, as a global public good, necessitates global collective action for its production and dissemination. The A2K movement has emerged to support the knowledge commons in favour of the developing world.

2.2. Structure of Knowledge

Having a dyadic structure, knowledge exists in two distinct forms, namely, codified knowledge and tacit knowledge. The former exists in documents, can easily be encoded, and is transmittable in formal, systematic language, while the latter indicates the knowledge that is not codified and can be accumulated through interactions and discussions within a group or community. Tacit knowledge can be defined as knowledge that is inarticulate and can only be gained through direct personal experience.[12] Unlike codified knowledge, tacit knowledge or implicit knowledge cannot be commodified and exchanged in the market. For the true development of any society, both tacit and codified knowledge are indispensable, if not merely for economic development. Some scholars have lamented that 'the terminology and meaning of "tacitness" in the economics literature have drifted far from its original epistemological and psychological moorings and have become unproductively amorphous'.[13]

Because codified knowledge or explicit knowledge can be converted into a commodity, copyright law significantly contributes to providing protection for knowledge goods.[14] On the other hand, copyright has no

[11] Adam Smith, 'Part III – Of the Expense of Public Works and Public Institutions' in *The Wealth of Nations* (2nd edn, OUP 1880).

[12] Ikujiro Nonaka, 'A Dynamic Theory of Organizational Knowledge Creation' [1994] 5 Organization Sci 14, 37; see also R. Cowan, P.A. David, and D. Foray, 'The Explicit Economics of Knowledge Codification and Tacitness' [2000] 9 Ind Corp Change 211, 253.

[13] R. Cowan, P.A. David, and D. Foray, 'The Explicit Economics of Knowledge: Codification and Tacitness' [2000] 9 Ind Corp Change 211, 253.

[14] Jia Wang, *Conceptualizing Copyright Exceptions in China and South Africa: A Developing View from the Developing Countries* (Springer Nature 2018) 36.

role in the protection of tacit knowledge as it lacks expression and fixation. When a professor explains a concept to his class from his mind, the idea–expression dichotomy comes into play, and the knowledge shared fails to receive copyright protection due to the lack of expression. If the professor imparts the same concept to the class through his writings, the knowledge becomes commodifiable and falls under the subject matter of copyright.[15]

Ancori et al. reflect upon the significance of codification through the transformation of knowledge into information for the economy:

> To be treated as an economic good, knowledge must be put in a form that allows it to circulate and be exchanged. The main transformation investigated by economists is the transformation of knowledge into information, i.e., the codification of knowledge. The process of codification allows them to treat knowledge-reduced-to-information according to the standard tools of economics.[16]

3. Information and Knowledge

While discussing the categories of knowledge, it becomes unavoidable to examine the concept of 'information', especially when information and knowledge are seen as virtual equivalents in common parlance. Does this interchangeable use signify that 'access to information' is an implicit strand in 'access to knowledge'? If yes, then why is the 'Access to Knowledge' movement not named 'Access to Information and Knowledge'? If not, then does it purport that only knowledge is inaccessible, and that information is easily affordable? To map the A2K movement, it is necessary to explore the distinction between different types of information and knowledge.

Neoclassical economists have argued that information and knowledge are similar to an extent. It has also been pointed out by many that information and knowledge are far from identical, not merely an etymological

[15] Reto Hilty, 'Copyright law and Scientific Research' in Paul Torremans (ed), *Copyright Law: A Handbook of Contemporary Research* (Edward Elgar 2007) 331.

[16] B. Ancori, A. Bureth, and P. Cohendet, 'The Economics of Knowledge: the Debate About Codification and Tacit Knowledge' [2000] 9 Ind Corp Change 255, 287.

distinction. Adolf and Stehr say that it would be 'misleading to say' that there is just one distinction between information and knowledge.[17] A vast body of literature exists on the relationship between data, information, and knowledge. The relationships between the three are intertwined and uneven; data is transformed into information, and information is further transformed into knowledge.[18]

Distinguishing knowledge from information is a highly complex task. As Adolf and Stehr write, the substance of information refers to attributes of 'product or outcome', while knowledge is concerned about characteristics of 'processes or inputs'.[19] Benkler has given an account of the distinction between the two:

> I use 'information' here colloquially, to refer to raw data, scientific reports of the output of scientific discovery, news, and factual reports. I use 'knowledge' to refer to the set of cultural practices and capacities necessary for processing the information into either new statement in the information exchange, or more important in our context, for practical use of the information in appropriate ways to produce more desirable actions or outcomes from action.[20]

He further categorizes information into three kinds that are important for development purposes: scientific publications, scientific and economic data, and news and factual reports. Apart from the differences, knowledge and information share many common attributes. Often, information is defined as 'knowledge reduced and converted into messages that can be communicated easily among decision agents'.[21] Many scholarly writings conceptualize information as a subset of knowledge

[17] Marian Adolf and Nico Stehr (eds) *Knowledge: Is Knowledge Power?* (2nd edn, Routledge 2017) 21.

[18] Dick Stenmark, 'The Relationship between Information and Knowledge' [2001] in Proceedings of IRIS 24.

[19] Marian Adolf and Nico Stehr (eds) *Knowledge: Is Knowledge Power?* (2nd edn, Routledge 2017) 22.

[20] Yochai Benkler, *The Wealth of Networks: How Social Production Transforms Markets and Freedom* (Yale University Press 2006) 313.

[21] Partha S. Dasgupta and Paul A. David, 'Toward a New Economics of Science' [1994] 23 Res Policy 487, 521.

that contains 'relevant meaning, implication, or input for decision and/or action'[22] and knowledge is defined as 'a cumulative stock of information'.[23]

Brown and Duguid have highlighted three fundamental differences between information and knowledge: 'first, knowledge usually entails a knower, second, knowledge is harder to detach from information, third, knowledge requires a greater effort of assimilation, i.e., knowledge is something we digest rather than merely hold'.[24] Information, hence, can be processed data about something, while knowledge refers to information gathered through experiences or learning. In a narrower sense, the information pertains to processed data, whereas knowledge refers to the capacity to utilize that data in a specific context to create new information. Information can be understood as the building block, while knowledge is the building itself, i.e., know-how. Know-how means 'the accumulated practical skill or expertise that allows one to do something smoothly and efficiently'.[25] Here, the term 'accumulated' refers to the knowledge that is acquired through learning.

There were discussions regarding the adoption of the term 'knowledge' or 'information' in the A2K movement. Abdel Latif gives an account that 'at the conceptual level, knowledge, rather than information, is at the heart of the empowerment of individuals and societies. While information is certainly a prerequisite in the generation of knowledge, the acquisition of knowledge remains the ultimate goal. Knowledge processes information to produce ideas, analysis, and skills that ideally should contribute to human progress and civilisation'. He further adds that access to knowledge suitably responds to the term 'knowledge economy'.[26]

[22] Anthony Liew, 'Understanding Data, Information, Knowledge and their Inter-Relationships' [2007] 8 J Knowl Manag Pract 1, 16.

[23] Alan Burton Jones, *Knowledge Capitalism: Business, Work and Learning in the new Economy* (OUP 1999) 5.

[24] John Seeley Brown and Paul Duguid, *The Social Life of Information* (Harvard Business School Press 2002) 120.

[25] Eric Von Hippel, *The Sources of Innovation* (MIT Press 1988) 76.

[26] Eric Von Hippel, *The Sources of Innovation* (MIT Press 1988) 76.

3.1. Access to Knowledge vis-à-vis Copyright

Libraries exist to be used, and their successful use involves copying, with the length and precision depending on the requirements and interests of the user.[27] When the need and interest are significant, mechanical copying would be laborious, and so electronic copying is resorted to. There is a considerable shift in means of copying from pen, parchment, pencil, and paper to photocopying machines. When the copying was done with pen and paper, it remained limited to just a few pages at a time. Then, typewriters accelerated the process of copying, but the advent of photostat machines in 1954 marked a radical change in the copying industry. Literary work was of no particular interest to the law until a century ago, when it gave rise to the mass production sector. The advent of the printing press not only facilitated mass reproduction, making literature readily available, but also promised greater accuracy.[28] Printing technology also contributed to preserving numerous works from extinction.[29] Scholars were allowed to channel the same amount of time and energy into more productive research and writing, rather than slavishly copying documents.[30]

Copyright owners are indeed adversely affected by technological advancements that have made it easier to copy their works. Hence, it became necessary to develop laws that balance the interests of publishers, authors, and book readers. Copyright confers the exclusive right to multiply, publish, or sell copies of the copyrighted original work.[31]

Copyright law is aimed at promoting the utilitarian goal of adding to the available pool of creative works for the public's enrichment. To achieve this goal, states grant economic incentives to creators and monopolistic privileges for a limited period to ensure that they receive a fair return for their intellectual efforts. Copyright law seeks to strike a balance

27 Verner W. Clapp, 'Library Photocopying and Copyright: Recent Developments' [1962] 55 Law Libr J 10, 12.

28 Craig W. Dallon, 'The Problem with Congress and Copyright Law: Forgetting the Past and Ignoring the Public Interest' [2004] 44 Santa Clara L Rev 365; Leonardas Vytautas Gerulaitis, *Printing and Publishing in Fifteenth-Century Venice* (American Library Association 1976) 9–10.

29 Craig W. Dallon, 'The Problem with Congress and Copyright Law: Forgetting the Past and Ignoring the Public Interest' [2004] 44 Santa Clara L Rev 365.

30 Elizabeth L. Eisenstein, *The Printing Revolution in Early Modern Europe* (CUP 1983) 17.

31 *Goldstein v California* 412 U.S. 546, 555, rehearing denied, 414 U.S. 883 (1973); *Bobbs-Merrill Co. v Straus*, 147 F. 15, 19 (2d Cir. 1906).

between the competing interests of authors and users. On the one hand, some are creators and seek creative control and commercial returns over their works. On the other hand, there are the interests of users who seek to use the existing works. The debate is not about the rationality of the concept of balance, but rather how to strike the proper balance. Lord Mansfield in 1785 rightly identified the necessity of balancing the divergent interests underlying copyright law:

> We must take care to guard against two extremes equally prejudicial; the one, that men of ability, who have employed their time for the service of the community, may not be deprived of their just merits, and the reward of their ingenuity and labour; the other, that the world may not be deprived of improvements, nor the progress of the arts be retarded.[32]

Copyright is limited in scope and duration precisely to balance the costs that the public must bear, for using the copyrighted work, with the benefit that it seeks.[33] But the optimal balance between incentives and access remains the central problem in copyright law,[34] as was also stated by former Senator Kenneth B. Keating, while speaking on behalf of publishers before the House Committee on the Judiciary:

> The new technology, the photocopying machinery, the information storage and retrieval systems, which make rapid access to material available to the user without requiring the purchase of the books written by the authors and published by the publishers, raise a serious and essential question. Should our copyright law provide that we feed the maws of this machinery by conscripting to this wonderful new machinery the

[32] *Sayre v Moore* (1785) 102 Eng Rep 139 (KB).

[33] F.M. Scherer, *Industrial Market Structure and Economic Performance* (2nd edn, Houghton Mifflin 1980) 450–51.

[34] William M. Landes and Richard A. Posner, 'An Economic Analysis of Copyright Law' [1989] 18 J Legal Stud 325, 326.

Landes and Posner argue that:

> Copyright protection—the right of the copyright's owner to prevent others from making copies—trades off the costs of limiting access to a work against the benefits of providing incentives to create the work in the first place. Striking the correct balance between access and incentives is the central problem in copyright law. For copyright law to promote economic efficiency, its principal legal doctrines must, at least approximately, maximize the benefits from creating additional works minus both the losses from limiting access and the costs of administering copyright protection.

services of authorship and book publishers without remuneration to them...?[35]

Copyright rules that cater to the interests of authors often upset the public by restricting the mobility of knowledge. Copyright maximalism seeks absolute control over the dissemination of copyrighted works and is opposed to any limitations, exceptions, and fair uses of its monopolistic copyright. There are three groups at the core of copyright policy: users, creators, and publishers. There is much in the copyright history to support each of these elements. It has always been the responsibility of the legislature to resolve the clash of interests by maintaining the appropriate balance between these three constituent groups. This can be described as striking a proper balance between copyright and user rights.

Initially, the primary concern of lawmakers was to shield the interests of publishers because 'books are commercially viable properties only after they pass through the hands of publishers, printers, and booksellers'.[36] Scholars have argued that authors' rights were nearly non-existent.[37] By the end of the twentieth century, they were afforded some protection under the law.

In 1710, the Statute of Anne intended to maintain a balance between rewards and incentives to foster learning, as the title sets out its underlying objective: *An Act for the Encouragement of Learning by Vesting the Copies of Printed Books in the Authors or Purchasers of such Copies, during the Times herein Mentioned*.[38] However, the current copyright law appears to deviate from the utilitarian principles outlined in the Statute of Anne, which aims to promote social utility and public interest considerations.

[35] Hearings on H.R. 4347, H.R. 5680, H.R. 6831 & H.R. 6835 Before Subcomm. No. 3 of the House Comm. on the Judiciary, 89th Congress, 1st Session, at 63 (1965).

[36] John Feather, 'From Rights in Copies to Copyright: The Recognition of Authors' Rights in English Law and Practice in the Sixteenth and Seventeenth Centuries' [1922] 10 Cardozo Arts & Ent LJ 455; also J. Feather, 'The Book Trade in Politics: The Making of the Copyright Act 1710' [1980] 8(2) Publishing History 19; see also A. Birrell, *Seven Lectures on the Law and History of Copyright in Books* (Cassell 1899); L.R. Patterson, *Copyright in Historical Perspective* (Vanderbilt University Press 1968).

[37] John Feather, 'From Rights in Copies to Copyright: The Recognition of Authors' Rights in English Law and Practice in the Sixteenth and Seventeenth Centuries' [1992] 10 Cardozo Arts & Ent LJ 455.

[38] 8 Anne c. 19 (1710).

4. Scepticism About IP: A Historical View

Historically, there has been considerable criticism and scepticism of monopolistic rights, to the extent that many scholars considered IPR to be 'necessary evils' that needed to be circumscribed by law in terms of duration and scope.[39] It is essential to cite the comments of a few scholars, who expressed concerns that inventions should not be granted proprietary rights for the long term. In 1813, Thomas Jefferson, an American statesman who served as the third president of the United States, expressed in a letter to Isaac McPherson:

> It has been pretended by some, (and in England especially,) that inventors have a natural and exclusive right to their inventions, and not merely for their own lives, but inheritable their heirs. But while it is a moot question whether the origin of any kind of property is derived from nature at all, it would be singular to admit a natural and even a hereditary right to inventors. It is agreed by those who have seriously considered the subject, that no individual has, of natural right, a separate property in an acre of land, for instance . . . if nature has made any one thing less susceptible than all others of exclusive property, it is the action of the thinking power called an idea, which an individual may exclusively possess as long as he keeps it to himself; but the moment it is divulged, it forces itself into the possession of every one, and the receiver cannot dispossess himself of it. Its peculiar character, too, is that no one possesses the less, because every other possesses the whole of it. He who receives an idea from me, receives instruction himself without lessening mine; as he who lights his taper at mine, receives light without darkening me. That ideas should freely spread from one to another over the globe, for the moral and mutual instruction of man, and improvement of his condition, seems to have been peculiarly and benevolently designed by nature, when she made them, like fire, expansible over all space, without lessening their density in any point, and like the air in which we breathe, move, and have our physical being, incapable of

[39] Thomas B. Macaulay, 'A Speech Delivered in the House of Commons on Feb. 5, 1841' in *VIII The Life And Works of Lord Macaulay* (Longmans, Green, and Co. 1897) 201.

> confinement or exclusive appropriation. Inventions then cannot, in nature, be a subject of property.[40]

Jefferson's metaphoric 'taper', which illuminates others without diminishing its own light,[41] illustrates the non-rivalrous and non-excludable attributes of knowledge transmission. He expressed vehement opposition to the monopolistic treatment of inventions as natural rights and apprehended the jeopardy that may occur due to an excessively long term of protection.[42] Macaulay also emphasized the need to circumscribe the duration and scope of IP protection legally.[43] Macaulay's speech of 1841 in the British parliament resonates with how imperative it is to limit the monopoly:

> It is good that authors should be remunerated, and the least exceptionable way of remunerating them is by a monopoly. Yet monopoly is an evil. For the sake of the good, we must submit to the evil; but the evil ought not to last a day longer than is necessary for the purpose of securing the good.[44]

Macaulay was specifically sceptical about the power that is passed on with 'transferable and inheritable monopoly'.[45] He also had a specific concern that granting a monopoly even after death poses a threat to the collective culture of society. These eighteenth- and nineteenth-century anti-monopolistic critics warned against IP-created artificial scarcity, high prices, and low quality.[46] Because of these concerns, Madison

[40] 'Letter from Thomas Jefferson to Isaac McPherson' (13 August 1813) in *The Writings of Thomas Jefferson* (Thomas Jefferson Memorial Association of the United States 1907) 326–334.

[41] Abby Smith Rumsey, *When We Are No More: How Digital Memory Is Shaping Our Future* (Bloomsbury 2016).

[42] 'Monopolies may be allowed to persons for their own productions in literature, and their own inventions in the arts, for a term not exceeding __ years, but for no longer term, and no other purpose.' 'Letter from Thomas Jefferson to James Madison' (28 August 1789) in *The Writings Thomas of Jefferson* (Thomas Jefferson Memorial Association of the United States 1907) 444, 451.

[43] Catherine Seville, *Literary Copyright Reform Early Victorian England: In the Framing of the 1842 Copyright Act* (CUP 1999) 46–48.

[44] Thomas B. Macaulay, 'A Speech Delivered in the House of Commons on Feb. 5, 1841' in *VIII The Life and Works of Lord Macaulay* (Longmans, Green, and Co. 1897) 201.

[45] Thomas B. Macaulay, 'A Speech Delivered in the House of Commons on Feb. 5, 1841' in *VIII The Life and Works of Lord Macaulay* (Longmans, Green, and Co. 1897) 201.

[46] James Boyle, 'The Second Enclosure Movement and the Construction of the Public Domain' [2003] 66 Law & Contemp Probs 57.

emphasized the need to have a definite limit on the scope and term of IP.[47] It is noticeable that all these scholars shared a similar concern that an IP monopoly leads to certain tendencies towards corruption, besides economic loss. Some of these criticisms from the eighteenth and nineteenth centuries against IP monopolies subsist even today.

4.1. Thematic Overview

Over the last three decades or so, a phenomenal expansion of IPR at the national and international levels has taken place.[48] The subject matter of IP has mushroomed significantly,[49] and the rights conferred upon owners have become more robust.[50] At the international level, multilateral agreements require member states to implement high standards of substantive IP protection. In response to this, several groups have appeared to challenge the strengthening of the scope of IPR [51] and 'the legitimation of this expansion by courts and legislatures'.[52]

The A2K movement is inherently pluralistic and takes diverse movements and approaches into its fold.[53] It is a movement that contains heterogeneous groups, civil society groups, non-governmental organizations (NGOs), scientific groups, consumer groups, scientists, and academics. The principles of the A2K movement can be characterized by positive concepts of freedom, cooperation, access, openness, and a commitment to the principles of sharing.

[47] James Madison, 'Monopolies, Perpetuities, Corporations, Ecclesiastical Endowments, in Aspects of Monopoly One Hundred Years Ago' [1914] Harper's Magazine 489, 90.

[48] Mark A. Lemley, 'Property, Intellectual Property, and Free Riding' [2005] 83 Tex L Rev 1031, 1042.

[49] Shuhba Ghosh, 'Deprivatizing Copyright' [2004] 54 Case Western Reserve L Rev 387, 390.

[50] Amy Kapczynski, 'The Access to Knowledge Mobilization and the New Politics of Intellectual Property' [2008] 117 Yale LJ 804, 822; see also Jessica Litman, 'Copyright Legislation and Technological Change' [1989] 68 Oregon L Rev 233.

[51] Amy Kapczynski, 'The Access to Knowledge Mobilization and the New Politics of Intellectual Property' [2008] 117 Yale LJ 804, 825.

[52] Jack M. Balkin and Reva B. Siegel, 'Principles, Practices, and Social Movements' [2006] 154 University of Pennsylvania L Rev 927, 949.

[53] Frederick Noronha and Jeremy Malcolm, *Access to Knowledge: A Guide for Everyone* (Consumers International 2010) 2–4; see also Gaëlle Krikorian, 'Access to Knowledge as a Field of Activism' in Amy Kapczynski and Gaëlle Krikorian (eds) *Access to Knowledge in the Age of Intellectual Property* (Zone Books 2010).

There are many possible arguments apart from the international human rights framework to advance the right of access to knowledge. Other good arguments are distributive justice, social justice, equality of opportunities, and economic efficiency. But the problems of inequality and exclusion can be better highlighted in the human rights framework, as it also includes the most marginalized and vulnerable groups.[54] The UN General Assembly adopted the Universal Declaration of Human Rights (UDHR) on 10 December 1948. Article 26 of the document speaks about the right to education for everyone. It stipulates:[55]

1. Everyone has the right to education. Education shall be free, at least in the elementary and fundamental stages. Elementary education shall be compulsory. Technical and professional education shall be made generally available, and higher education shall be equally accessible to all on the basis of merit.
2. Education shall be directed to the full development of the human personality and to the strengthening of respect for human rights and fundamental freedoms. It shall promote understanding, tolerance, and friendship among all nations, racial or religious groups, and shall further the activities of the United Nations for the maintenance of peace.
3. Parents have a prior right to choose the kind of education that shall be given to their children.

The text of Article 26 covers three basic aspects: first, the use of the terms 'elementary' and 'fundamental' stages of education denotes the right to basic education for everyone.[56] The second segment of Article 26 advances to the next level of basic education, ensuring that education is aimed at promoting overall development, tolerance, respect, and the upholding of all other human rights.[57] The third aspect focuses on parental

[54] James Nickel, *Making Sense of Human Rights: Philosophical Reflections on the Universal Declaration of Human Rights* (University of California Press 1987) 4.
[55] United Declaration of Human Rights 1948, Art 26.
[56] Douglas Hodgson, *The Human Right to Education* (Ashgate Publishing 1998) 11.
[57] Audrey Osler, 'Universal Declaration of Human Rights and education' in J.A. Banks (ed) *Encyclopaedia of Diversity in Education* (Sage 2012) 12.

role and clearly defines the right of parents to have their say in the education of their child.[58]

This recognition of the right to education was later included in Article 13 of the International Covenant on Economic, Social and Cultural Rights (ICESCR) of 1966.[59] The right to education is addressed in two separate articles of the ICESCR, namely Articles 13 and 14. Article 13(2)(a) provides that 'primary education shall be compulsory and available free to all'. Subclauses (a), (b), and (c) of Article 13(2) provide for primary, secondary, and higher education respectively. General Comment 13 is of immense use in understanding the provisions of Article 13. The UN Committee on Economic, Social and Cultural Rights (CESCR) mentioned that primary education is the 'main delivery system' aimed at providing basic education.[60] The General Comment explains the concept and scope of the right to education through the concept of

[58] Jost Delbruck, 'The Right to Education as an International Human Right' [1992] 35 German YB Int'l L 92, 97.

[59] International Covenant on Economic, Social and Cultural Rights 1966, Art 13, provides as:

1. The States Parties to the present Covenant recognize the right of everyone to education. They agree that education shall be directed to the full development of the human personality and the sense of its dignity, and shall strengthen the respect for human rights and fundamental freedoms. They further agree that education shall enable all persons to participate effectively in a free society, promote understanding, tolerance and friendship among all nations and all racial, ethnic or religious groups, and further the activities of the United Nations for the maintenance of peace.
2. The States Parties to the present Covenant recognize that, with a view to achieving the full realization of this right:
   (a) Primary education shall be compulsory and available free to all;
   (b) Secondary education in its different forms, including technical and vocational secondary education, shall be made generally available and accessible to all by every appropriate means, and in particular by the progressive introduction of free education;
   (c) Higher education shall be made equally accessible to all, on the basis of capacity, by every appropriate means, and in particular by the progressive introduction of free education;
   (d) Fundamental education shall be encouraged or intensified as far as possible for those persons who have not received or completed the whole period of their primary education;
   (e) The development of a system of schools at all levels shall be actively pursued, an adequate fellowship system shall be established, and the material conditions of teaching staff shall be continuously improved...

[60] *CESCR General Comment No. 13: The Right to Education*, UN Doc E/C.12/1999/10 (1999) para 9.

four 'A's.[61] It devised a '4A' formula—standing for availability, accessibility, acceptability, and adaptability—to analyse the elements of the right to education and the state obligations resulting from it, with these representing the minimum core content of education.[62] Accessibility entails that 'educational institutions and programmes have to be accessible to everyone, without discrimination, also implying physical and economic accessibility'.[63] The Special Rapporteur states that the 'simple 4A scheme structures governmental human rights obligations to making education available, accessible, acceptable and adaptable . . . captures both horizontal and vertical division of competence in education'.[64]

The text of Article 26 UDHR and Article 13 ICESCR emphasizes education that leads to the complete development of human personality, tolerance, and respect for human beings and for other racial, ethnic, or religious groups.[65] The right entitles every person to have access to and to receive adequate education to be provided by the state, and, hence, the right entails 'state involvement'.[66] The right to education as a 'second generation' human right demands an active role from the state in terms of providing educational infrastructure, financial resources, and access to learning materials.[67] This aspect of the provision highlights the state's positive obligations, which require states to make education more accessible, available, and affordable.[68]

4.2. Development and Education

The right to education is a 'multiplier human right' that leads to the realization of other rights. Denial of the right to education results in the

[61] Azubike Onuora-Oguno, *Development and the Right to Education in Africa*, Palgrave Macmillan (2019) 36.

[62] *Preliminary Report of the Special Rapporteur on the right to education*, UN Doc E/CN.4/1999/49, Ch. II (1999).

[63] *CESCR General Comment No. 13: The Right to Education*, UN Doc E/C.12/1999/10 (1999) para 6.

[64] Katrina Tomasevski, *Manual on Rights-Based Education: Global Human Rights Requirements made Simple* (UNESCO 2004).

[65] Jost Delbruck, 'The Right to Education as an International Human Right [1992] 35 German YB Int'l L 92.

[66] Jost Delbruck, 'The Right to Education as an International Human Right [1992] 35 German YB Int'l L 104.

[67] Jost Delbruck, 'The Right to Education as an International Human Right [1992] 35 German YB Int'l L 104.

[68] Fons Coomans, 'Exploring the Normative Content of the Right to Education as a Human Right: Recent Approaches' [2004] 50 *Persona Y Derecho* 61, 64.

underdevelopment of individuals, as it possesses the latent transformative potential that allows individuals to fully participate in society. The origin of the word 'education' has its roots in the Latin term *educare*, which means 'to bring up, to lead out, to raise, and to educate ... in its original sense, to educate means acting to lead out fully all the potential of individuals.'[69] To justify the liberalization of copyright policies to make works accessible, it is necessary first to establish the relationship between development and the right to education. The nexus between education and development is inextricable as the education process is one of continual reorganising, reconstruction, and transformation.[70]

'Basic education' is defined as 'education up to a level of functional literacy, in other words, reading, writing, arithmetic, and an elementary knowledge or awareness of economics, culture, and politics',[71] while 'education' is more about the acquisition of knowledge, values, beliefs, and attitudes. This book focuses on education at all levels, not just basic or elementary knowledge.

Development, as a concept, is understood in different ways. The concept of 'development' flourished after World War II. It is seen as more than 'improved material conditions' and has expanded considerably over recent years to embrace human development or sustainable development in its ambit. Article 1(1) of the UN Declaration on the Right to Development says that the 'right to development is an inalienable human right by virtue of which every human person and all peoples are entitled to participate in, contribute to, and enjoy economic, social, cultural and political development, in which all human rights and fundamental freedoms can be fully realised'. The exercise of the right to development implies full realization of peoples' right to self-determination, with the sovereign use of natural resources.[72]

The Human Development Report, 1991, provides that 'the basic objective of human development is to enlarge the range of people's choices to make development more democratic and participatory. These choices should include access to income and employment opportunities,

[69] Alice A. Jekayinfa and D.O. Kolawole, 'Conceptual Background to Education' in J.O.O. Abiri and A.A. Jekafnfa (eds), *Perspective on the History of Education in Nigeria* (Bamitex 2010) 3.

[70] James Bowen and Peter R. Hobson, *Theories of Education: Studies of Significant Innovation in Western Educational Thoughts* (2nd edn, John Wiley & Sons 1987) 18.

[71] W. Bray, *Human Rights in Education* (Centre for Education Law and Policy 2008) 83.

[72] Declaration on the Right to Development 1986, Art 1(2).

education and health, and a clean and safe physical environment. Each individual should also have the opportunity to participate fully in community decisions and to enjoy human, economic, and political freedoms.'[73]

Education plays an indispensable role in concretizing the global development goals. Universal primary education has been identified as one of the Millennium Development Goals 2000, as a target for the year 2015. It is also notable that the UN's Human Development Index (HDI) assesses the development of countries. The HDI measures development through three indicators, including education, life expectancy, and GNI (Gross National Income) per capita.

Education is an attitudinal concept, and different actors have varying interests in education as a basic right. Some may advocate for basic education as a human right for children, while researchers, scientists, and academics may have interests in education beyond the elementary level, contributing to holistic development. There is a plethora of literature on the realization of the right to basic education and the role of institutions, but the education interests beyond 'basic education' remain understated and out of focus. A change is required in the vision towards education; we should not confine the emphasis to primary education. At present, the knowledge-driven economies demand access to quality education and learning outcomes at all levels.

The UN's Sustainable Development Goals (SDGs) have aimed for lifelong learning opportunities for all. These goals are contained in the declaration titled 'Transforming our World: The 2030 Agenda for Sustainable Development', which the UN General Assembly adopted through a Resolution in September 2015.[74] The seventeen SDGs are built on the Millennium Development Goals and target action on these goals over the next fifteen years. Goal 4 contains the aim for education:

> Goal 4: Ensure inclusive and equitable quality education and promote lifelong learning opportunities for all.

[73] UNDP, *Human Development Report 1991* (OUP 1991) 1.

[74] *Transforming Our World: The 2030 Agenda for Sustainable Development*, UN Doc A/RES/70/1 (UN General Assembly 21 October 2015) <www.un.org/en/development/desa/population/migration/generalassembly/docs/globalcompact/A_RES_70_1_E.pdf> accessed 18 August 2025.

> 4.1 By 2030, ensure that ALL girls and boys have access to free, equitable and quality primary and secondary education leading to relevant and effective learning outcomes.[75]

Furthermore, Goal 4.3 also aims beyond primary education and seeks to ensure equal access for all women and men to affordable and quality technical, vocational, and tertiary education, including higher education at the university level.

In the Doha Plan of Action, the Group of 77 and China emphasized the need to have affordable access to essential basic educational tools and the importance of preserving and nurturing the policy space for developing states to realize their development goals.[76]

While exploring the nexus between education and development, it is inevitable to consider the role that institutions play in promoting and monitoring the effective implementation of rights and the development agenda. While social actors, lawyers, and organizations are the forefront players in the education agenda, the courts also play an extensive range of roles to ensure access to education. Apart from the usual adjudicational role, courts can go further by being anticipatory and instructive in function. Courts

[75] *Transforming Our World: The 2030 Agenda for Sustainable Development*, UN Doc A/RES/70/1 (UN General Assembly 21 October 2015) para 17 <www.un.org/en/development/desa/population/migration/generalassembly/docs/globalcompact/A_RES_70_1_E.pdf> accessed 18 August 2025.

[76] *Doha Plan of Action*, Second South Summit of the Group of 77 (G-77/SS/2005/2) (12–15 June 2005) para 8(vii) <www.g77.org/southsummit2/doc/Doha%20Plan%20of%20Action%20(English).pdf> accessed 18 August 2025. Para 8(vii) reads as:

> [T]o enhance the development dimension of the international Intellectual Property Rights system, taking into account the different levels of development of developing countries with a view to ensuring affordable access to necessary basic products, including medicines and educational tools and software, the transfer of knowledge, the promotion of research and stimulation of innovation and creativity, and in this regard, we call:
>
> a. for action to accelerate the work on the development related mandate concerning the TRIPS Agreement and the implementation related issues in the Doha Ministerial Declaration, especially on the issues of making intellectual property rules of TRIPS supportive of the objectives of the Convention on Biological Diversity;
>
> b. on WIPO, as a UN Agency, to include in all its future plans and activities including legal advice a development dimension that includes promoting development and access to knowledge for all, pro-development norm setting, establishing development friendly principles and guidelines for the provisions of technical assistance and the transfer and dissemination of technology . . .

provide plenteous guidance in establishing the link between the right to education and access to adequate resources to support effective learning.

5. Copyright Globalization and *Unequal* Access

The developing world's growth and welfare depend to a large extent on access to knowledge and its mobility. The international IP 'top-down approach' has better served the interests of IP-rich states but has failed to fulfil the social welfare goals of developing countries, especially in respect of human development interests.[77] There are many developing and least developed countries that lack access to textbooks and other learning materials. The lack of the 'substantive equality principle' in IP globalization has hindered human development capabilities.[78] Policymakers seek an appropriate balance between the right to exclude others and access to work by framing limitations and exceptions to IPR. The distributive justice problem remains largely unaddressed by the international copyright regime. Global public goods scholars, under the 'rubric' of global knowledge goods, focus not only on the inadequate supply of public goods but also on unequal access to public goods.[79] Chon mentions an 'IP from below' approach that fulfils the distributive justice purposes of IP in a better way, particularly in terms of access to knowledge and its dissemination.[80]

Access to knowledge comprises 'essential needs' of the developing countries, in the same way as access to life-saving drugs.[81] Knowledge

[77] Olufunmilayo B. Arewa, 'Piracy, Biopiracy and Borrowing: Culture, Cultural Heritage and the Globalization of Intellectual Property' *Case Research Paper Series in Legal Studies*, Working Paper No. 04-19 (2006) 79–80.

[78] Margaret Chon, 'Intellectual Property and the Development Divide' [2006] 27 Cardozo L Rev 2821, 2823 (suggests incorporation of substantive equality principle into international IP regime, which would be corollary to the formal equality principle of national treatment and minimum standards).

[79] Margaret Chon, 'Intellectual Property and the Development Divide' [2006] 27 Cardozo L Rev 2821, 2823.

[80] Margaret Chon, 'Intellectual Property "from Below": Copyright and Capability for Education' [2007] 40 UC Davis L Rev 803, 817 (stating *that this approach responds to the imbalance that observers in both the North* and the South are identifying in both domestic and global IP policymaking settings).

[81] Peter Drahos, 'An Alternative Framework for the Global Regulation of Intellectual Property Rights' [2005] 21 Australian J Dev Stud 44. For developing countries, the coming century of knowledge-based growth raises two basic development priorities. The first is that these

infrastructure directly impacts the level of education in any society, and education, in turn, helps in the production of more knowledge goods.[82] But the issue of educational materials has remained less focused as compared to musical and other entertainment works, which have gained far more attention.[83]

The issue of distributive justice can be viewed from different angles; the political view renders an approach of division of public goods among those who have a share in the constitution.[84] It focuses on 'how a society or group should allocate its scarce resources or product among individuals with competing needs or claims'.[85] It has been a significant challenge to address the pervasive inequalities in the international IP regime.

The principles of international IP need to be steered by foundational human development capabilities. The provisions for access to education must be the subject of primary concern, because human capabilities are crucially founded on education and hence the technological progress that is the ultimate rationale of the TRIPS Agreement.[86] There are allusions in the TRIPS Agreement of particular importance to overall development: Preamble, Article 7,[87] and Article 8.[88] These development-friendly provisions seem to strengthen the position of developing and least developed countries.[89] The objectives stated in the TRIPS Agreement emphasize

countries must give more urgent attention to encouraging investment in human capital. This essentially translates into investment in health and education. Without growth in human capital, developing countries will be left to participate in simple commodities markets rather than the knowledge economy.

[82] Martha Nussbaum, 'Capabilities and Human Rights' [1997] 66 Fordham L Rev 273, 287.

[83] Peter K. Yu, 'From Pirates to Partners: Protecting Intellectual Property in China in the Twenty-First Century' [2001] 50 American University L Rev 131; see generally Peter K. Yu, 'Four Common Misconceptions About Copyright Piracy' [2003] 26 Loyola LA Int'l & Comp L Rev 127.

[84] Frank J. Garcia, *Trade, Inequality, And Justice: Toward A Liberal Theory of Just Trade* (Transnational Publishers 2003) 49.

[85] Siva Vaidhyanathan, 'Copyrights and Copywrongs' [2002] 15 Harvard JL & Tech 453, 496 [citing John E. Roemer, *Theories of Distributive Justice of Distributive Justice* (1996)].

[86] Joseph Stiglitz, 'Learning to Learn, Localized Learning and Technological Progress' in Partha Basgupta and Paul Stoneman (eds) *Economic Policy and Technological Performance* (CUP 1987).

[87] Article 7 emphasizes the promotion of technological innovation that is conducive to social and economic welfare and to a balance of rights and obligations.

[88] Article 8 emphasizes the adoption of such measures that promote the public interest in sectors of vital importance to their socio-economic development.

[89] Peter K. Yu, 'The Objectives and Principles of the TRIPS Agreement' [2009] 46 Houston L Rev 979, 1023 (discussing how Articles 7 and 8 can be used as a seed for the development

'social and economic welfare' and the need to balance the rights and obligations. The TRIPS resource book provides guidance on Article 7, through a detailed analysis:

> Article 7 makes clear that TRIPS negotiators did not mean to abandon a balanced perspective on the role of intellectual property in society. TRIPS is not intended only to protect the interests of right holders. It is intended to strike a balance that more widely promotes social and economic welfare.[90]

Use of the term 'development' in the TRIPS Agreement inherently incorporates the social distributive justice nuance. As per the Vienna Convention on the Law of Treaties, the terms of the treaty shall be given the ordinary meaning in their context and in the light of its object and purpose.[91] It has also been stated by one of the WTO settlement panels that 'the text of the treaty must, of course, be read as a whole. One cannot simply concentrate on a paragraph, an article, a section, a chapter or a part.'[92] Moreover, the Doha Declaration on Public Health also stipulated that 'the TRIPS Council shall be guided by the objectives and principles set out in Articles 7 and 8 of the TRIPS Agreement and shall take fully into account the development dimension.'[93] The reference to 'development' incorporated the access to knowledge in the TRIPS preamble and objectives. Despite featuring 'development' provisions in the TRIPS Agreement, development interests remain largely marginalized, and TRIPS seems to have poorly served the development-related interests of

of new international IP norms); see also J.H. Reichman, 'The TRIPS Agreement Comes of Age: Conflict or Cooperation with the Developing Countries' [2000] 32 Case Western Reserve J Int'l L 441, 462; see also Ruth Okediji, 'Toward an International Fair Use Doctrine' [2000] 39 Colum J Transnat'l L 167, 168 (stating how Articles 7 and 8 can be used to justify the fair use privilege under the TRIPS Agreement).

[90] UNCTAD-ICTSD, *Resource Book on TRIPS and Development* (CUP 2005) 126.

[91] Vienna Convention on the Law of Treaties 1969, Art 31(1).

[92] *United States-Section 110(5) of the US Copyright Act*, WTO doc WT/DS 160/R (15 June 2000) (Report of the Panel) 17 <www.wto.org/english/tratop_e/dispu_e/1234da.pdf> accessed 18 August 2025; see also *United States-Standards for Reformulated and Conventional Gasoline*, WTO doc WT/DS2/AB/R (Report of the Appellate Body) (29 April 1996) (announcing that the General Agreement is not to be read in clinical isolation from public international law); Daniel J. Gervais, 'Intellectual Property, Trade & Development: The State of Play' [2005] 74 Fordham L Rev 505, 528.

[93] *Doha Ministerial Declaration of 14 November 2001*, WTO doc WT/MIN(01)/DEC/1 (WTO 2002) 19.

the 'Global South'.[94] Reichman has expressed the difficulty inherent in maintaining a balance in dual layers, first, balancing the interests of creators and users of IP at the national level, and second, balancing the welfare interests of developing and developed states.[95]

In developing and least developed nations, the distributive justice principle suggests the full realization of the Berne-endorsed exceptions. The utilization of exceptions and limitations is a matter to be determined by domestic legislation. The lack of national institutional capacity and insufficient optimal policy space is reflected in the absence of enactments of provisions for educational exceptions and limitations.[96]

6. WIPO's Development Agenda

In August 2004, Argentina and Brazil circulated a proposal to establish a 'Development Agenda for WIPO'. The agenda aimed to balance the system of IP protection in a way that serves the interests of all sectors of society.[97] The proposal calls for a reformed role of WIPO in the future that facilitates the development of interests more earnestly. The Development Agenda appeared in response to 'an agenda of *under*development'[98] that was characterized by an imbalance of rights throughout the twentieth century, which Vera Franz describes as a crisis of imbalance between 'privatised knowledge that which is controlled by the intellectual property rights holder and the knowledge commons that which is owned by the public'.[99] The agenda aimed for WIPO to focus on 'broad development goals' rather than limiting itself to the promotion of IP protection.

94 'Global South' is a term used by the World Bank to denote the subset of developing countries that are below the median in terms of development indicators.

95 Jerome H. Reichman, 'The TRIPS Agreement Comes of Age: Conflict or Cooperation with the Developing Countries?' [2000] 32 Case Western Reserve J Int'l L 441.

96 Ruth L. Okediji, 'Africa and the Global Intellectual Property System: Beyond the Agency Model' [2006] 12 Afr YB Int'l L 207, 241.

97 *Proposal by Argentina and Brazil for the Establishment of a Development Agenda for WIPO*, WIPO Doc WO/GA/31/11 (WIPO 27 August 2004) <www.wipo.int/meetings/en/doc_details.jsp?doc_id=31737> accessed 14 August 2025.

98 Peter Drahos and John Braithwaite, *Information Feudalism: Who Owns the Knowledge Economy?* (Earthscan 2002) 12.

99 Becky Hogge and Vera Franz, 'The Rise of the Access to Knowledge Movement: An Interview with Vera Franz' *Open Society Foundations* (02 February 2011) <www.opensocietyfoundations.org/voices/rise-access-knowledge-movement-interview-vera-franz> accessed 16 August 2025.

Latif has likened A2K to a double sided coin, where one side of the coin, under the heading 'A2K for development', is advocating for the curtailment of IP policies to advance the access concerns of developing states, while the other side of the coin, under the label 'A2K for innovation and creativity', embarks upon supporting high IP standards in developed nations.[100] Hence, the movement aims to achieve a proper balance between the two faces of a coin. In the movement, developing states and NGOs in the capacity of importers of knowledge have a common aim, that is, the goal of bringing such a balance between IP and development that advances access to knowledge and information.[101]

This proposal was strongly supported by many policymakers, business representatives, members of civil society, NGO representatives, academics, and scientists, who signed the 'Geneva Declaration on the Future of the World Intellectual Property Organization'.[102] The declaration campaigned for access to essential medicines, knowledge, education, technology, and free software, as well as Creative Commons. Signed by more than five hundred, the declaration proclaims: 'Humanity faces a global crisis in the governance of knowledge, technology and culture. The crisis is manifest in many ways.'[103] Realizing the 'grave social and economic cost' of expansion of monopolistic privileges, the treaty claims that 'WIPO needs to enable its members to understand the real economic and social consequences of excessive intellectual property protections, and the importance of striking a balance between the public domain and competition on the one hand, and the realm of property rights on the other'.[104] It goes on to resist the one-size-fits-all

[100] Ahmed Abdel Latif, 'The Emergence of the A2K Movement: Reminiscences and Reflections of a Developing-Country Delegate' in Gaëlle Krikorian and Amy Kapczynski (eds) *Access to Knowledge in The Age of Intellectual Property* (Zone Books 2010) 117.

[101] Ahmed Abdel Latif, 'The Emergence of the A2K Movement: Reminiscences and Reflections of a Developing-Country Delegate' in Gaëlle Krikorian and Amy Kapczynski (eds) *Access to Knowledge in The Age of Intellectual Property* (Zone Books 2010) 117.

[102] 'Geneva Declaration on the Future of the World Intellectual Property Organization' (September 2004) <www.cptech.org/ip/wipo/futureofwipodeclaration.pdf> accessed 16 August 2025.

[103] 'Geneva Declaration on the Future of the World Intellectual Property Organization' (September 2004) <www.cptech.org/ip/wipo/futureofwipodeclaration.pdf> accessed 16 August 2025.

[104] 'Geneva Declaration on the Future of the World Intellectual Property Organization' (September 2004) 2 <www.cptech.org/ip/wipo/futureofwipodeclaration.pdf> accessed 16 August 2025.

mantra of IP because it fails to address the needs of developing countries. The Geneva Declaration campaigned that WIPO take 'a more balanced and realistic view of the social benefits and costs of intellectual property rights as a tool, but not the only tool, for supporting creative intellectual activity'.[105] The declaration also called for a 'Treaty on Access to Knowledge and Technology'.[106] By May 2005, the draft of the Access to Knowledge Treaty was ready.[107] The treaty was proposed with an aim 'to protect and enhance access to knowledge, and to facilitate the transfer of technology to developing countries'.[108] It discusses deploying minimum exceptions and limitations with respect to IP in the educational sector.

WIPO entered into force on 26 April 1970,[109] and its objective was to 'promote the protection of intellectual property throughout the world through cooperation among states and, where appropriate, in collaboration with any other international organisation'.[110] WIPO was affiliated with the UN as a specialized agency on 17 December 1974, after being approved by the General Assembly, and, in that capacity, it was required to contribute towards the UN's global development mandate.[111] The UN recognized WIPO as its specialized agency 'for promoting creative intellectual activity and for facilitating the transfer of technology related to industrial property to the developing countries to accelerate economic, social and cultural development'.[112] But, WIPO's primary obsession with strong IPR posed a great challenge to achieving its UN-mandated

[105] 'Geneva Declaration on the Future of the World Intellectual Property Organization' (September 2004) <www.cptech.org/ip/wipo/futureofwipodeclaration.pdf> accessed 16 August 2025.

[106] 'Geneva Declaration on the Future of the World Intellectual Property Organization' (September 2004) 3 <www.cptech.org/ip/wipo/futureofwipodeclaration.pdf> accessed 16 August 2025.

[107] Draft Treaty on Access to Knowledge <www.cptech.org/a2k/a2k_treaty_may9.pdf> accessed 17 August 2025.

[108] Draft Treaty on Access to Knowledge, Art 1-1 <www.cptech.org/a2k/a2k_treaty_may9.pdf> accessed 17 August 2025.

[109] *Convention Establishing the World Intellectual Property Organization*, 828 Treaty Series (UN 1972) 7 <https://treaties.un.org/doc/Publication/UNTS/Volume%20828/v828.pdf>.

[110] *Convention Establishing the World Intellectual Property Organization*, 828 Treaty Series (UN 1972) 11; <https://treaties.un.org/doc/Publication/UNTS/Volume%20828/v828.pdf>.

[111] Jeremy De Beer, 'Defining WIPO's Development Agenda' in Jeremy De Beer (ed) *Implementing WIPO's Development Agenda* (Wilfrid Laurier University Press 2009) 4.

[112] Agreement between the United Nations and the World Intellectual Property Organization, Art 1, WIPO Doc TRT/UN-WIPO/001 (17 December 1974) <www.wipo.int/treaties/en/text.jsp?file_id=305623> accessed 17 August 2025.

development goals. At one time, in WIPO, protection of IP was a synonym for 'development'.[113] WIPO defines IP primarily as a means to 'economic growth' instead of 'development'.[114] However, economic growth, as a central metric to gauge development, is not the only development indicator; Amartya Sen, in one of his acclaimed works, presented the concept of development as having an essential nexus to freedom.[115] Sen has argued why freedom needs to be positioned as the main element of development. WIPO always stayed committed to the idea that IP is the only appropriate tool to realize economic growth. The idea appeared to change when developing states began questioning the suitability of IP policies in relation to their local social, economic, and cultural interests.

Furthermore, TRIPS did not prove itself to be a success for the development of developing countries; hence, the Development Agenda emerged as a result of dissatisfaction on the part of developing countries. The organizations in favour of the Development Agenda aimed not to displace WIPO but to make some fundamental reforms with a 'more balanced and realistic view of the social benefits and costs of intellectual property rights as a tool, but not the only tool, for supporting creative intellectual activity'.[116]

The Geneva Declaration recommended that WIPO should:

- Enable its member states to understand the significance of balancing the public domain, on one hand, and the realm of property rights, on the other.
- Oust the one-size-fits-all approach that results in more unjust and burdensome outcomes for the developing and least developed countries.
- Address the substantive concerns of society and public interest groups, such as the protection of human rights.

[113] Jeremy De Beer, 'Defining WIPO's Development Agenda' in Jeremy De Beer (ed) *Implementing WIPO's Development Agenda* (Wilfrid Laurier University Press 2009) 4, 5.
[114] Kamil Idris, *Intellectual Property – A Power Tool for Economic Growth* (2nd edn, WIPO 2003).
[115] Amartya Sen, *Development as Freedom* (Alfred Knopf 1999).
[116] 'Geneva Declaration on the Future of the World Intellectual Property Organization' (30 September 2004) <www.cptech.org/ip/wipo/futureofwipodeclaration.pdf> accessed 18 August 2025.

- Help developing countries to incorporate the limitations and exceptions in the copyright laws that are required for fairness, development, and innovation.
- Create standing committees and working groups on technology transfer and development-related issues.
- Consider a Treaty on Access to Knowledge and Technology.[117]

The Geneva Declaration was signed by hundreds of academicians, scientists, NGOs, and members of civil society with the hope that WIPO would adopt a sympathetic approach towards developing countries while protecting IP and, at the same time, balancing it with their developmental interests.[118]

Following the adoption of the Doha Declaration, there was a need to reject the 'one size fits all' approach and adopt a system that allowed for flexibility in its implementation, responding to the specific needs of countries. In October 2004, the General Assembly of WIPO welcomed the proposal and convened a series of intergovernmental meetings between future sessions.[119] WIPO's role is not merely to protect IP, but, as a UN specialized agency, it is also mandated to take into consideration the development-related commitments and resolutions of the UN system as a whole.[120] In response to the proposal, WIPO stated that:

> IP for Development is an emphatic articulation of the notion that IP is not an end in itself but rather is a tool that could power countries' growth and development. WIPO, as the lead United Nations agency mandated to promote the protection of intellectual property through cooperation among states and in collaboration with other international organizations, is committed to ensuring that all countries are

[117] 'Geneva Declaration on the Future of the World Intellectual Property Organization' (30 September 2004) <www.cptech.org/ip/wipo/futureofwipodeclaration.pdf> accessed 18 August 2025.

[118] Debora J. Halbert, 'The World Intellectual Property Organization: Past, Present and Future' [2007] 54 J Copyright Soc'y USA 275.

[119] *Report Adopted by WIPO General Assembly*, WIPO Doc WO/GA/31/15 (5 October 2004) <www.wipo.int/edocs/mdocs/govbody/en/wo_ga_31/wo_ga_31_15.pdf> accessed 18 August 2025.

[120] *Proposal by Argentina and Brazil for the Establishment of a Development Agenda for WIPO*, WIPO Doc WO/GA/31/11 (27 August 2004) <www.wipo.int/meetings/en/doc_details.jsp?doc_id=31737> accessed 18 August 2025.

able to benefit from the use of IP for economic, social, and cultural development.[121]

Over the next three years, the proposal led to intense discussions and debates in the Provisional Committee on Proposals Related to a WIPO Development Agenda and the Inter-sessional Inter-Governmental Meeting on a Development Agenda for WIPO, over the relation of IP and development. The Group of Friends of the Development Agenda (GFD) desired to bring development-oriented IP trends into any negotiation involving the IP systems.[122] The GFD emphasized the need for a more balanced approach to protect IP and facilitate access to knowledge for developing countries and least developed countries.[123] In September 2007, a set of forty-five recommendations was unanimously adopted by WIPO's General Assembly.[124] To arrive at a consensus on forty-five recommendations was never an easy task. Delegates from the member states discussed, debated, and categorized the proposal in six thematic clusters, in which recommendations reflected upon the focus area:

Cluster A technical assistance and capacity building;
Cluster B norm setting, flexibilities, public policy, and public domain;
Cluster C technology transfer, information and communication technologies, and access to knowledge;
Cluster D assessment, evaluation, and impact studies;

[121] WIPO, 'Intellectual Property for Development' <www.wipo.int/ip-development/en/agenda/> accessed 19 August 2025.

[122] *Proposal to Establish a Development Agenda for WIPO*, WIPO Doc WO/GA/31/11 (6 April 2005) <www.wipo.int/edocs/mdocs/mdocs/en/iim_1/iim_1_4.pdf> accessed 19 August 2025.

[123] *Proposal to Establish a Development Agenda for WIPO*, WIPO Doc WO/GA/31/11 (6 April 2005) 4 <www.wipo.int/edocs/mdocs/mdocs/en/iim_1/iim_1_4.pdf> accessed 19 August 2025. The Proposal states:

> In order to ensure the credibility of the IP system, however, more has to be done in order to ensure that peoples all over the world have access to knowledge and technological development. We believe WIPO could have a new role as a relevant actor in this context if it incorporates the development dimension into its work.

[124] *The Forty-Five Adopted Recommendations under the WIPO Development Agenda* (WIPO 2007) <www.wipo.int/ip-development/en/agenda/recommendations.html> accessed 20 August 2025.

Cluster E institutional matters, including mandate and governance; and
Cluster F other issues.

Cluster F of the agenda calls upon WIPO to cover 'other issues', whose implications must not be underrated. Recommendation No. 45 reads as:

> To approach intellectual property enforcement in the context of broader societal interests and especially development-oriented concerns, with a view that 'the protection and enforcement of intellectual property rights should contribute to the promotion of technological innovation and to the transfer and dissemination of technology, to the mutual advantage of producers and users of technological knowledge and in a manner conducive to social and economic welfare, and to a balance of rights and obligations', in accordance with Article 7 of the TRIPS Agreement.[125]

It is noteworthy to mention Recommendation No. 10, which emphasizes achieving a 'fair balance between IP protection and the public interest'.[126] Recommendation Nos. 17 and 19 require WIPO to 'take into account the flexibilities in international IP agreements, especially those which are of interest to developing countries and least developed countries' and to 'facilitate access to knowledge and technology for developing countries'.[127]

The developing and the least developed countries have much faith in the realization of the WIPO Development Agenda. But, the year 2007 cannot be said to be the first time in history when countries have demanded reform while addressing the concerns and needs of developing countries.[128] Peter Yu emphasizes that it was not the first

[125] *The Forty-Five Adopted Recommendations under the WIPO Development Agenda* (WIPO 2007) recommendation no. 45 <www.wipo.int/ip-development/en/agenda/recommendations.html> accessed 20 August 2025.

[126] *The Forty-Five Adopted Recommendations under the WIPO Development Agenda* (WIPO 2007) recommendation no. 10 <www.wipo.int/ip-development/en/agenda/recommendations.html> accessed 20 August 2025.

[127] *The Forty-Five Adopted Recommendations under the WIPO Development Agenda* (WIPO 2007) recommendation nos. 17 and 19 <www.wipo.int/ip-development/en/agenda/recommendations.html> accessed 20 August 2025.

[128] Debora J. Halbert, 'The World Intellectual Property Organization: Past, Present and Future' [2007] 54 J Copyright Soc'y USA 275.

development agenda in the field of IP, and it will not be the last.[129] The WIPO Development Agenda's evolution began nearly two decades ago, aiming to ensure that WIPO integrates development concerns into its work.

[129] Peter K. Yu, 'A Tale of Two Development Agendas' [2009] 35 Ohio Northern University L Rev 465, 512 (explains the earlier development agenda established in the pre- and post-TRIPS era). Yu categorizes the Stockholm Protocol (1967), WIPO as a UN specialized agency (1974), and the Paris Convention (1967) as the Old Development Agenda and categorizes the Doha Development Agenda (2001) and the WIPO Development Agenda (2004) as the New Development Agendas. See also Peter K. Yu, 'Five Decades of Intellectual Property and Global Development' [2016] 8 WIPO Journal 1.

2

International Copyright Law

1. Introduction

The principle of territoriality in intellectual property (IP) negates the existence of anything like international copyright law.[1] The territoriality principle makes the enforcement of IP rights limited only to the territory of the country that grants such rights. However, with the escalation in cross-border exploitation of copyrights, it cannot be asserted that infringements are restricted solely within sealed domestic boundaries. Uses made in one state affect the rights in other states and impair the policies that were designed to protect the rights. Hence, a need to protect authors from the threats posed by transborder infringements was realized. International copyright protection became necessary to protect authors in foreign lands because of the expansion of knowledge goods globally and how technology disseminates copyrighted works in all corners of the world. After the invention of the printing press by Gutenberg in 1436, there was a proliferation in copying and publishing globally at a much faster pace.[2] The need for international copyright protection was realized in the nineteenth century when publishers in the United States, the Netherlands, Belgium, and Holland pirated French and British works.[3] France was one of the most affected states at that time because French works were widely pirated in

[1] D.J. Llewelyn Davies, 'The Influence of Huber's de Conflictu Legum on English Private International Law' [1937] 18 Brit YB Int'l L 49, 63 (citing Ulrik Huber's reflection of concept of territoriality: (1) a state's laws have force only within the state's boundaries; (2) anyone found within the state's boundaries is subject to the state's authority; and (3) comity will discipline sovereign exercises of authority so that the territorial effect of each state's laws is respected).

[2] Edward W. Ploman and L. Clark Hamilton, *Copyright: Intellectual Property in the Information Age* (Routledge 1980) 9–18.

[3] Paul Goldstein and Bernt Hugenholtz, *International Copyright: Principles, Law and Practice* (OUP 2010) 10.

Access to Knowledge in the Developing World. Vandana Mahalwar, Oxford University Press.
 DOI: 10.1093/9780198986782.003.0002

Belgium and Holland.[4] International piracy was the fundamental reason for the emergence of international relations among nation-states. As a result, many European countries established international relations through reciprocity treaties and bilateral agreements, which protected works of both contracting parties.[5] The emergence of international copyright relations occurred through bilateral agreements rather than the multilateral treaties that are prevalent today. France signed many treaties between 1843 and 1851 with Sardinia, Hanover, Portugal, and Great Britain without any requirement of reciprocity,[6] followed by the French Decree of 28 March 1852, which extended protection to all works irrespective of the place of origin of work or nationality of the author.[7] International copyright emerged with the bilateral treaty between Sardinia and Austria in 1840, followed by eighty-four more bilateral treaties among different nations till 1886, when the Berne Convention for the Protection of Literary and Artistic Works ('Berne Convention') was signed.[8] Berne was the first multilateral convention on copyright in the world, and at that time, thirty-three bilateral agreements were in force.[9] Then, it was followed by the TRIPS Agreement in 1994 and two WIPO treaties in 1996.

2. Historical Overview

Before the advent of the printing press, booksellers had to manually copy the books, which was a lengthy and time-consuming task.[10] Use of

[4] Edward W. Ploman and L. Clark Hamilton, *Copyright: Intellectual Property in the Information Age* (Routledge 1980) 20 (France unsuccessfully attempted to persuade Holland and Belgium to enter into reciprocity treaties).

[5] George Putnam, 'Literary Property: An Historical Sketch' in G. Putnam (ed) *The Question of Copyright* (G.P. Putnam's Sons 1904) 359; see also Stephen P. Ladas, *The International Protection of Literary and Artistic Property* (Macmillan 1938).

[6] Cécile Cottenet, *Literary Agents in the Transatlantic Book Trade: American Fiction, French Rights and the Hoffman Agency* (Taylor and Francis 2017) (France was 'the undisputed ruler of the bilateral universe' and it played the key role in advent of international copyright and protection of literary and artistic property).

[7] Harry G. Henn, 'Quest for International Copyright Protection' [1954] 39 Cornell LQ 43, 45; W. Briggs, *The Law of International Copyright* (Stevens & Haynes 1906).

[8] Jorgen Blomqvist, *Primer on International Copyright and Related Rights* (Edward Elgar 2014) 8.

[9] Jorgen Blomqvist, *Primer on International Copyright and Related Rights* (Edward Elgar 2014) 10.

[10] Richard Adelstein and Steven Peretz, 'The Competition of Technologies in Markets for Ideas: Copyright and Fair Use in Evolutionary Perspective' [1985] 5 Int'l Rev L & Econ 209,

the printing press helped the booksellers to recover the cost of printing the press and the author's manuscript by selling copies of the books.[11] But, there was a negative side to the printing press, which equipped pirates to copy and publish books unauthorizedly. The pirated copies were sold by pirates at relatively much lower prices than the actual cost of the books.[12] The legitimate booksellers, who were authorized by the authors to publish books, had no recourse against such illegitimate copying practices of the pirates, and some kind of protection was much needed.[13] Such pirated copies of books were affecting booksellers more than authors, because booksellers' monetary interest was hugely involved in it. Booksellers were then granted the 'privilege', which was an exclusive right to print and sell the author's manuscript for a specific time period. Hence, publishers were conferred the limited monopoly to publish manuscripts.[14]

The privileges system was abolished about 200 years after it was introduced.[15] There were numerous reasons for the abolition of privileges. First, the booksellers were abusing the monopoly given to them; second, the need for censorship started diminishing as the government grew more mature. Third and most important was that authors began to press for the protection of their own rights.

After the abolition of the privileges system, a new system emerged that, for the first time, gave statutory protection to the authors. England became the first country that introduced, through the Statute of Anne in

226; W. Briggs, *The Law of International Copyright* (Stevens & Haynes 1906) 27–28; Edward W. Ploman and L. Clark Hamilton, *Copyright: Intellectual Property in the Information Age* (Routledge 1980) 9–18; George Putnam, 'Literary Property: An Historical Sketch' in G. Putnam (ed) *The Question of Copyright* (G.P. Putnam's Sons 1904) 359.

[11] Peter Burger, 'The Berne Convention: Its History and Its Key Role in the Future' [1988] 3 JL & Tech 1, 3.

[12] Richard Adelstein and Steven Peretz, 'The Competition of Technologies in Markets for Ideas: Copyright and Fair Use in Evolutionary Perspective' [1985] 5 Int'l Rev L & Econ 209, 224.

[13] Steven M. Stewart, *International Copyright and Neighboring Rights* (Butterworths 1983) 15; W. Briggs, *The Law of International Copyright* (Stevens & Haynes 1906); Edward W. Ploman and L. Clark Hamilton, *Copyright: Intellectual Property in the Information Age* (Routledge 1980); Brander Matthews, 'The Evolution of Copyright' in G. Putnam (ed) *The Question of Copyright* (G.P. Putnam's Sons 1904) 330.

[14] Edward W. Ploman and L. Clark Hamilton, *Copyright: Intellectual Property in the Information Age* (Routledge 1980) 9; see also Steven M. Stewart, *International Copyright and Neighboring Rights* (Butterworths 1983) 16.

[15] W. Briggs, *The Law of International Copyright* (Stevens & Haynes 1906) 28; Stephen P. Ladas, *The International Protection of Literary and Artistic Property* (Macmillan 1938) 19.

1709, a replacement of the privileges system.[16] When there was a shift in copyright from bookseller to author, a new debate started regarding the origin of the right. Many philosophers advocated that authors' rights should be unlimited in time, as they are the main creators of books and ideas emanate from them. These philosophers based their argument on natural law theory. They contended that copyright must be viewed as a naturally given right, rather than a statutory right,[17] because statutes merely recognize already existing rights.[18] But this natural right justification could not hold good in the United States and Great Britain, and authors were given protection for only those rights that were mentioned in the legislative acts.[19] In continental Europe, however, the natural rights approach was adopted, and authors' moral rights were protected, even if they had transferred their economic rights to the publisher.[20] These differences between the natural rights approach (the author's right approach) and the Anglo-American approach (statutory right approach) created a divide at the international level as well.[21] The countries in favour of natural law philosophy, called *droit d'auteur*, lay an emphasis on authors' rights, while the Anglo-American countries stress copyright owners, be they authors or publishers. The natural right philosophy best justified the international copyright law because natural rights are never hermetically bound within domestic territories; they belong to every human being. Hence, it is clear that the states that founded their copyright law on a natural law approach were the early nations to apply their copyright laws to foreign works, while the Anglo-American countries did not extend their copyright laws to anyone other than national authors.[22] The difference in these approaches did not gain much significance during the late

[16] W. Briggs, *The Law of International Copyright* (Stevens & Haynes 1906) 32.

[17] Stephen P. Ladas, *The International Protection of Literary and Artistic Property* (Macmillan 1938) 22.

[18] Stephen P. Ladas, *The International Protection of Literary and Artistic Property* (Macmillan 1938) 22.

[19] Stephen P. Ladas, *The International Protection of Literary and Artistic Property* (Macmillan 1938) 24–25.

[20] Stephen P. Ladas, *The International Protection of Literary and Artistic Property* (Macmillan 1938) 32.

[21] Stephen P. Ladas, *The International Protection of Literary and Artistic Property* (Macmillan 1938) 33–35.

[22] Stephen P. Ladas, *The International Protection of Literary and Artistic Property* (Macmillan 1938) 37.

eighteenth century due to the limited transboundary sales of the books.[23] The need for international copyright protection was realized in late nineteenth century when books of one country were being purchased in other countries.[24] With the rise in the level of international piracy, countries started entering into bilateral agreements based on the condition of material reciprocity. As per the principle of reciprocity, country A accords the same protection to authors of country B that country B accords to authors of country A.

France's policy of unilateral grant of protection is a kind of 'pragmatic altruism' that encouraged countries to make agreements with France.[25] By 1886, Belgium was the only country to follow France's way of granting unilateral protection to foreign works.[26]

2.1. The Early Bilateralism in Copyright

In the nineteenth century, most countries were quite restrictive as they limited the availability of copyright protection only to national works, and if they protected foreign works, they conditioned the protection on the criterion of nationality of the author and the place of publication of the work.[27] Prussia was the first to enter into bilateral agreements (with some thirty-two German states in 1827, 1828, and 1829) on the basis of formal reciprocity, to abolish the distinctions between national and foreign authors.[28] The early bilateral arrangements were mostly entered into between the countries that were major copyright exporters. The United Kingdom and France, being major copyright exporters of the nineteenth century, were the protagonists in early bilateralism. After enjoying little

[23] Stephen P. Ladas, *The International Protection of Literary and Artistic Property* (Macmillan 1938) 38.

[24] Stephen P. Ladas, *The International Protection of Literary and Artistic Property* (Macmillan 1938) 39.

[25] Sam Ricketson and Jane C. Ginsburg, *International Copyright and Neighbouring Rights: The Berne Convention and Beyond* (OUP 2005) 23.

[26] Belgian Law of 1886, Art 38.

[27] Paul Goldstein and P. Bernt Hugenholtz, *International Copyright: Principles, Law and Practice* (OUP 2010) 31; see also Sam Ricketson and Jane C. Ginsburg, *International Copyright and Neighbouring Rights: The Berne Convention and Beyond* (OUP 2005) 24.

[28] W. Briggs, *The Law of International Copyright* (Stevens & Haynes 1906) 66.

success from the decree of 1852 in securing foreign protection, France entered into a bilateral copyright agreement with Belgium, which was the main market for pirated copies of French works, and it also led to the rapid increase in bilateral treaties between other European states.[29] After the 1846 convention with Prussia, the UK concluded several bilateral treaties with European states. But the UK did not conclude a treaty with the United States, which was a major source of pirated copies of English works.[30] Germany also signed bilateral treaties with Belgium, France, Italy, Switzerland, and the UK.[31]

On the whole, each convention was founded on the governing principle of national treatment. But the bilateral agreements varied widely in their scope of rights recognized, the term of protection, and the required formalities.[32] Due to these differences, the task of ascertaining the entitlements of an author of country A in countries B, C, and D became more strenuous and cumbersome.[33] These conventions were subject to two more shortcomings: first, that treaties had uncertain duration and could be denunciated by either contracting state party on a notice of one year;[34] second, was the 'most-favoured nation'[35] clause in the agreements. Such clauses made the treaties uncertain because it was easier for the contracting parties to abrogate the terms and adopt the terms of the treaty that was concluded between the second contracting state and the

[29] Sam Ricketson and Jane C. Ginsburg, *International Copyright and Neighbouring Rights: The Berne Convention and Beyond* (OUP 2005) 29–30 (France entered into bilateral agreements with Austria-Hungary, Belgium, the newly constituted state of Italy, Luxembourg, the Netherlands, Portugal, Prussia, the Russian Empire, Spain, and the Swiss Confederation).

[30] Paul Goldstein and P. Bernt Hugenholtz, *International Copyright: Principles, Law and Practice* (OUP 2010) 32; Sam Ricketson and Jane C. Ginsburg, *International Copyright and Neighbouring Rights: The Berne Convention and Beyond* (OUP 2005) 29 (the UK signed treaties with Hanover, France, Belgium, Spain, and Sardinia-Italy).

[31] Sam Ricketson and Jane C. Ginsburg, *International Copyright and Neighbouring Rights: The Berne Convention and Beyond* (OUP 2005) 30.

[32] Stephen P. Ladas, *The International Protection of Literary and Artistic Property* (Macmillan 1938) 55–57.

[33] Stephen P. Ladas, *The International Protection of Literary and Artistic Property* (Macmillan 1938) 66.

[34] Stephen P. Ladas, *The International Protection of Literary and Artistic Property* (Macmillan 1938) 67.

[35] A 'most-favoured nation' clause provides that if there is a convention between country A and country B, and country A signs a treaty with any third country C and offers a higher level of protection to it, then country B can claim the same higher treatment which is accorded to country C.

third state. Hence, the 'most-favoured nation' clause kept shaking the level of protection whenever a contracting country signed a new bilateral treaty,[36] and it 'added greatly to the complications of international copyright protection in the pre-Berne period'.[37]

2.2. Origin of Multilateralism

Though the existence of bilateralism prior to 1886 was extensive, it led to a complicated situation, with varying copyright protection between different countries. The differences in the subject matter in bilateral treaties led to the need for a uniform and more comprehensive solution. This need for multilateral copyright sowed the seeds of justice for authors and added a chapter to the progressive history of international copyright law.

2.2.1. Brussels Congress of Authors and Artists, 1858

On 27 September 1858, the International Congress of Authors and Artists held its first meeting in Brussels. The Congress was international in nature, attended by authors, artists, journalists, librarians, and lawyers from different countries representing different interests.[38] The agenda of the Congress was broadly divided into five categories, namely, 'international questions', 'property in literary and artistic works in general', 'dramatic and musical works', 'artistic works', and 'economic questions'. However, while there was unanimity for international copyright protection, the members differed on the term of protection. A difference of opinion existed between perpetuity and a fixed term, but the majority favoured a definite term of protection, bearing in mind the general interests of the public.[39] The Congress passed five resolutions, which entailed

[36] Stephen P. Ladas, *The International Protection of Literary and Artistic Property* (Macmillan 1938) 66.

[37] Sam Ricketson and Jane C. Ginsburg, *International Copyright and Neighbouring Rights: The Berne Convention and Beyond* (OUP 2005) 39.

[38] Stephen P. Ladas, *The International Protection of Literary and Artistic Property* (Macmillan 1938) 72.

[39] Sam Ricketson and Jane C. Ginsburg, *International Copyright and Neighbouring Rights: The Berne Convention and Beyond* (OUP 2005) 45.

a foundational outline of international copyright protection.[40] The Congress met again in 1877, requesting the *Institut de droit Internationale* to draft the world law for the protection of artistic works, but the institute never completed it, and eventually, the draft work was carried out by the International Literary Association.

The movement for international protection gathered momentum at the International Literary Association, which was formed in 1878, under the presidency of Victor Hugo.[41] The association, comprising distinguished authors and literary societies, passed five resolutions[42] wherein the last two resolutions pointed at the national treatment and simplification of formalities.

[40] The resolutions were:

(1) That the principle of international recognition of copyright in favor of authors must be made part of the legislation of all civilized countries.
(2) This principle must be admitted regardless of reciprocity.
(3) The assimilation of foreign to national authors [national treatment] must be absolute and complete.
(4) Foreign authors should not be required to comply with any particular formalities for the recognition and protection of their rights, provided they have complied with the formalities required in the country where publication first took place.
(5) It is desirable that all countries adopt uniform legislation for the protection of literary and artistic works.

[41] Stephen P. Ladas, *The International Protection of Literary and Artistic Property* (Macmillan 1938) 72; Sam Ricketson and Jane C. Ginsburg, *International Copyright and Neighbouring Rights: The Berne Convention and Beyond* (OUP 2005) 49.

[42] The Literary Congress passed the following five resolutions:

1. The right of an author in his work does not constitute a grant of law, but one of the forms of property which the legislator must guarantee.
2. The right of the author and of his heirs and legal representatives is perpetual.
3. After the expiration of the period fixed for the duration of the author's right by the laws in force in the various countries, any person may freely reproduce a literary work, subject to payment of a royalty to the author or his legal representatives. The rights recognized in favor of heirs cannot prevent the publication of a new edition provided this is accurate; this new edition must be preceded by real offers of payment of an indemnity and two summonses repeated at intervals of six months. Nevertheless, the heir will be deemed bound by the wishes of the author whenever he may justify this.
4. Every literary, scientific or artistic work shall be treated in the countries other than the country of origin in the same way as works of national origin. This shall also apply to the execution of dramatic and musical works.
5. In order that this protection be secured, it will be sufficient for the author to have complied with the ordinary formalities in the country where the work was first published.

2.2.2. ALAI Conference, 1883

The International Literary Association was later named as *L'Association Litteraire et Artistique Internationale* (ALAI), which agreed to 'constitute a general Union for the protection of rights of authors in their literary works and manuscripts'.[43] The Conference held its first meeting on 10 September 1883, and the participants drafted a ten-article treaty. The primary focus of the treaty was on national treatment and the abolition of formalities as a condition to copyright protection.

2.2.3. Diplomatic Conference, 1884

Following favourable responses to the draft treaty, the Swiss government invited various governments to meet at the Diplomatic Conference in Berne on 8 September 1884.[44] Eleven countries agreed to be represented there.[45] Before the discussion began, a German delegation proposed abandoning the principle of national treatment,[46] but the participating countries responded negatively and decided to incorporate the national treatment approach.[47] In the draft, the principle of national treatment was retained in almost the same manner as in the ALAI draft. The drafting commission made the principle of national treatment subject to a temporal limitation, which provided that the protection would last for the duration the protection subsists in the author's own country or the country of origin.[48] The conferees rejected the French proposal to adopt the full-term protection of translation rights; instead, an exclusive

[43] Sam Ricketson and Jane C. Ginsburg, *International Copyright and Neighbouring Rights: The Berne Convention and Beyond* (OUP 2005) 54.

[44] Sam Ricketson and Jane C. Ginsburg, *International Copyright and Neighbouring Rights: The Berne Convention and Beyond* (OUP 2005) 58.

[45] Argentina, Colombia, France, Germany, Guatemala, Italy, Luxembourg, Norway, Salvador, Sweden, and the UK.

[46] The German delegation proposed the idea to Conference:

> Instead of concluding a convention based on the principle of national treatment, would it not be preferable to aim for a codification, in the framework of a convention, regulating in a uniform manner for the whole projected Union, and in the framework of a convention, the totality of dispositions relating to the protection of copyright.

[47] Sam Ricketson and Jane C. Ginsburg, *International Copyright and Neighbouring Rights: The Berne Convention and Beyond* (OUP 2005) 59.

[48] Sam Ricketson and Jane C. Ginsburg, *International Copyright and Neighbouring Rights: The Berne Convention and Beyond* (OUP 2005) 65.

translation right for ten years following the first publication of the work was adopted.[49]

In Article 8 of the draft, the contracting states were to permit, reciprocally, the publication of, 'excerpts, fragments or whole passages of a literary or artistic work' that had first appeared in another Union country, provided that this publication was specially made and adopted for educational purposes or had a scientific character.[50] Likewise, chrestomathies compiled of passages from different authors were to be protected. All these reproductions were subject to the condition of acknowledging the name of the author of the work.[51] Article 9 of the draft provided a limitation in public interest that articles extracted from newspapers or periodicals might be reproduced.[52]

Article 9 provided that:[53]

> Articles excerpted from newspapers or periodical journals published in one of the countries of the Union may be reproduced, in the original or in translation, in the other countries of the Union.
>
> This right shall not, however, extend to the reproduction, in the original or in translation, of serialized novels or articles on science or art.

There was a proposal for the deletion of the word 'science' from the second paragraph of Article 9. Voting was also taken on the said proposal, but the proposal was rejected, and the term 'science' was retained in the draft. On the whole, the draft of 1883 did not appear to be as protective of authors' rights.

2.2.4. Conference of 1885

In the Conference of 1885, the draft of 1884 received considerable amendments. The Conference amended the provision governing 'the

[49] Sam Ricketson and Jane C. Ginsburg, *International Copyright and Neighbouring Rights: The Berne Convention and Beyond* (OUP 2005) 67.

[50] Draft Convention Concerning the Creation of a General Union for the Protection of Authors' Rights 1884, Art 8 para 1.

[51] Draft Convention Concerning the Creation of a General Union for the Protection of Authors' Rights 1884, Art 8, para 3.

[52] Sam Ricketson and Jane C. Ginsburg, *International Copyright and Neighbouring Rights: The Berne Convention and Beyond* (OUP 2005) 68.

[53] Arpad Bogsch, *First Hundred Years of Berne Convention for the Protection of Literary and Artistic Works* (International Bureau of Intellectual Property WIPO 1986).

reproduction of articles of newspapers and periodicals'. The British delegation proposed to delete this article altogether, as the article stood in contradiction to the domestic law of Great Britain, which required the sources of excerpts from newspapers to be indicated.[54] The Committee rejected the British proposal and agreed on:[55]

> Articles from newspapers or periodical journals published in one of the countries of the Union may be reproduced, in the original or in translation, except where the authors of publishers thereof have expressly prohibited it. For journals, it may be sufficient for the prohibition to be stated in a general way at the head of each issue of the journal.

This prohibition may not in any case apply to articles of political discussion, or to the reproduction of news of the day or miscellaneous information.

Another significant amendment was made to the provision governing lawful borrowings from literary and artistic works. Article 8, which dealt with borrowings, was discussed at length, where the French and British delegations asked for its deletion. But the Committee decided that the regulation of lawful borrowing should be left to domestic legislation. The Committee adopted the wording:[56]

> With regard to the right to make lawful borrowings from literary or artistic works for publications intended for education or of scientific character, or for chrestomathies, the effect of the legislation of the countries of the Union and of special arrangements existing or to be concluded between them is reserved.

It is pertinent to note that in relation to the above article, the Spanish delegation proposed to add the words 'or study' to 'especially intended for education'. The Committee responded negatively to this amendment,

[54] Arpad Bogsch, *First Hundred Years of Berne Convention for the Protection of Literary and Artistic Works* (International Bureau of Intellectual Property WIPO 1986) 120.

[55] Arpad Bogsch, *First Hundred Years of Berne Convention for the Protection of Literary and Artistic Works* (International Bureau of Intellectual Property WIPO 1986) 121.

[56] Arpad Bogsch, *First Hundred Years of Berne Convention for the Protection of Literary and Artistic Works* (International Bureau of Intellectual Property WIPO 1986) 121.

as the Committee had already agreed that the term 'education' applied both to elementary education and to higher education, and that works intended for self-teaching were covered by the words 'of scientific character'.[57]

2.2.5. Conference of 1886

The Diplomatic Conference of 1886 was a formal proceeding, where the 1885 draft was ratified and signed by participating countries as the Berne Convention. On 6 September 1886, the agreement was signed by France, Germany, Great Britain, Haiti, Holland, Italy, Liberia, Spain, Switzerland, and Tunisia.[58] The United States of America and Japan were represented as mere observers in the Conference.[59] A year later, on 6 September 1887, nine signatories met for the exchange of ratifications. Although the convention could not achieve all the objectives outlined in the Brussels Congress, it was a remarkable step towards international copyright protection for authors and artists.

3. International Copyright Instruments

3.1. The Berne Convention

The deliberations over the previous few years eventually resulted in the evolution of the Berne Convention. The main purpose of the Convention was to establish minimum standards that all member countries were required to recognize in their domestic laws. Even today, the Berne Convention continues to be the most significant multilateral treaty in world copyright law. One of the primary reasons for its continued influence is the periodic modernizations that took place

[57] Arpad Bogsch, *First Hundred Years of Berne Convention for the Protection of Literary and Artistic Works* (International Bureau of Intellectual Property WIPO 1986) 121.
[58] Arpad Bogsch, *First Hundred Years of Berne Convention for the Protection of Literary and Artistic Works* (International Bureau of Intellectual Property WIPO 1986) 130.
[59] Sam Ricketson and Jane C. Ginsburg, *International Copyright and Neighbouring Rights: The Berne Convention and Beyond* (OUP 2005) 82.

through revisions at Berlin in 1908,[60] Rome in 1928,[61] Brussels in 1948,[62] Stockholm in 1967,[63] and Paris in 1971.[64] The first convention had just a few minimum requirements; however, the number of minimum requirements expanded with successive revisions of the Berne Convention as the signatories wanted to achieve the goal of protection of authors' rights.

3.1.1. National Treatment Principle

The Berne Convention is based on the principle of national treatment,[65] which means that a member country will grant the same protection to the authors of other member countries of the Berne Convention as it accords to its own national authors. The principle remains the basic rule of international copyright even today, as it ensures that there is no discrimination against authors of other contracting states. The national treatment principle does not apply to the term of protection. Instead, the work is protected in other Berne Convention countries as long as the work is protected by the country of origin.

3.1.2. Points of Attachment

For a work to be entitled to protection, the author or their legal representative has to be a national of a Union country (i.e. a country to which the Convention applies). However, two points of attachment entitle a work to protection in a Union country other than the country of origin: if the author of the work is a national or domiciliary of a member country,[66] or

[60] UNESCO, *Copyright Laws & Treaties of the World, Berne Copyright Union*, Item C-1 Berlin Convention (1908).

[61] UNESCO, *Copyright Laws & Treaties of the World, Berne Copyright Union*, Item E-1 Rome Convention (1928).

[62] UNESCO, *Copyright Laws & Treaties of the World, Berne Copyright Union*, Item F-1 Brussels Convention (1948).

[63] UNESCO, *Copyright Laws & Treaties of the World, Berne Copyright Union*, Item G-1 Stockholm Act (1967).

[64] UNESCO, *Copyright Laws & Treaties of the World, Berne Copyright Union*, Item H-1 Paris Act (1971).

[65] UNESCO, *Copyright Laws & Treaties of the World, Berne Copyright Union*, Item A-1 Berne Convention, Art. 2 (1886).

[66] Berne Convention 1971 (Paris Text), Arts 3(1)(a) and 3(2).

if there has been a 'first publication' or 'simultaneous publication'[67] of the work in a Union country.[68] The Paris Act 1971 does not require any formalities to enjoy and exercise the copyright.[69]

In case of published works, the Paris Act defines the 'country of origin' of a particular work as the country where the work was first published.[70] If the work was simultaneously published in several Union countries, the country of origin is 'the country whose legislation grants the shortest term of protection'.[71] For unpublished works, the country of origin is 'the country of the Union of which the author is a national'.[72]

3.1.3. Term

The Act prescribes the term of protection as the 'life of the author and fifty years after his death'.[73] However, Article 7*bis* provides that in a work of joint authorship, the term shall be measured from the death of the last surviving author. In case of anonymous or pseudonymous works, Article 7(3) prescribes the term of 'fifty years after the work has been lawfully made available to the public'.

3.1.4. Works

The Paris Act 1971 has provided a minimum standard of protection in the form of an encompassing list of works that the member countries are required to protect. Article 2(1) of the Act defines the 'literary and artistic works' as including 'every production in the literary, scientific and artistic domain, whatever may be the mode or form of its expression'. The list includes: 'books, pamphlets and other writings; lectures, addresses, sermons and other works of the same nature; dramatic or dramatico-musical works; choreographic works and entertainments in dumb show; musical compositions with or without words; cinematographic works to which are assimilated works expressed by a process analogous to

[67] Berne Convention 1971 (Paris Text), Art 3(4) reads as: 'A work shall be considered as having been published simultaneously in several countries if it has been published in two or more countries within thirty days of its first publications.'
[68] Berne Convention 1971 (Paris Text), Art 3(1)(b).
[69] Berne Convention 1971 (Paris Text), Art 3(2).
[70] Berne Convention 1971 (Paris Text), Art 4(a).
[71] Berne Convention 1971 (Paris Text), Art 4(a).
[72] Berne Convention 1971 (Paris Text), Art 4(c).
[73] Berne Convention 1971 (Paris Text), Art 7(1).

cinematography; works of drawing, painting, architecture, sculpture, engraving and lithography; photographic works to which are assimilated works expressed by a process analogous to photography; works of applied art; illustrations, maps, plans, sketches and three-dimensional works relative to geography, topography, architecture or science.' The Act gives discretion to the member states to prescribe the fixation requirement.[74] In addition to this, the Act provides protection to translations, adaptations, arrangements of music, and other alterations of literary or artistic works, such as encyclopaedias and anthologies, as original works.[75] The member countries are also given the discretion to determine the protection of 'official text of a legislative, administrative and legal nature, and to official translations of such texts'.[76]

3.1.5. Exclusive Rights

The Paris Act protects both moral and economic rights of authors. It establishes minimum standards for various exclusive economic rights, namely, the right to reproduce a literary or artistic works in any manner or form,[77] the right to make adaptations, arrangements or other alterations of their work,[78] the right to make translations of their work throughout the term of protection of their rights in the original works,[79] the right to make public performance in the case of dramatic, dramatico-musical and musical works,[80] the right to broadcast in the case of literary and artistic works,[81] the right to recite the work publicly,[82] and the right to make cinematographic adaptations and reproductions and to distribute and publicly perform the works thus adapted or reproduced.[83]

Article 6*bis* of the Act protects moral rights of authors by providing that 'the author shall have the right to claim authorship of the work and to object to any distortion, mutilation or other modification of, or other

[74] Berne Convention 1971 (Paris Text), Art 2(2).
[75] Berne Convention 1971 (Paris Text), Arts 2(3) and (5).
[76] Berne Convention 1971 (Paris Text), Art 2(4).
[77] Berne Convention 1971 (Paris Text), Art 9(1).
[78] Berne Convention 1971 (Paris Text), Art 12.
[79] Berne Convention 1971 (Paris Text), Art 8.
[80] Berne Convention 1971 (Paris Text), Art 11(1).
[81] Berne Convention 1971 (Paris Text), Art 11*bis* (1).
[82] Berne Convention 1971 (Paris Text), Art 11*ter* (1).
[83] Berne Convention 1971 (Paris Text), Art 14.

derogatory action in relation to, the said work, which would be prejudicial to his honour or reputation'.

To balance private interests with public interests, the Paris Act permits each member country to legislate certain limitations and exceptions to these rights.[84] Limitations and exceptions are discussed at length later in this chapter.

3.2. Universal Copyright Convention

Despite the Berne Convention's grand success at the international level as the first multilateral copyright treaty, by 1948, only thirty-nine members had signed it. The United States, the Soviet Union, and several Asian and African countries were not members of the Berne Convention because of its higher standard of protection. The Berne Convention required these countries to bring massive changes to their national laws before they could comply with the Berne Convention. Hence, emphasizing the need for a global copyright system, UNESCO commenced negotiations with United Nations members to establish an effective multilateral treaty which would ensure in all countries copyright protection of literary, scientific, and artistic works, without replacing the Berne Convention.

The Universal Copyright Convention (UCC) emerged as a landmark multilateral agreement in the field of international copyright law.[85] Adopted under the aegis of UNESCO, the UCC was signed on 6 September 1952, in Geneva and came into effect on 16 September 1955. It adopted no new copyright norms, but rather harmonized the existing national systems, which were founded on the national treatment principle.[86] The preamble to UCC states that it came out as a copyright system 'in addition to, and without impairing, the international system already in force'.[87]

[84] Berne Convention 1971 (Paris Text), Art 9(2).

[85] Joseph Dubin, 'The Universal Copyright Convention' [1954] 42 Cal L Rev 89, citing John Schulman, 'A Realistic Treaty', *American Writer* (November 1952).

[86] Edward A. Sargoy, *Report of the Committee on International Copyrights to the Annual Meeting of the Section of Patents, Trademarks, and Copyright of the American Bar Association* (Boston, 1953).

[87] The UCC 1971 preamble states:

> The contracting States,
>
> Moved by the desire to assure in all countries copyright protection of literary, scientific and artistic works,

In UCC, the basic principle of national treatment and the protectible subject matter are similar to those of the Berne Convention. Article II of the UCC requires each contracting country to grant national treatment to the works of nationals of any other contracting state and works first published in that state. However, as a minimum, the contracting states are required to provide 'adequate and effective' protection and must ensure the exclusive right to reproduction, public performance, broadcasting,[88] and translation of works.[89]

There are some substantial differences between the Berne Convention and the UCC. The Berne Convention is known for providing strong and extended protection to authors, and it is based on the idea that copyright protection must not be conditioned upon formalities.[90] In contrast, the UCC provides for formalities like deposit, registration, notice, and the symbol © as conditions to protection. However, in cases where works are first published outside the territory and the author is non-national, then the formalities are considered to be satisfied if, from the time of first publication, all copies of the work bear a prescribed notice.[91] The UCC provides for a relatively shorter copyright term, i.e., twenty-five years after the death of the author or from the date of first publication,[92] while the Berne Convention has an extensive term of fifty years after the death of the author.

When the draft of the UCC was under construction, the representatives of the states that were Berne Convention members emphasized a condition of not requiring countries to withdraw from the Berne Union to join the UCC.[93] As a result, Article XVII was formulated with an

> Convinced that a system of copyright protection appropriate to all nations of the world and expressed in a universal convention, additional to, and without impairing international systems already in force, will ensure respect for the rights of the individual and encourage the development of literature, the sciences and the arts,
>
> Persuaded that such a universal copyright system will facilitate a wider dissemination of works of the human mind and increase international understanding

[88] The Universal Copyright Convention 1971 (Paris Text), Art IV bis (1).

[89] The Universal Copyright Convention 1971 (Paris Text), Art V(1).

[90] John Schulman, 'Another View of Article III of the Universal Copyright Convention' [1953] Wisc L Rev 297, 300.

[91] Universal Copyright Convention 1952 (Geneva Text), Art III(1).

[92] Universal Copyright Convention 1952 (Geneva Text), Art IV(2).

[93] Kelsey Martin Mott, 'The Relationship between the Berne Convention and the Universal Copyright Convention' [1966] 11 Patent, Trademark and Copyright J Res and Education 306, 307.

intention to 'avoid any conflict which might result from the co-existence of the Convention of Berne and the Universal Convention'. The UCC ensures, in Article XVII, that it does not conflict with the Berne Convention by stating that 'this convention shall not in any way affect the provisions of the Berne Convention for the Protection of Literary and Artistic Works or membership in the Union created by that Convention'.

3.3. The TRIPS Agreement

It is widely accepted that the Agreement on Trade Related Aspects of Intellectual Property Rights (TRIPS) ushered in a robust multilateral agreement in the new global copyright era. Until the Uruguay round, it could hardly be said that a global copyright system existed with a strong enforcement mechanism. Ginsberg rightly noted that 'at present we have a system of interlocking national copyrights, woven together by the principle of national treatment'.[94] Before TRIPS, the system that existed was a mere 'patchwork' of varying bilateral and multilateral arrangements, which remained ineffectual for want of enforcement measures. The pre-TRIPS era mirrored the chronic breaches of treaty obligations, and the International Court of Justice was the forum to adjudicate the disputes of such breaches.[95] With its jurisdiction to resolve disputes and to monitor the responsibilities of the TRIPS Council,[96] the WTO has effected an effective system for the advancement of international copyright law and policy.[97] The TRIPS Agreement stands distinct from other copyright

[94] Jane C. Ginsburg, 'International Copyright: From a Bundle of National Copyright Laws to a Supranational Code' [2000] 47 J Copyright Soc'y USA 265, 266. (noting 'international copyright, in the sense of a uniform law binding all nation states, does not exist').

[95] Berne Convention 1971 (Paris Text), Art 33.

[96] TRIPS Agreement 1994, Art 68 (the Council has the responsibility to monitor the operation of TRIPS Agreement and members' compliance with their obligations; it is under an obligation to carry out such other responsibilities as assigned to it by the members, and it shall, in particular, provide any assistance requested by them in the context of dispute settlement procedures); TRIPS Agreement 1994, Arts 63(1) and (2) (to receive notifications of laws and regulations from member states in order to review the operation of Agreement); TRIPS Agreement 1994, Art 71(1) (the Council is under obligation to review the implementation of this Agreement after the expiration of transitional period and at identical intervals thereafter).

[97] Ruth Okediji, 'TRIPs Dispute Settlement and the Sources of (International) Copyright Law' [2001] 49 J Copyright Soc'y USA 585, 586.

treaties in the sense that it covers both copyright and neighbouring rights.[98]

TRIPS brought many transformational aspects with it, but 'the Understanding on Rules and Procedures Governing the Settlement of Disputes', or Dispute Settlement Understanding (DSU), has been the most accomplished feature of it. A binding dispute settlement under TRIPS promotes 'harmonisation' of domestic laws by integrating various norms and policies.[99]

WTO's DSU dispute settlement mechanism aims to secure a 'positive solution to a dispute'.[100] It provides for consultation procedures in the event that any member breaches its obligations under the agreement, mandating that each member must accord sympathetic consideration to and afford adequate opportunity for consultation regarding any representations made by another member.[101] If no satisfactory adjustment is secured through consultations, the contracting parties may pursue mediation, good offices, or conciliation, or the complaining member may ask the Dispute Settlement Body (DSB) to establish a panel.[102] Such a request for the establishment of a panel must indicate whether consultations were held, identify the specific measures at issue, and provide a brief summary of the legal basis of the complaint sufficient to present clearly the problem of inconsistency with the trade agreements in question.[103] After the panel is formed, the panellists fix the timetable for the

[98] Axel Nordemann, 'Berne and Beyond: Understanding International Conventions Relating to Copyright Law' [2012] 59 J Copyright Soc'y USA 263, 264 (the Berne Convention, the UCC, the WIPO Copyright Treaty, and many bilateral agreements like the German–American Copyright Treaty of 1892 cover copyright works only, the neighbouring rights are covered by the Rome Convention, the Geneva Phonogram Convention, the Strasbourg Television Agreement, and the WIPO Performances and Phonograms Treaty).

[99] Ruth Okediji, 'TRIPs Dispute Settlement and the Sources of (International) Copyright Law' [2001] 49 J Copyright Soc'y USA 585, 616 (noting that '[h]armonization involves the progressive integration of norms and policies in a given area to produce a level of symmetry between domestic laws of Member states that is greater than one but less than 100').

[100] 'Understanding on Rules and Procedures Governing the Settlement of Disputes', Art 3(7), Annex II, the WTO Agreement 1994.

[101] 'Understanding on Rules and Procedures Governing the Settlement of Disputes', Art 4, Annex II, the WTO Agreement 1994.

[102] 'Understanding on Rules and Procedures Governing the Settlement of Disputes', Art 6, Annex II, the WTO Agreement 1994.

[103] 'Understanding on Rules and Procedures Governing the Settlement of Disputes', Art 6(2), Annex II, the WTO Agreement 1994.

panel process, in consultation with the parties to the dispute.[104] Then, the parties submit their written submissions comprising facts behind the complaint, procedural points at issue, and claims based on legal grounds. The first substantive meeting of the panel takes place one or two weeks after receipt of the respondent's written submission.[105] The DSU mandates that 'deliberations of a panel and documents submitted to it shall be kept confidential'.[106] At the first meeting, both parties make oral statements regarding their written submissions, which is followed by a question-and-answer session between both parties. After two or three months of the first meeting, the second substantive meeting takes place, which primarily focuses on the counterarguments against claims of the opposite party.[107] Following the hearing and deliberations, the panel issues its report, describing the findings and conclusions of the panel. Para 9 of Article 12 provides that the panel is to make an investigation within a period of six months.[108] The report is referred to the DSB for adoption and becomes legally binding on the parties once adopted by the DSB. If the DSB decides against adoption, the parties may seek review by the Appellate Body to examine the appropriateness of the legal interpretations employed by the panel.[109]

The DSU provides for prompt compliance with recommendations or rulings of the DSB.[110] Emphasizing the special interests of developing countries, para 2 of Article 21 provides that 'Particular attention should be paid to matters affecting the interests of developing country members with respect to measures which have been subject to dispute settlement'.

One significant IP dispute resolved by a WTO panel involved a 2007 complaint filed by the US against China, alleging that Article 4 of the Chinese Copyright Act violated Articles 9.1 and 41.1 of the TRIPS Agreement and Article 5(1) of the Berne Convention.[111] A 2007 WTO

[104] 'Understanding on Rules and Procedures Governing the Settlement of Disputes', Art 12(3), Annex II, the WTO Agreement 1994.
[105] The WTO Agreement 1994, annex II, appendix 3, para 12.
[106] The WTO Agreement 1994, annex II, appendix 3, para 3.
[107] The WTO Agreement 1994, annex II, appendix 3, para 7.
[108] The WTO Agreement 1994, annex II, Art 12, para 8.
[109] The WTO Agreement 1994, annex II, Art 17, para 4.
[110] The WTO Agreement 1994, annex II, Art 21, para 2.
[111] *China – Measures Affecting the Protection and Enforcement of Intellectual Property Rights*, WTO doc WT/DS362/15 (13 April 2010) (Report of the Panel) <www.wto.org/english/tratop_e/dispu_e/cases_e/ds362_e.htm> accessed 27 August 2025.

panel examined and deliberated upon the issues at length. Due to the complexities involved in the case, the panel informed the DSB on 16 July 2008 that it would not be able to complete the examination work within six months. The panel issued the report on 26 January 2009, which was circulated to its members. The panel ruled that Article 4(1) of the Chinese Copyright Law was inconsistent with China's obligations under Article 5(1) of the Berne Convention and Article 9(1) and 41(1) of the TRIPS Agreement. The DSB adopted the report on 20 March 2009. China informed the DSB that it would require a reasonable period of time to implement the recommendations and rulings. On 29 June 2009, the US and China informed the DSB that they had agreed upon a period of twelve months for China to implement the DSB recommendations and rulings. The twelve-month period was to expire on 20 March 2010. On 19 March 2010, China reported that the eleventh National People's Congress approved the amendments to the Chinese Copyright Act.

3.3.1. The National Treatment Principle

TRIPS adopted the national treatment clause as an effective tool for enabling right holders to get the same degree of protection as nationals, at least in those member states that protect IP rights.[112] The principle does not impact domestic laws because it has an obligation to give only formal equal treatment.[113] Hence, the member countries continue to enjoy their discretion in governing IP policies. Where domestic law protects the IP laws inadequately, the principle of national treatment alone cannot enhance the level of protection. Due to considerable differences in the levels of IP protection, the TRIPS Agreement, like other international treaties, contains the principle of material reciprocity as an exception to the principle of national treatment.[114] Material reciprocity as an exception to the principle of national treatment counteracts the chances of countries with a low level of protection benefitting from countries providing a higher level of protection.

[112] Peter-Tobias Stoll, Jan Busche, and Katrin Arend (eds) *WTO – Trade Related Aspects of Intellectual Property Rights* (Martinus Nijhoff Publishers 2009) 151.

[113] G.E. Evans, 'TRIPs and the Sufficiency of the Free Trade Principles' [1999] 2 JWIP 707, 711.

[114] As per material reciprocity, a non-national member can be denied national treatment in case his or her own national laws do not grant the claimed treatment.

Article 3 of the TRIPS Agreement provides that members shall accord to the nationals of other members the treatment no less favourable than that it accords to its own nationals with regard to the protection of IP. Footnote 3 of Article 3.1 clarifies that the term 'protection' shall include matters affecting 'the availability, acquisition, scope, maintenance and enforcement of intellectual property rights as well as those matters affecting the use of intellectual property rights specifically addressed in this Agreement'. Therefore, the national treatment principle extends to availability, acquisition, scope, maintenance, and enforcement of IP rights, which means that it is granted not merely in respect of legal provisions but also in relation to administrative actions and judicial practices.

3.3.2. Subject Matter: Works, Rights, and Term

Article 9.1 of the TRIPS Agreement mandates 'compliance' with Articles 1 to 21 of the Berne Convention (1971) and the Appendix thereto. The deliberate use of the term 'comply' makes it clear that each member country is required to change its national law to conform with the substantive provisions on economic rights. However, it does not obligate members to accede to the Berne Convention. The provision asks the members to comply with Article 1 to 21 of the Berne Convention (1971). Footnote 2 to Article 1.3 of the TRIPS Agreement elucidates the distinction between 'Berne Convention' and 'Berne Convention (1971)'.[115] Hence, it can be concluded that any subsequent revision to the Berne Convention (1971) would not affect the member countries' obligations.

Second sentence of Article 9.1 follows a 'Berne-minus' approach[116] by using the language of explicit exclusion of moral rights pursuant to Article 6*bis* of the Berne Convention.[117]

Article 9.2 expresses that '[c]opyright protection shall extend to expressions and not to ideas, procedures, methods of operation or mathematical

[115] TRIPS Agreement 1994, footnote 2 to Art 1.3 provides that 'Berne Convention' refers to the Berne Convention for the Protection of Literary and Artistic Works; 'Berne Convention (1971)' refers to the Paris Act of this Convention of 24 July 1971.

[116] TRIPS Agreement, Art 9.1 reads as: 'Members shall not have rights or obligations under this Agreement in respect of the rights conferred under Article 6*bis* of that Convention or of the rights derived therefrom.'

[117] Peter-Tobias Stoll, Jan Busche, and Katrin Arend (eds) *WTO – Trade Related Aspects of Intellectual Property Rights* (Martinus Nijhoff Publishers 2009) 208.

concepts as such'. Unlike the EU Database Directive, Article 9.2 of the TRIPS Agreement does not prescribe *sui generis* protection for databases. The demarcation that Article 9.2 draws between copyright protected expressions and free ideas in the public domain, reflects the concern about preserving the freedom of expression.[118]

The significance of Article 9 is twofold: first, it brought the Berne Convention under the WTO dispute settlement mechanism[119] and strengthened it through the normative force of a binding interpretation. Second, in the pre-TRIPS era, the binding exceptions to copyrightability were never configured. Until the TRIPS Agreement was concluded, there had been a common denominator among national systems that 'copyright protects the expression of ideas, not ideas per se', but there existed no international binding provision.[120]

As per Article 9, TRIPS has incorporated not only exclusive rights of a copyright nature but also limitations thereupon. Article 13 permits the members to provide for *a numerus clausus of limited exceptions to exclusive rights* of a copyright nature. Limitations and exceptions are discussed at length later in this chapter.

Article 12 of the TRIPS Agreement provides that any work other than photographs and applied arts, for which the term of protection is calculated on a basis other than a natural life, the term shall not be less than fifty years from the year of publication, or if the work is not published within fifty years, then fifty years from the year it was created.[121] TRIPS has explicitly excluded the photographs and works of applied arts. Hence, these two works shall be governed as per Article 7.4 of the Berne Convention, which says that the minimum term of protection for the works envisaged by this provision is 25 years from their making.[122]

[118] Daniel Gervais, *The TRIPS Agreement: Drafting History and Analysis* (4th edn, Sweet & Maxwell 2012) 245.

[119] Berne Convention 1886, Art 33(1) mentions that a dispute between members may be submitted to International Court of Justice, which has never been done.

[120] Claude Masouyé, *Guide to the Berne Convention for the Protection of Literary and Artistic Works (Paris Act 1971)* WIPO Publication No 615(E) (WIPO 1978).

[121] TRIPS Agreement 1994, Art 12.

[122] Berne Convention 1886, Art 7.4 states: 'It shall be a matter for legislation in the countries of the Union to determine the term of protection of photographic works and that of works of applied art in so far as they are protected as artistic works; however, this term shall last at least until the end of a period of twenty-five years from the making of such a work.'

3.4. The WIPO Copyright Treaty

In global copyright history, the TRIPS Agreement emerged as an era-defining instrument[123] that brought radical changes to the institutional structure of the IP system. But the WIPO Copyright Treaty (WCT) has played a cardinal role in shaping the future of international copyright by giving, for the first time, an explicit recognition to the concept of 'balance' that is integral to copyright law. No doubt the concept of balance had already gained some attention before 1996[124] but the clear language of 'balance' was framed in 1996 in the WCT for the first time.[125]

Article 1 of the WCT says that it is a 'special agreement' within the meaning of Article 20 of the Berne Convention, to provide more extensive rights to its members.[126] It ensures that nothing in it shall derogate from contracting states' obligations under the Berne Convention[127] and shall not prejudice any other rights and obligations under any other treaties.[128] WCT comprises twenty-five articles and the Agreed Statements Concerning the WIPO Copyright Treaty, which offers an explanation to the articles of the treaty. Article 2 offers a more elaborate scope of protection than the Berne Convention by stating that the protection 'extends to expressions and not to ideas, procedures, methods of operation or mathematical concepts as such.' Article 3 of the treaty has incorporated Articles 2 to 6 of the Berne Convention, which comprises

[123] Graeme B. Dinwoodie, 'The Institutions of International Intellectual Property Law: New Actors, New Institutions, and New Sources' [2008] in 98th Proceedings of the Annual Meeting of the American Society of International Law 213.

[124] Ruth L. Okediji, 'Sustainable Access to Copyrighted Digital Information Works in Developing Countries' in Keith E. Maskus and Jerome H. Reichman (eds) *International Public Goods and Transfer of Technology Under A Globalized Intellectual Property Regime* (CUP 2005) 148 (the 1967 Stockholm Revision of the Berne Convention Protocol Regarding Developing Countries reflected the concern for 'balance' by emphasizing greater access to copyrighted works).

[125] Julie S. Sheinblatt, 'The WIPO Copyright Treaty' [1998] 13 Berkeley Tech LJ 535.

[126] Berne Convention 1886, Art 20 reads as: 'The Governments of the countries of the Union reserve the right to enter into special agreements among themselves, in so far as such agreements grant to authors more extensive rights than those granted by the Convention, or contain other provisions not contrary to this Convention. The provisions of existing agreements which satisfy these conditions shall remain applicable.'

[127] WIPO Copyright Treaty 1996, Art 1(2).

[128] WIPO Copyright Treaty 1996, Art 1(1).

mainly the provisions on points of attachment,[129] protected works,[130] possible limitation of protection, and rights guaranteed to authors.[131]

WCT has adopted the Berne-plus approach in the protectible subject matter list. Though Article 2 of the Berne Convention has not listed computer programs in its non-exhaustive list,[132] Article 4 of WCT expands its definition of literary works by stating that 'computer programs are protected as literary works within the meaning of Article 2 of the Berne Convention'. Another Berne-plus feature is embodied in Article 5 of the WCT, which protects the original compilations of data (databases) in any form, by virtue of the compilation's selection or arrangement of the content.[133] The protection of a database is 'without any prejudice to any copyright subsisting in the data or material contained in the compilation' and does not extend to the data itself.[134] Unlike Article 7(4) of the Berne Convention, the treaty expressly states not to give any special term of protection to photographic works.[135] Article 10 of the treaty allows the contracting states to provide for 'limitations of or exceptions to the rights granted to authors' that do not conflict with a normal exploitation of the work and unreasonably prejudice the legitimate interests of the author.

4. Limitations and Exceptions for Educational Use under International Copyright: A Historical and Legal Analysis

John Locke maintains in §27 of *The Second Treatise of Government* that an individual's ability to acquire private property in the state of nature is not unlimited and private owners have some natural law obligations:

[129] Berne Convention 1886, Art 3.
[130] Berne Convention 1886, Art 2.
[131] Berne Convention 1886, Art 5.
[132] Berne Convention 1886, Art 2(1) uses the term 'such as' in its enumerated list of literary works.
[133] The idea of protecting databases was already reflected in the landmark case *Feist Publications Inc. v Rural Telephone Service Company Inc.* 111 S Ct 1282 (1991), where the Supreme Court addressed the issue of the degree of creativity to sustain copyright in a compilation.
[134] WIPO Copyright Treaty 1996, Art 5.
[135] WIPO Copyright Treaty 1996, Art 9.

> Whatsoever then he removes out of the state that nature hath provided, and left it in, he hath mixed his labour with, and joined to it something that is his own, and thereby makes it his property. It being by him removed from the common state nature hath placed it in, it hath by this labour something annexed to it, that excludes the common right of other men: for this labour being the unquestionable property of the labourer, no man but he can have a right to what that is once joined to, at least where there is enough, and as good, left in common for others.[136]

In a contextualist approach, Locke's pragmatic view appears compatible with the need to balance public welfare against private interests. But will it fulfil the objectives of copyright policies, if enough is not left for others? Locke's idea of leaving plenty for others is a necessary condition to private appropriation. Locke's rhetoric of '*enough and as good*' is embedded deep in the approach to the determination of limitations and exceptions in the copyright law.

It is thus necessary to explore how the international copyright framework sought to reflect a 'balance' between copyright and access for educational purposes. This part of the book analyses the limitations and exceptions in international instruments, commonly called the 'three-step test'. The three-step test is an effective way of preventing the excessive application of limitations and exceptions to exclusive rights, ensuring a proper balance of interests is achieved.

4.1. Historical Background

To examine and analyse the relation between the three-step test and access to knowledge, it becomes imperative to trace the historical background of the three-step test. A general right of reproduction was introduced in the Berne Convention during the 1967 Revision Conference at Stockholm.[137] Before that, there was no explicit provision regarding reproduction rights in the Berne Convention; however, the majority of the nations

[136] John Locke, *Two Treatise of Government* (CUP 1960).
[137] Berne Convention 1886, Art 9(1).

had already recognized reproduction rights in their domestic laws. The question of adding a general right of reproduction was first considered at the Brussels Conference, but the proposal was eventually withdrawn and was not pursued by the Conference. However, in the 1964 report, the Study Group finally arrived at the decision to recognize that a provision on the general right of reproduction must be proposed.[138] The Study Group added that bringing the reproduction right to the conventions meant that 'satisfactory formula would have to be found for the inevitable exceptions to this right'.[139] Individually, most of the Union members had crafted some exceptions to their reproduction rights as per their own interests.[140]

The Study Group, set up by BIRPI (the predecessor of WIPO) and the government of Sweden, developed the document for revision of the Berne Convention in 1967. The Study Group observed that:

> On one hand, it was obvious that all the forms of exploiting a work which had, or were likely to acquire, considerable economic or practical importance must in principle be reserved to the authors; exceptions that might restrict the possibilities open to authors in these respects were unacceptable. On the other hand, it should not be forgotten that domestic laws already contained a series of exceptions in favour of various public and cultural interests and that it would be vain to suppose that countries would be ready at this stage to abolish these exceptions to any appreciable extent.[141]

The most recognized exceptions in the members countries were related to uses such as for public speeches, quotations, school books, newspaper articles, reporting current events, private use, reproduction by

[138] *Records of the Intellectual Property Conference of Stockholm, June 11 to July 14, 1967* (WIPO 1971) 111.

[139] *Records of the Intellectual Property Conference of Stockholm, June 11 to July 14, 1967* (WIPO 1971) 111.

[140] Susan Isiko Straba, *International Copyright Law and Access to Education in Developing Countries* (Martinus Nijhoff Publishers 2012) 54 (culturally developed countries like France and Germany provided narrower exceptions while countries who were culturally not so developed provided wide exceptions). Articles 53 and 54 of the German Copyright Law and Article 41 of the French Copyright Law provided exceptions strictly for personal use.

[141] *Records of the Intellectual Property Conference of Stockholm, June 11 to July 14, 1967* (WIPO 1971) 111–12.

photocopying in libraries, reproduction in special characters for the use of the blind, sound recordings of literary works for the use of the blind, texts of songs, sculptures on permanent display in public places, reproduction in the interests of public safety.[142]

After considering a few probable solutions, the Study Group made a suggestion with respect to exceptions that:

> [I]t shall be a matter for legislation in the countries of the Union, having regard to the provisions of this Convention, to limit the recognition and the exercising of that right, for specified purposes and on the condition that these purposes should not enter into economic competition with these works.[143]

This restricted the ability of Union members to make exceptions, in three ways: (1) while drafting exceptions, the already existing provisions of the Convention are to be respected; (2) exceptions can only be made for specified purposes, which means that there can be no exceptions without mentioning specific purposes such as teaching, quotation, etc.; (3) exceptions to the reproduction rights should not 'enter into economic competition with' protected works.[144]

4.2. Rules of Interpretation

The text of Article 9(2) of the Berne Convention and Article 13 of the TRIPS Agreement contains the three-step test to evaluate the validity of limitations and exceptions on exclusive rights.[145] Both articles are based on the idea that, though a well-laid-out list of exceptions is not necessary,

[142] *Records of the Intellectual Property Conference of Stockholm, June 11 to July 14, 1967* (WIPO 1971) 112.

[143] *Records of the Intellectual Property Conference of Stockholm, June 11 to July 14, 1967* (WIPO 1971) 112.

[144] *Records of the Intellectual Property Conference of Stockholm, June 11 to July 14, 1967* (WIPO 1971) 112.

[145] Peter-Tobias Stoll, Jan Busche, and Katrin Arend (eds) *WTO – Trade Related Aspects of Intellectual Property Rights* (Martinus Nijhoff Publishers 2009) 279 (an exception eliminates an existing exclusive right, while a limitation restricts such a right to a certain extent)

some of the circumstances can be determined under which the member countries can make their own limitations and exceptions. The incorporation of the test in the TRIPS Agreement advances members' desire to 'promote effective and adequate protection of intellectual property rights' enshrined in its preamble and in its objectives and principles expressed in Articles 7 and 8. The three-step test is an attempt to fulfil the objective of 'promotion of technological innovation' and 'transfer and dissemination of technology' in such a way that contributes to the social and economic welfare and 'to a balance of rights and obligations'.[146] The test significantly advances the intention of members contained in Article 8 'to promote the public interest in sectors of vital importance to their socio-economic and technological development'.

To maintain a balance between rights of authors and larger public interests, the limitations on and exceptions to copyright have been included in various international conventions and treaties: Berne Convention (Article 9(2)), TRIPS Agreement (Article 13), WCT (Article 10(1) and (2)), and WIPO Performances and Phonograms Treaty (Article 16(2)). Unlike the provisions relating to limitations and exceptions in national law, the limitations and exceptions provisions in international instruments are open-ended and more general, which requires interpretation. For the interpretation of these treaties, there are some generally accepted rules of interpretation in customary public international law.[147] Articles 31 and 32 of the Vienna Convention on the Law of Treaties have been applied to the interpretation of WTO agreements as per the provision in Article 3(2) of the DSU, which provides that WTO agreements are to be construed 'in accordance with customary rules of interpretation of public international law'. Article 31 of the Vienna Convention is worth considering here:

> (1) A treaty shall be interpreted in good faith in accordance with the ordinary meaning to be given to the terms of the treaty in their context and in the light of its object and purpose.

[146] TRIPS Agreement 1994, Art 7.

[147] Sam Ricketson, *WIPO Study on Limitations and Exceptions of Copyright and Related Rights in the Digital Environment*, WIPO Doc SCCR/9/7 (5 April 2003) 5.

Article 31(2) and (3) further adds to the meaning of 'context' in clause (1), by providing that the 'context' shall comprise the text itself, the preamble, annexes, any ancillary and subsequent agreements made by the parties, their subsequent practice in relation to treaty obligation, and any such rules of international law as may be applicable to their interpretation. Hence, the TRIPS Agreement has to be interpreted in light of its preamble, objective, and purposes. In *United States-Section 110(5) of the US Copyright Act*,[148] a dispute resolution panel of the WTO in June 2000 relied upon Vienna Convention principles, specifically Article 31(2)(a) of the Vienna Convention.

Article 32 of the Vienna Convention stipulates the rule of supplementary means of interpretation, which can be applied when the interpretation in accordance with Article 31 leaves 'the meaning ambiguous or obscure' or 'leads to a result which is manifestly absurd or unreasonable'. The two specific means which can be employed for interpretation are: (1) 'preparatory work of the treaty' and (2) 'circumstances of its conclusion'.

4.3. International Treatment of Education-Related Limitations and Exceptions

The terms 'limitation' and 'exception' are often used interchangeably. The limitations can be understood as a liability rule that makes acts permissible subject to an obligation, while 'exceptions' are the outright exemptions from the copyright liability. Different legal systems have employed various terms to describe limitations and exceptions. In the United Kingdom, the Copyright, Designs and Patents Act 1988 uses the term 'acts permitted' in chapter III, while India has used the term 'certain acts' in section 52 of the Copyright Act, 1957. The United States has employed the term 'fair use' to examine whether the use of copyrighted work has infringed copyright or not. Here, the 'limitations and exceptions' are discussed in relation to the Berne Convention and the TRIPS Agreement framework.

[148] *United States-Section 110(5) of the US Copyright Act*, WTO doc WT/DS 160/R (15 June 2000) (Report of the Panel).

The Berne Convention embodies two kinds of limitations and exceptions: compensated limitations and uncompensated limitations. Compensated limitations are those in which the user does not require permission of the copyright owner, and the owner is authorized to receive remuneration for the use made. These compensated limitations are positioned somewhere between the exclusive rights of the owner and absolute exemptions on copyright.[149] The Berne Convention recognizes compensated limitations (statutory licences) for broadcasting and cable retransmission (Article 11*bis* (2)) and mechanical recording of musical works (Article 13). Moreover, the Berne Appendix provides some special provisions for compulsory licensing for translation and reproduction of printed works, which can be invoked by developing countries. But unfortunately, these provisions have remained unused due to the complexities of the provisions and administrative burden on the users.[150]

On the other hand, uncompensated limitations are meant for those uses which are not 'considered part of the legitimate scope of the author's proprietary grant'.[151] Uncompensated limitations are mainly concerned with the activities that aim at 'promoting or securing liberty interests'.[152] These limitations ensure that certain uses of copyrighted works are beyond the owner's control and can be undertaken by users at no cost.[153] The Berne Convention has some provisions for uncompensated limitations on exclusive rights which include: disseminations of public lectures and addresses (Article 2*bis*(2)), quotations (Article 10(1)), teaching purposes (Article 10(2)), reproduction by the press (Article 10*bis* (1)), reporting of current events (Article 10*bis* (2)), and ephemeral recordings by broadcasting organizations (Article 11*bis* (3)). These provisions

[149] Paul Goldstein and P. Bernt Hugenholtz, *International Copyright: Principles, Law and Practice* (OUP 2010) 361.

[150] Adolf Dietz, 'Intellectual Property and Desocialization in Eastern Europe' [1995] 26 Int'l Rev Industrial Property & Copyright L 851, 868.

[151] Paul Goldstein and P. Bernt Hugenholtz, *International Copyright: Principles, Law and Practice* (OUP 2010) 360.

[152] Ruth L. Okediji, 'The Limits of International Copyright Exceptions for Developing Countries' [2019] 21 Vanderbilt J Ent & Tech L 689, 711.

[153] Ruth L. Okediji, 'The Limits of International Copyright Exceptions for Developing Countries' [2019] 21 Vanderbilt J Ent & Tech L 711 (uncompensated limitations encourage the liberal exercise of personal freedoms and encourage markets for book reviews, commentary, and criticism, which leaves the basic building blocks of creativity in the public domain).

merely address the purpose of use and leave the member states at their discretion to implement at the national level.

In addition to the explicit provisions on permissible limitations and exceptions that are contained in the Berne Convention, there are some exceptions that are implied.[154] Such exceptions are known as 'minor reservations' or 'minor exceptions', and they largely concern *de minimus* uses such as the use of works during religious ceremonies or use by military bands.[155] Minor reservations fall into two categories: (1) in relation to performing, recitation, broadcasting, recording, and cinematographic rights, and (2) in relation to translation.[156]

Since this book deals with access to knowledge, it is a must to examine how limitations and exceptions in the international framework, in particular the Berne Convention and the TRIPS Agreement, have addressed the needs of education. Education occupies one of the most important places in the field of public interest. The WCT, in its preamble, refers to education as being in the public interest, stating that there is 'the need to maintain a balance between the rights of authors and the larger public interest, particularly education, research and access to information, as reflected in the Berne Convention'.[157] Through revisions, the Berne Convention has created some exceptions and limitations to foster educational uses for the benefit of a larger section of society. Despite the efforts made by the Convention, educational limitations and exceptions fail to prepare citizens for a knowledge economy.[158]

There exists not even a single exception for 'education' in the Berne/TRIPS framework.[159] Yet, some limitations and exceptions concern the activities related to education, such as making quotations from a work already lawfully made available to the public,[160] and for teaching

[154] *United States-Section 110(5) of the US Copyright Act*, WTO doc WT/DS 160/R (15 June 2000) (Report of the Panel) paras 6.48–6.49 ('This possibility, available to all Berne Union members, to provide exceptions to certain exclusive rights is most often referred to as "minor reservations" doctrine').

[155] Martin Senftleben, *Copyright, Limitations and the Three-Step Test* (Kluwer 2004) 198–201.

[156] Martin Senftleben, *Copyright, Limitations and the Three-Step Test* (Kluwer 2004) 198–201.

[157] WIPO Copyright Treaty 1996, preamble.

[158] William McGeveran and William W. Fisher, *The Digital Learning Challenge: Obstacles to Educational Uses of Copyrighted Material in the Digital Age* (Berkman Centre for Internet and Society. Harvard University 2006) 22.

[159] Ruth L. Okediji, 'The Limits of International Copyright Exceptions for Developing Countries' [2019] 21 Vanderbilt J Ent & Tech L 689, 726.

[160] Berne Convention 1886, Art 10(1).

purposes.[161] Moreover, there are some limitations and exceptions that provide for compulsory licensing for educational reproduction and translations.[162] However, there is no particular provision for educational institutions to reproduce or distribute work in the form of instructional material. Moreover, there are no provisions for the circumvention of technological protection measures or rights management information for educational purposes.[163]

It is a must to begin with identifying and then analysing the 'education-related' limitations and exceptions in the Berne/TRIPS framework. The following subsections discuss the provisions that inadequately and remotely serve the learning needs of countries.

4.3.1. Quotation

A quotation or an excerpt is an integral part of education and is required 'to illustrate a theme or defend some proposition or to review or criticise the work quoted'.[164] The provision allowing the use of quotations was added in the Brussels revision of 1948, where contracting states agreed that 'it shall be permissible in all countries of the Union to make short quotations from newspaper articles and periodicals' as well as to include them in press summaries, along with the requirement to acknowledge the source of the quotation or excerpt and the name of the author. In 1967, the Stockholm revision extended the right to use quotations to all works, provided that the use was compatible with fair practice and the extent of use was justified by purpose.[165]

Under Article 10(1) of the Berne Convention, it is mandatory for members to provide for an exception for quotation.[166] The Convention

[161] Berne Convention 1886, Art 10(2).

[162] Daniel Seng, *Draft Study on Copy Right Limitations and Exceptions for Educational Activities*, WIPO Doc SCCR/33/6 (WIPO 2016) <www.wipo.int/edocs/mdocs/copyright/en/sccr_33/sccr_33_6.pdf> accessed 30 August 2025.

[163] Ruth L. Okediji, 'The Limits of International Copyright Exceptions for Developing Countries' [2019] 21 Vanderbilt J Ent & Tech L 689, 727.

[164] Claude Masouyé, *Guide to the Berne Convention for the Protection of Literary and Artistic Works (Paris Act 1971)* WIPO Publication No 615(E) (WIPO 1978) 58.

[165] Arpad Bogsch, *First Hundred Years of Berne Convention for the Protection of Literary and Artistic Works* (International Bureau of Intellectual Property WIPO 1986) 233.

[166] Berne Convention 1886, Art 10(1) provides: 'It shall be permissible to make quotations from a work which has already been lawfully made available to the public, provided that their making is compatible with fair practice, and their extent does not exceed that justified by the purpose, including quotations from newspaper articles and periodicals in the form of press summaries.'

has imposed three limitations on the use. First, the work must have been lawfully made available to the public, which means that the provision does not give the right to make quotations from unpublished works.[167] Second, the use must be compatible with fair use.[168] Third, the extent of the quotation must 'not exceed that justified by the purpose'.[169] The provision does not limit the use of quotation to literary work; it can be from 'a lecture, performance or broadcast, as in a material form such as a book, Article or visual work of art'.[170] Though Article 10(1) states a mandatory limitation, the member countries are free to impose their own conditions to permit the use of quotations of copyrighted works.

4.3.2. Teaching

The most straightforward exception to educational use is the teaching exception, given in Article 10(2) of the Berne Convention. Just like Article 10(1), this provision was introduced in the Brussels revision in 1948, and some further changes were brought in the Stockholm Conference 1948. Article 10(2) of the Berne Convention provides as follows:

> It shall be a matter for legislation in the countries of the Union, and for special agreements existing or to be concluded between them, to permit the utilization, to the extent justified by the purpose, of literary or artistic works by way of illustration in publications, broadcasts or sound or visual recordings for teaching, provided that such utilization is compatible with fair practice.

[167] Claude Masouyé, *Guide to the Berne Convention for the Protection of Literary and Artistic Works (Paris Act 1971)* WIPO Publication No 615(E) (WIPO 1978) 58.

[168] Claude Masouyé, *Guide to the Berne Convention for the Protection of Literary and Artistic Works (Paris Act 1971)* WIPO Publication No 615(E) (WIPO 1978) 58; Paul Goldstein and P. Bernt Hugenholtz, *International Copyright: Principles, Law and Practice* (OUP 2010) 379.

[169] Claude Masouyé, *Guide to the Berne Convention for the Protection of Literary and Artistic Works (Paris Act 1971)* WIPO Publication No 615(E) (WIPO 1978) 59 (the word 'short', which appeared in the Brussels text of 1948, disappeared later. The quotations were not meant to be long works; but 'it is a question of proportion and there are cases where quite large extracts from articles or speeches fall to be quoted'); Sam Ricketson, *WIPO Study on Limitations and Exceptions of Copyright and Related Rights in the Digital Environment*, WIPO Doc SCCR/9/7 (5 April 2003) 12 (at present, no limitation is placed on the length of quotation although it is subject to the general criterion of purpose and fair practice; sometimes, lengthy quotations are consistent with the criterion of fair practice as in the case of critical review or work of scholarship).

[170] Sam Ricketson, *WIPO Study on Limitations and Exceptions of Copyright and Related Rights in the Digital Environment*, WIPO Doc SCCR/9/7 (5 April 2003) 12.

The provision permits the use of literary and artistic works as illustrations for the purpose of teaching.[171] The provision leaves it to the discretion of members to decide the 'utilization . . . of works for teaching'.[172] The limitation permits the use of literary and artistic works at all levels of education, provided the use made is compatible with fair practice.[173]

As in Article 10(1), the conditions imposed in Article 10(2) are also general and open-ended, stating no mandatory quantitative limitations. The provision requires that the permitted use of literary or artistic work must be in consonance with 'fair practice'. The term 'fair practice' has not been defined in the Berne Convention. However, the Guide to the Berne Convention explains that 'compatibility with fair practice' means an 'objective appreciation of what is normally considered admissible'.[174] The fairness has to be ultimately decided by courts, which considers the question of proportionality of the extracts of the actual work and the extent to which the new work competes with old works in terms of its sales and circulation.[175] The concept of fair practice needs to be interpreted in the light of the three-step test given in Article 9(2) of the Berne Convention for a better understanding.

Moreover, Article 10(3) re-states the moral rights and requires the legislation to have a condition that the source of the work has to be cited, if it appears in the work.[176] Article 6*bis*(1) gives the right of attribution

[171] Muhammad Masum Billah and Saleh Albarashdi, 'Fair or Free Use of Copyrighted Materials in Education and Research and the Limit of Such Use' [2018] 17 Chicago-Kent Journal of Intellectual Property 422, 424.

[172] Sam Ricketson, *WIPO Study on Limitations and Exceptions of Copyright and Related Rights in the Digital Environment*, WIPO Doc SCCR/9/7 (5 April 2003) 14.

[173] Arpad Bogsch, *First Hundred Years of Berne Convention for the Protection of Literary and Artistic Works* (International Bureau of Intellectual Property WIPO 1986) 1148. (Records from the Stockholm Conference (1967) reveal the views of Committee: '[I]t should be made clear in this Report that the word "teaching" was to include teaching at all levels–in educational institutions and universities, municipal and State schools, and private schools. Education outside these institutions, for instance general teaching available to the general public but not included in the above categories, should be excluded'.)

[174] Claude Masouyé, *Guide to the Berne Convention for the Protection of Literary and Artistic Works (Paris Act 1971)* WIPO Publication No 615(E) (WIPO 1978) 59.

[175] Muhammad Masum Billah and Saleh Albarashdi, 'Fair or Free Use of Copyrighted Materials in Education and Research and the Limit of Such Use' [2018] 17 Chicago-Kent Journal of Intellectual Property 422, 428; Claude Masouyé, *Guide to the Berne Convention for the Protection of Literary and Artistic Works (Paris Act 1971)* WIPO Publication No 615(E) (WIPO 1978) 59.

[176] Berne Convention 1886, Art 10(3) reads as: 'Where use is made of works in accordance with the preceding paragraphs of this Article, mention shall be made of the source, and of the name of the author if it appears thereon.'

and integrity to authors.[177] This tautology raises a question of whether Article 10 is excluded from the applicability of Article 6*bis*, though the delegates agreed at the 1967 Revision Conference that 'Article 6*bis* applied in respect of exceptions authorized by the Convention, including Article 10'.[178]

However, the reason for a separate provision on moral rights in Article 10 can also be concluded from the fact that modifications and alterations are required in a work for teaching purposes, and unlike Article 6*bis*, the right of integrity is not promised under Article 10. Moreover, Article 10(3) requires not merely attribution of the author's name but also acknowledgement of the full publication details, including the name of the volume in which it appears. Hence, Article 6*bis* is insufficient to serve the teaching purposes of Article 10.

4.3.3. Private Use

The Berne/TRIPS framework does not address the 'personal use' limitation directly. Nevertheless, it is regarded as the most far-reaching limitation to the reproduction right. Most of the Berne Union members have recognized this limitation in their national copyright legislation. Some countries have construed this limitation to include 'research purposes'. In contrast, other countries went ahead to distinguish between 'private' and 'personal research purposes' and whether the research involves any commercial purposes.[179] Section 178 of the Copyright, Designs and Patents Act 1988 defines 'private study' as excluding study conducted for any direct or indirect commercial purpose.

The records of the Conference and various proposals by the delegation indicate that they were considering the expression 'private use' to

[177] Berne Convention 1886, Art 6bis (1), reads as: 'Independently of the author's economic rights, and even after the transfer of the said rights, the author shall have the right to claim authorship of the work and to object to any distortion, mutilation or other modification of, or other derogatory action in relation to, the said work, which would be prejudicial to his honor or reputation.'

[178] *Records of the Intellectual Property Conference of Stockholm, June 11 to July 14, 1967* (WIPO 1971) 1165.

[179] Ruth L. Okediji, 'The International Copyright System: Limitations, Exceptions and Public Interest Considerations for Developing Countries' [2006] International Centre for Trade and Sustainable Development (ICTSD) and United Nations Conference on Trade and Development (UNCTAD) 20.

be incorporated as an exception under Article 9(2). To this end, the Committee suggested the draft of Article 9(2) as follows:

> It shall be a matter for legislation in the countries of the Union to permit the reproduction of such works: (a) *for private use*; (b) for judicial or administrative purposes; (c) in certain particular cases where the reproduction is not contrary to the legitimate interests of the author.[180]

The 'private use' limitation appears in a variety of forms at the national level, fulfilling a variety of functions, including research. The Copyright Act, 1957 of India permits 'fair dealing with any work, not being a computer programme, for private or personal use – including research'.[181] The Chinese Copyright Act allows a work to be exploited without permission for the 'purposes of the user's own private study, research or entertainment'.[182] The Japanese Copyright Law permits reproducing a work for 'personal use, family use, or similar uses within a limited circle'.[183] The Italian law allows reproduction of a work 'when made by hand or by means of reproduction unsuitable for marketing or disseminating the work in public'.[184] German law allows single copies of a work to be made for 'personal scientific use' and 'other private use'.

The Berne/TRIPS framework does not encompass an adequate number of limitations for educational purposes while national laws have a broader range of limitations and exceptions related to educational uses, including: private or personal use (for personal education and research purpose), quotations, reproduction for educational purpose, educational publications (in the form of instructional material by the educational institution), school performances, educational communications (which

180 *Records of the Intellectual Property Conference of Stockholm, June 11 to July 14, 1967* (WIPO 1971) 857. During the Sixth meeting of the Main Committee, France made a proposal that the expression 'private use' should be replaced by 'personal use' because the term 'private' may give way to an extensive interpretation. The United Kingdom expressed that the use of the term 'private use' in paragraph II carries many dangers for authors and publishers because the majority of books are for private purposes and the term 'private use' can allow the wholesale use of copyrighted material, without any payment, by large industrial organizations or for government educational systems.

181 The Copyright Act 1957, s 52.

182 Copyright Law of the People's Republic of China 2010, sec 4, Art 22.

183 Copyright Act 1970, Art 30.

184 Italian Copyright Statute 1941, Art 68(1).

include broadcasts, cable transmissions, the making of recordings of such communications and performances, and online distance learning), and compulsory licensing for reproduction and translation.[185]

4.4. The Three-Step Test

Apart from the expressed limitations recognized in the Berne Convention, Article 9(2) of the Berne Convention contains a provision for unspecified limitations subject to a loosely circumscribed standard, called the 'three-step test'. In the Stockholm revision of the Berne Convention, the 'three-step test' was invented to limit the extent to which members could create limitations and exceptions to the right to reproduce.[186] Article 9(2) of the Berne Convention provides that:

> It shall be a matter for legislation in the countries of the Union to permit the reproduction of such works in certain special cases, provided that such reproduction does not conflict with a normal exploitation of the work and does not unreasonably prejudice the legitimate interests of the author.

Inspired by the Berne Convention, a similar provision in Article 13 of the TRIPS Agreement reads as:

> Members shall confine limitations or exceptions to exclusive rights to certain special cases which do not conflict with a normal exploitation of the work and do not unreasonably prejudice the legitimate interests of the right holder.

Both provisions are worded in general terms and create difficulty in interpreting the scope of the provision and the meaning of the three

[185] Daniel Seng, *Draft Study on Copy Right Limitations and Exceptions for Educational Activities*, WIPO Doc SCCR/33/6 (WIPO 2016) <www.wipo.int/edocs/mdocs/copyright/en/sccr_33/sccr_33_6.pdf> accessed 30 August 2025.

[186] Ruth L. Okediji, 'Reframing International Copyright Limitations and Exceptions as Development Policy' in Ruth Okediji (ed) *Copyright Law in an Age of Limitations and Exceptions* (CUP 2017) 444.

distinct conditions stipulated in the provision.[187] Article 9(2) of the Berne Convention and Article 13 of the TRIPS Agreement are known to be the most controversial provisions, and there have been extensive debates across the world on their exact meaning.[188]

4.5. Article 13 of TRIPS vis-a-vis Article 9(2) of the Berne Convention

Although Article 13 of the TRIPS Agreement is inspired by Article 9(2) of the Berne Convention and has employed similar language, there exist some key differences between the two provisions that affect the applicability of the limitations and exceptions by the member countries.

The first difference is that the Berne Convention permits limitations and exceptions to the reproduction rights of literary and artistic works, while Article 13 of the TRIPS Agreement is not limited merely to reproduction rights but rather covers all exclusive rights, including the rental rights conferred in TRIPS, hence it broadens the scope of exceptions beyond what the Convention provides for.[189]

For the first time, this difference was acknowledged by the WTO panel in *United States – Section 110(5) of the US Copyright Act*.[190] This provision

[187] Carlos M. Correa, *Trade Related Aspects of Intellectual Property Rights: A Commentary on the TRIPS Agreement* (OUP 2007) 135; Christophe Geiger, Daniel Gervais, and Martin Senftleben, 'The Three-Step Test Revisited: How to Use the Test's Flexibility in National Copyright Law' [2014] 29 American University Int'l L Rev 581, 612.

[188] G. Dworkin, 'Exceptions to Copyright Exclusivity: Is Fair Use Consistent with Article 9.2 Berne and the New International Order?' in H Hansen (ed) *International Intellectual Property Law & Policy* (Juris Publishing 2001) 66.

[189] Carlos M. Correa, *Trade Related Aspects of Intellectual Property Rights: A Commentary on the TRIPS Agreement* (OUP 2007) 136. In addition to reproduction right, Article 13 of TRIPS includes: translation [Article 8], public performance [Article 11], broadcasting and other communications [Article 11*bis*], public recitation [Article 11*ter*], and adaptation [Article 12]; Sam Ricketson, *The Three-Step Test, Deemed Quantities, Libraries and Closed Exceptions* (Centre for Copyright Studies 2002) 42; Bruno de Vuyst Lic R, Alea M Fairchild, and Gunther Meyer Lic R, 'Exceptions to Intellectual Property Rights: Lessons from WTO – Trips Panels' [2003] 10 Murdoch University Electronic JL 31; Daniel Gervais, 'The Three-step test' in *(Re)structuring Copyright A Comprehensive Path to International Copyright Reform* (Edward Elgar Publication 2017) 6.

[190] *United States-Section 110(5) of the US Copyright Act*, WTO doc WT/DS 160/R (15 June 2000) (Report of the Panel) para 6.72 ('The language used in Article 13 of the TRIPS Agreement has its origins in the similar language used in Article 9(2) of the Berne Convention (1971), although the latter only applies in the case of the reproduction right'); para 6.74 ('the main

can be viewed as a 'Berne-minus' approach of the TRIPS Agreement that diminishes the rights granted under the Berne Convention. In respect of other Berne Convention rights (exclusive rights apart from the right to reproduction), Article 13 of TRIPS allows the member countries to legislate similar limitations and exceptions in the same manner as given in Article 9(2), provided they conform to Article 2(2) of the TRIPS Agreement[191] and Article 20 of the Berne Convention.[192]

Second, although both provisions are considerably similar in language, Article 13 deviates from Article 9(2) in the opening words. Article 13 limits the use of exceptions by employing the term 'shall confine' limitations or exceptions to exclusive rights, while Article 9(2) of the TRIPS Agreement, and the Berne Convention, allows countries to permit limitations and exceptions in their national legislation.[193] Nowhere has the Berne Convention used the terms 'exceptions' or 'limitations', nor do these expressions exist in any other provision of the Convention.[194] This provision is more rigid than Article 9(2) in the sense that it limits the limitations.[195] The WTO panel expressed its opinion on the scope of the provision by stating that:

> It may be noted at the outset that Article 13 cannot have more than a narrow or limited operation. Its tenor, consistent as it is with the

difference between Article 9(2) of the Berne Convention (1971) and Article 13 of the TRIPS Agreement is that the former applies only to the reproduction right').

[191] TRIPS Agreement1994, art2(2) reads as:

> Nothing in Parts I to IV of this Agreement shall derogate from existing obligations that Members may have to each other under the Paris Convention, the Berne Convention, the Rome Convention and the Treaty on Intellectual Property in Respect of Integrated Circuits.

[192] Berne Convention 1886, Art 20 reads as:

> The Governments of the countries of the Union reserve the right to enter into special agreements among themselves, in so far as such agreements grant to authors more extensive rights than those granted by the Convention, or contain other provisions not contrary to this Convention. The provisions of existing agreements which satisfy these conditions shall remain applicable.

[193] Susan Isiko Straba, *International Copyright Law and Access to Education in Developing Countries* (Martinus Nijhoff Publishers 2012) 63.

[194] Sam Ricketson, *The Three-Step Test, Deemed Quantities, Libraries and Closed Exceptions* (Centre for Copyright Studies 2002) 44.

[195] Susan Isiko Straba, *International Copyright Law and Access to Education in Developing Countries* (Martinus Nijhoff Publishers 2012) 63.

provisions of Article 9(2) of the Berne Convention (1971), discloses that it was not intended to provide for exceptions or limitations except for those of a limited nature.[196]

Third, the last segment of the Berne Convention provision refers to the 'legitimate interests of the author', which means it includes both economic (monetary interests) and moral rights (non-monetary interests) of the author and successor in title.[197] The TRIPS provision has broadened the interests of users by referring to the term 'legitimate interests of the right holder'. Following this difference, it is possible that an exception to the reproduction right under Article 13 of TRIPS can be violative of Article 9(2) of the Berne Convention, as it does not require the attribution of authorship.[198] It is important to consider Article 2(2) of the TRIPS Agreement, which underlines the intention of members not to derogate from their existing obligations under the Berne Convention. Reading Article 2(2) along with Article 9(1) of TRIPS makes it clear that any such exception would not contravene Article 13 *simpliciter*, but it is certainly a derogation from the existing obligations given under Article 6*bis* of the Berne Convention. Hence, it would be in contravention of the Berne Convention if such a country were a member of the Berne Convention but not of TRIPS.[199]

As per Article 2(2) of TRIPS and Article 20 of the Berne Convention, any limitation or exception under Article 13 of TRIPS has to be in consonance with Articles 1 to 21 of the Berne Convention.[200] Any Berne Convention member framing its limitations and exceptions, which is also a member of the TRIPS Agreement, has to be consistent with the express and implied exceptions mentioned in the Berne Convention.[201]

[196] *United States-Section 110(5) of the US Copyright Act*, WTO doc WT/DS 160/R (15 June 2000) (Report of the Panel) para 6.97.

[197] Carlos M. Correa, *Trade Related Aspects of Intellectual Property Rights: A Commentary on the TRIPS Agreement* (OUP 2007) 136; Sam Ricketson, *The Three-Step Test, Deemed Quantities, Libraries and Closed Exceptions* (Centre for Copyright Studies 2002) 5.

[198] Sam Ricketson, *WIPO Study on Limitations and Exceptions of Copyright and Related Rights in the Digital Environment*, WIPO Doc SCCR/9/7 (5 April 2003) 49.

[199] Sam Ricketson, *WIPO Study on Limitations and Exceptions of Copyright and Related Rights in the Digital Environment*, WIPO Doc SCCR/9/7 (5 April 2003) 49.

[200] Paul Goldstein and P. Bernt Hugenholtz, *International Copyright: Principles, Law and Practice* (OUP 2010) 364.

[201] Sam Ricketson, *WIPO Study on Limitations and Exceptions of Copyright and Related Rights in the Digital Environment*, WIPO Doc SCCR/9/7 (5 April 2003) 50 (already established

However, in light of Articles 2(2) and 9(1) of the TRIPS Agreement, the limitations contemplated in the Convention would always prevail, in case of any deviation from them.[202]

This interpretation further leads us to a crucial issue: Does Article 13 of TRIPS make any extra addition to the limitations and exceptions that are permissible under Articles 1 to 21 of the Berne Convention? Ricketson analyses how 'provisions that extend the scope of existing Berne limitations and exceptions, even though otherwise sustainable under Article 13 of TRIPS', will not be acceptable and will stand in violation of Article 2(2) of the Berne Convention.[203]

Article 13 is referred to as a 'Berne-plus' element because of its close connection with Article 20 of the Berne Convention.[204] As already emphasized, Article 20 of the Berne Convention plays an important role in the TRIPS Agreement as its provisions are to be interpreted in a way that does not contravene the Berne standards. Senftleben refers to Article 13 as 'an additional hurdle which exemptions from exclusive rights have to surmount to be permissible'. Holding a different view on Article 13, Correa stated:

> The argument that Article 13 would be an additional requirement, a 'Berne plus' solution, would also certainly defeat those who have argued for keeping (if not expanding) the room for socially valuable acts, such as fair use. Despite its narrow wording, Article 13 is the only window left in Section 1 of the TRIPS Agreement for allowing members certain flexibility in recognizing and enforcing rights covered (through

exceptions—such as teaching, news reporting exceptions under Article 10 and 10 *bis*, restrictions on broadcasting under Article 11*bis* (2), and the 'minor exceptions' which are implied exceptions in the text of Convention—have to be conformed to by any country framing its limitations and exceptions under Article 13 of TRIPS).

[202] Carlos M. Correa, *Trade Related Aspects of Intellectual Property Rights: A Commentary on the TRIPS Agreement* (OUP 2007) 138.

[203] Sam Ricketson, *WIPO Study on Limitations and Exceptions of Copyright and Related Rights in the Digital Environment*, WIPO Doc SCCR/9/7 (5 April 2003) 51 (Ricketson applies the legal maxim *ex specialis legi generali deroga*, which means that a specific law can override the general law, not vice versa).

[204] Christophe Geiger, Daniel Gervais, and Martin Senftleben, 'The Three-Step Test Revisited: How to Use the Test's Flexibility in National Copyright Law' [2014] 29 American University Int'l L Rev 581 (authors refer to Article 13 as an 'additional safeguard').

> incorporation of the Berne Convention) in the Agreement, and the capacity to balance private and public interests.[205]

Reflecting upon the function of copyright law, Correa expresses that copyright law aims not at ensuring a maximum monetary profit to the owner, but at balancing the rights of authors to obtain a fair return and society's interest in access to and use of information.[206]

4.6. Interpretation of Three Criteria

After evaluating the relation between Article 13 of the TRIPS Agreement and Article 9(2) of the Berne Convention, the task of interpreting each of the three criteria must be fulfilled. For a limitation or exception to be consistent with the three-step provision of the Berne/TRIPS Agreement, all three conditions must be fulfilled cumulatively. The interpretative analysis of the expressions 'certain special cases', 'conflict with a normal exploitation of the work', and 'unreasonably prejudice the legitimate interests of the authors' follows.

4.6.1. Certain Special Cases

Before analysing the first prong, it must be noted that during the Stockholm Conference, the Committee received a proposal from the Drafting Committee that the second condition must be placed before the first one because it would offer a more logical sequence for the interpretation of the rule. The Committee expressed that:

> If it is considered that reproduction conflicts with the normal exploitation of the work, reproduction is not permitted at all. If it is considered that reproduction does not conflict with the normal exploitation of the work, the next step would be to consider whether it does not unreasonably prejudice the legitimate interests of the author. Only if such is not

[205] Carlos M. Correa, *Trade Related Aspects of Intellectual Property Rights: A Commentary on the TRIPS Agreement* (OUP 2007) 140.
[206] Carlos M. Correa, *Trade Related Aspects of Intellectual Property Rights: A Commentary on the TRIPS Agreement* (OUP 2007) 140.

> the case would it be possible in certain special cases to introduce a compulsory license, or to provide for use without payment.[207]

The three-step test finds its expression in Article 9(2) of the Berne Convention, in the wording 'It shall be a matter for legislation in the countries of the Union to permit the reproduction of such works in certain special cases'. Similar language is contained in Article 13 of the TRIPS Agreement: 'Members shall confine limitations or exceptions to exclusive rights to certain special cases.' The first prerequisite for limitations is that the reproductions may be allowed only in 'certain special cases'. It leads to the question: What would be the meaning of the term 'certain' in context? The first step is to ascertain the ordinary meaning of the word 'certain'. The ordinary meaning of 'certain' is fixed, settled, assured in mind or action. The WTO panel in *United States-Section 110(5) of the US Copyright Act* expressed that 'certain' means 'known and particularized, but not explicitly identified, determined, fixed, not variable; definitive, precise, exact'.[208] It was expressed that the member countries must clearly define their limitations or exceptions. The panel further elaborated that it is not required 'to identify each and every possible situation to which the exception could apply, provided that the scope of the exception is known and particularized'.[209]

As far as the term 'special' is concerned, it connotes 'not ordinary or usual', 'having a particular purpose', 'distinguished by some unusual quality', unique, extraordinary, distinctive in some way, or exceptional in quality or degree. The WTO panel explained the meaning of 'special':

> The term 'special' connotes 'having an individual or limited application or purpose', 'containing details; precise, specific', 'exceptional in quality or degree; unusual; out of the ordinary' or 'distinctive in some way'. This term means that more is needed than a clear definition to meet the

[207] Arpad Bogsch, *First Hundred Years of Berne Convention for the Protection of Literary and Artistic Works* (International Bureau of Intellectual Property WIPO 1986) 1145.
[208] *United States-Section 110(5) of the US Copyright Act*, WTO doc WT/DS 160/R (15 June 2000) (Report of the Panel) para 6.108.
[209] *United States-Section 110(5) of the US Copyright Act*, WTO doc WT/DS 160/R (15 June 2000) (Report of the Panel) para 6.108.

> standard of the first condition. In addition, an exception or limitation must be limited in its field of application or exceptional in its scope. In other words, an exception or limitation should be narrow in quantitative as well as a qualitative sense. This suggests a narrow scope as well as an exceptional or distinctive objective. To put this aspect of the first condition into the context of the second condition ('no conflict with a normal exploitation'), an exception or limitation should be the opposite of a non-special, i.e., a normal case.[210]

The panel explained the ordinary meaning of the third element 'case' as:

> an 'occurrence', 'circumstance' or 'event' or 'fact' [footnote omitted]. For example, in the context of the dispute at hand, the 'case' could be described in terms of beneficiaries of the exceptions, equipment used, types of works, or by other factors.[211]

Hence, the two adjectives in the first filter require the limitation and exception to be clearly defined (certain) and narrow in its scope and reach (special). This interpretation sounds harmonious with the purpose of the Berne Convention established in Article 1 that the 'countries to which this Convention applies constitute a Union for the protection of the rights of authors in their literary and artistic works'.[212] Ricketson makes a detailed analysis of the first filter; his analysis is a two-prong reading: first, the exceptions should be for a specific purpose and should not consist of a broad range of subject matter, and second, the exception must be founded on a clear reason of public policy or some other exceptional circumstances.[213] Ricketson contended:

210 *United States-Section 110(5) of the US Copyright Act*, WTO doc WT/DS 160/R (15 June 2000) (Report of the Panel) para 6.109.
211 *United States-Section 110(5) of the US Copyright Act*, WTO doc WT/DS 160/R (15 June 2000) (Report of the Panel) para 6.110.
212 Sam Ricketson, *The Three-Step Test, Deemed Quantities, Libraries and Closed Exceptions* (Centre for Copyright Studies 2002) 33. Ricketson, *WIPO Study on Limitations and Exceptions of Copyright and Related Rights in the Digital Environment*, WIPO Doc SCCR/9/7 (5 April 2003) 22.
213 Sam Ricketson, *The Berne Convention for the Protection of Literary and Artistic Works: 1886-1986* (Kluwer 1987).

> Does the phrase 'certain special cases' also require that there should be some 'special purpose' or justification underlying the exceptions that are made in a national law? This has been suggested by several commentators, including myself, but is a matter on which other commentators are silent. Furthermore, although the WTO panel on the 'homestyle' exception used the adjectives 'exceptional' and 'distinctive' in this context (see the passage quoted above), it nonetheless took some pains to indicate that it was not thereby equating the term 'certain special cases' with 'special purpose'. While the panel was dealing here with a different international agreement, namely TRIPS, the language of Article 13 is the same as Article 9(2) and a number of commentators have argued that the first step should receive the same interpretation under both instruments.[214]

Relying on the WTO panel's decision, Ginsburg rejects 'certain special cases' as a normative connotation, noting that 'Art. 9(2) creates a hierarchy of analysis—that is, step one is the threshold to be crossed before analysis of the other criteria may be undertaken—an adjudicator would not need to reach the question of "normal exploitation" if the "certain special cases" condition were not satisfied'.[215] It is worth noting that subsequent to the panel report, Ricketson changed his view and agreed with Ginsburg that 'special cases' should not be interpreted as requiring 'special purpose' underlying it.[216]

The next question is whether 'open-ended exceptions' like the fair use doctrine would be compatible with the first step or not? The flexible and multipurpose fair use doctrine is recognized to have a qualitatively broader scope of limitations and exceptions, which leaves to courts the job of elaborating what is permissible on specific occasions.[217] There are

[214] Sam Ricketson, *The Three-Step Test, Deemed Quantities, Libraries and Closed Exceptions* (Centre for Copyright Studies 2002) 29.

[215] Jane C. Ginsburg, 'Toward Supranational Copyright Law? The WTO Panel Decision and The "Three-Step Test" For Copyright Exceptions' [2001] *Revue Internationale Du Droit D'auteur* 12. See also *United States-Section 110(5) of the US Copyright Act*, WTO doc WT/DS 160/R (15 June 2000) (Report of the Panel) para 6.160.

[216] Sam Ricketson, *WIPO Study on Limitations and Exceptions of Copyright and Related Rights in the Digital Environment*, WIPO Doc SCCR/9/7 (5 April 2003) 22.

[217] Carlos M. Correa, *Trade Related Aspects of Intellectual Property Rights: A Commentary on the TRIPS Agreement* (OUP 2007) 141; Paul Goldstein and P. Bernt Hugenholtz, *International Copyright: Principles, Law and Practice* (OUP 2010) 362 (the narrower fair dealing provisions in

various opinions on fair use exceptions, which also reveal their impact on the interests of larger sections of society. Professor Okediji has observed that 'the fair use doctrine is a broad exception to the rights granted to authors under the Copyright Act; it clearly is not limited to 'special' cases, unless one argues that special cases are of an ilk that has to do with an identified important policy objective'. Professor Correa argued that the US has stoutly defended the compatibility of the fair use doctrine with the TRIPS Agreement.[218] Some have viewed the fair use doctrine as a rule allowing courts to craft exceptions in different instances.[219] A suggestion made by Gervais is worth nothing, namely that an open-ended exception in US copyright law may seem semantically incompatible with the first filter of the test, but it does not mean that it is normatively incompatible.[220] Hence, we need to view the test as three steps forming a whole, for justifying the legislative perspective on open-ended limitations or exceptions.[221]

While discussing the fair use doctrine, it would be equally important to examine the fair dealing provisions in India and the UK. In these countries, fair dealing of copyrighted works is permitted for purposes such as research or private study, criticism and review, and for reporting current events. These provisions deal with those instances that are specifically regulated in the Berne Convention, viz. Article 10(1) and Article 10*bis* of the Convention and have been merged in the fair dealing provision.[222] Senftleben elucidates that as far as the making use of quotations for the purpose of reviewing, criticism, and the reporting of current events is concerned, it 'automatically' establishes itself as a special case for the

the common law countries do not confer upon courts the same open-ended authority to resolve cases outside the specific categories).

[218] Carlos M. Correa, *Trade Related Aspects of Intellectual Property Rights: A Commentary on the TRIPS Agreement* (OUP 2007) 142.

[219] Pamela Samuelson, 'Unbundling Fair Uses' 77 Fordham L Rev 2537 (2009); Justin Hughes, 'Fair Use and its Politics – At Home and Abroad' In Ruth Okediji (ed) *Copyright in an Age of Exceptions and Limitations* (CUP 2017).

[220] Daniel Gervais, *The TRIPS Agreement: Drafting History and Analysis* (4th edn, Sweet & Maxwell 2012) 283.

[221] Christophe Geiger, Daniel Gervais, and Martin Senftleben, 'The Three-Step Test Revisited: How to Use the Test's Flexibility in National Copyright Law' 29 American University Int'l L Rev 581–626 (2014).

[222] Martin Senftleben, *Copyright, Limitations and the Three-Step Test* (Kluwer 2004) 165.

purpose of the three-step test.[223] For research and private study purposes, Senftleben relies on his conclusion about personal use, wherein he mentions that limitations allowing the use of work for 'personal study, learning and enjoyment in privacy' can be qualified as a special case.[224] Therefore, dealing with copyrighted works for the purpose of research and private study will fall under 'strictly personal use' and pass the first filter of the test.

4.6.2. Conflict with the Normal Exploitation of the Work

Limitations that are 'certain special cases' must not 'conflict with normal exploitation of work'. Applying the same form of analysis, it is necessary to ascertain what constitutes normal exploitation. Relying on the Oxford Dictionary meaning, the WTO panel defined 'exploitation' as 'making use of' or 'utilising for one's own ends'.[225] The term 'normal' is defined as 'constituting or conforming to a type or standard; regular, usual, typical, ordinary, conventional'.[226] These definitions take us to a tricky question: What would be a 'normal exploitation'? The WTO panel expressed that there are two connotations of the word 'normal'. The first one has an empirical nature, i.e., what is regular, usual, typical, or ordinary. The other one appears to have a normative nature, i.e., conforming to a type or standard.[227] Instead of adopting any single approach, the panel preferred to adopt a harmonious interpretation by combining empirical with a normative approach.[228]

To understand the meaning of 'normal exploitation', it would be pertinent to know the views of the Committee of the Stockholm Conference 1967, which expressed its apprehension that private copying can erode

[223] Martin Senftleben, *Copyright, Limitations and the Three-Step Test* (Kluwer 2004) 165.
[224] Martin Senftleben, *Copyright, Limitations and the Three-Step Test* (Kluwer 2004) 162.
[225] *United States-Section 110(5) of the US Copyright Act*, WTO doc WT/DS 160/R (15 June 2000) (Report of the Panel) para 165 (the panel illustrated that 'exploitation' of a musical work would mean any activity by which copyright owner employs his exclusive right to make monetary profits out of it).
[226] *United States-Section 110(5) of the US Copyright Act*, WTO doc WT/DS 160/R (15 June 2000) (Report of the Panel) para 6.166.
[227] *United States-Section 110(5) of the US Copyright Act*, WTO doc WT/DS 160/R (15 June 2000) (Report of the Panel) para 6.166.
[228] *United States-Section 110(5) of the US Copyright Act*, WTO doc WT/DS 160/R (15 June 2000) (Report of the Panel) para 6.166.

the reproduction right.[229] The panel considered the views of Main Committee I during the Stockholm Conference 1967 and concluded that normal exploitation is not equivalent to full use of an exclusive right, as this would question the nature of the exception.[230]

Regarding the second requirement, Paul Goldstein has expressed that it aims to 'fortify authors' interests in their accustomed markets against local legislative inroads'.[231] Similarly, Ricketson also stated that an exception would not conflict with normal exploitation of a work if it does not enter into economic competition (present or potential) with the non-exempted use.[232]

4.6.3. Unreasonable Prejudice to the Legitimate Interests

Apart from not being in conflict with the normal exploitation of a work, the use must also not unreasonably prejudice the legitimate interests of the right holder. The last criterion is framed differently in the Berne Convention and the TRIPS Agreement. Article 9(2) of the Berne Convention provides that the use in order to be permissible must not unreasonably prejudice the legitimate interests of the author, while Article 13 of the TRIPS Agreement refers to the expression 'legitimate interests of the right holders'. At times, an author and right holder can be the same person, but in many cases, it will not be so, and this inconsistency between the two provisions impacts the application of the three-step test. This step is comprised of three elements. First, it concerns the author's

[229] Arpad Bogsch, *First Hundred Years of Berne Convention for the Protection of Literary and Artistic Works* (International Bureau of Intellectual Property WIPO 1986) 1145. The Committee stated:

> A practical example may be photocopying for various purposes. If it consists of producing a very large number of copies, it may not be permitted, as it conflicts with a normal exploitation of the work. If it implies a rather large number of copies for use in industrial undertakings, it may not unreasonably prejudice the legitimate interests of the author, provided that, according to national legislation, an equitable remuneration is paid. If a small number of copies is made, photocopying may be permitted without payment, particularly for individual or scientific use.

[230] *United States-Section 110(5) of the US Copyright Act*, WTO doc WT/DS 160/R (15 June 2000) (Report of the Panel) para 6.167 (stating that 'normal' exploitation clearly means something less than full use of an exclusive right).

[231] Paul Goldstein and P. Bernt Hugenholtz, *International Copyright: Principles, Law and Practice* (OUP 2010) 295.

[232] Sam Ricketson, *The Three-Step Test, Deemed Quantities, Libraries and Closed Exceptions* (Centre for Copyright Studies 2002) 33.

and right holder's interests, not their rights. Second, the ambit of interests is funnelled down to legitimate ones only. Third, prejudice to the legitimate interests *is* permissible to the extent they are not unreasonable.[233]

The term 'legitimate' can be understood in two ways: something which is permitted or authorized by law, or that which is normal, regular, or conformable to a regular standard type.[234] The WTO panel adjudicating on the *United States – Section 110(5)* case holds a legal positivist approach (authorized by law) and normative approach (justifiable and rightful) to interpret the term 'legitimate'. The WTO panel observed that the term 'legitimate':

> relates to lawfulness from a legal positivist perspective, but it has also the connotation of legitimacy from a more normative perspective, in the context of calling for the protection of interests that are justifiable in the light of the objectives that underlie the protection of exclusive rights.[235]

As to the term 'interest', the panel opined that it means a legal right or title to a property or to the use or benefit of a property, but it is not limited to actual or potential value.[236] Hence, the panel intended to include both economic and moral interests, despite an explicit exclusion of Article 6*bis* from the TRIPS Agreement.[237]

Now, the meaning of the last element, i.e., 'unreasonable prejudice', needs to be examined. Relying on the dictionary meaning, the WTO panel defined 'prejudice' as damage, harm, or injury, and prejudice as being 'unreasonable' when it is unequitable, unjustifiable, or unfair because of not being 'proportionate' or 'within the limits of reason, not

[233] Martin Senftleben, *Copyright, Limitations and the Three-Step Test* (Kluwer 2004) 210.

[234] *United States-Section 110(5) of the US Copyright Act*, WTO doc WT/DS 160/R (15 June 2000) (Report of the Panel) para 6.224; see also Daniel J. Gervais, *(Re)structuring Copyright: A Comprehensive Path to International Copyright Reform* (Edward Elgar 2019) 67 (the panel illustrated that it is possible to estimate in economic terms the value of exercising an exclusive right, e.g., by licensing such rights).

[235] *United States-Section 110(5) of the US Copyright Act*, WTO doc WT/DS 160/R (15 June 2000) (Report of the Panel) para 6.224.

[236] *United States-Section 110(5) of the US Copyright Act*, WTO doc WT/DS 160/R (15 June 2000) (Report of the Panel) para 6.223.

[237] Jane C. Ginsburg, 'Toward Supranational Copyright Law? The WTO Panel Decision and the "Three-Step Test" for Copyright Exceptions' [2001] *Revue Internationale Du Droit D'auteur* 8–9.

greatly less or more than might be thought likely or appropriate' or 'of a fair, average or considerable amount or size'.[238] For instance, in the case of photocopies made in large numbers, there would be 'unreasonable' prejudice to the legitimate interests of the author if there is no provision for adequate remuneration to be paid to the author.[239] It would be pertinent to note that during the Stockholm Conference, the Committee used the French expression '*ne cause pas un prejudice injustifie*', which literally means 'does not cause an unjustified prejudice', but the Committee translated the expression as 'does not cause an unreasonable prejudice'.[240] Use of the term 'unreasonable' in the last step clearly envisages the need to balance the public interests with the rights of authors. In this vein, this step serves the public interest and advances the purpose of maintaining a balance between the rights of authors and the larger public interest, particularly education, research, and access to information. It is pertinent to note that the 'public interest' and 'users' needs' are not the same. Gervais has rightly stated that there must be a 'public interest' justification to limit a copyright.[241]

[238] *United States-Section 110(5) of the US Copyright Act*, WTO doc WT/DS 160/R (15 June 2000) (Report of the Panel) para 6.225.

[239] *Records of the Intellectual Property Conference of Stockholm, June 11 to July 14, 1967* (WIPO 1971) 883.

[240] *Records of the Intellectual Property Conference of Stockholm, June 11 to July 14, 1967* (WIPO 1971) 1145.

[241] Daniel J. Gervais, *(Re)structuring Copyright: A Comprehensive Path to International Copyright Reform* (Edward Elgar 2019) 69.

3

Access to Knowledge in the Developing World and International Copyright Law

1. Introduction

The emergence of third-world countries after World War II has added a new chapter to international copyright law. This aspect of international law is a principal area of concern in the developing world, as it governs the global distribution of knowledge, and developing countries are heavily dependent on foreign learning materials. Discussions in developing countries have raised issues of distributive justice to enhance global social welfare and meet human development needs, particularly in the field of education. Pragmatically, copyright law raises distributive issues in both developed and developing countries due to the unequal distribution of consumers across every country.[1] However, the impact of the prohibitive prices of learning materials in developing countries is more adverse than the relative impact on consumers in developed countries. In this vein, it is a must to consider 'what do developing nations hope for under the multilateral copyright system?' Regarding access to knowledge goods, the needs of developing countries differ from those of developed countries. To this end, the provisions of the Berne Appendix provide some remedies for developing countries, including some compulsory licensing provisions. The question is whether the special provisions for developing countries address the radical inequalities on the

[1] Margaret Chon, 'Intellectual Property "from Below": Copyright and Capability for Education' [2007] 40 UC Davis L Rev 803, 809 (considering the question whether the interests of poor users in a rich state are similar to poor users in a poor state); see also Peter Gerhart, 'The Tragedy of TRIPS' [2007] Michigan State L Rev 143, 158 ('Under any reckoning of distributive justice, some wealthy consumers in poor countries ought to be treated the same as wealthy consumers in rich countries').

Access to Knowledge in the Developing World. Vandana Mahalwar, Oxford University Press.
 DOI: 10.1093/9780198986782.003.0003

global copyright stage. This chapter outlines the special access needs of developing countries with respect to knowledge goods and how the international copyright system has responded to these needs. While speaking of 'needs', the author refers to the need for learning materials required to achieve educational goals.

2. Access from Below

The global copyright regime tends to reflect a 'top-down approach', which is skewed to primarily benefit the interests of developed economies.[2] Approaching the existing international copyright framework from a critical angle relates to the question of 'access from above or below'. To this end, I draw an analogy between 'access' and 'development', as the former leads to the latter. Where 'access from above' seeks to expand financial returns, 'access from below' alludes to just and equitable distribution of knowledge goods to satisfy basic needs and make people self-reliant.[3] While explaining the term 'from below', Margaret Chon rightly relates it to the term 'Global South', which is increasingly being used to denote that subset of developing countries located below the equator and also below the median in terms of development indicators, whether measured by GNI (Gross National Income) or HDI (Human Development Index).[4] Hence, considering the welfare concerns, the access needs of

[2] Margaret Chon, 'Intellectual Property "from Below": Copyright and Capability for Education' [2007] 40 UC Davis L Rev 803, 805 ('This approach fails to generate the full range of policy choices for both developed and developing countries to maximize global social welfare with respect to human development needs such as education'). See generally Olufunmilayo B. Arewa, 'Piracy, Biopiracy and Borrowing: Culture, Cultural Heritage and the Globalization of Intellectual Property' [2006] Case Research Paper Series in Legal Studies, Working Paper No. 04-19 79 (reflecting upon the TRIPS Agreement's top-down approach: 'Unless they incorporate substantially more flexibility than current TRIPS standards, such approaches, by applying a fairly unitary and uniform standard across different local communities, may have the ultimate effect of lessening local participation in questions of local knowledge'); see also Balakrishnan Rajagopal, *International Law Below: Development, Social Movements and Third World Resistance* (CUP 2003).

[3] Susan Healey, *The Case for Development from Below* (University of Guelph 2013) <www.paecon.net/studentessays/Healey1.htm> accessed 12 September 2025; Walter B. Stöhr and D.R. Fraser Taylor (eds) *Development from Above or Below? The Dialectics of Regional Planning in Developing Countries* (John Wiley and Sons 1981).

[4] Margaret Chon, 'Intellectual Property "from Below": Copyright and Capability for Education' [2007] 40 UC Davis L Rev 803, 813.

developing economies are more acute. The Education 2030 Incheon Declaration Framework for Action for the Implementation of Sustainable Development Goals highlights access to learning materials as a core element of the development goal on education:

> Education institutions and programmes should be adequately and equitably resourced, with safe, environment-friendly and easily accessible facilities; sufficient numbers of teachers and educators of quality using learner-centred, active and collaborative pedagogical approaches; and books, other learning materials, open educational resources and technology that are non-discriminatory, learning conducive, learner friendly, context specific, cost effective and available to all learners—children, youth and adults.[5]

The availability of textbooks and other learning materials has also been recognized as a 'fundamental prerequisite of education' and part of the state's obligation to provide free education.[6]

2.1. Price Barrier

Access to goods is attributed not merely by their availability but also by their affordability. The prohibitive cost of copyrighted educational materials in developing countries is well documented.[7] The higher cost of books and journals inhibits educational opportunities and results in the denial of the right to education. Access to learning materials must not be solely determined by an individual's capability to participate as a

[5] *Incheon Declaration and SDG4: Education 2030 Framework for Action*, UNES Doc ED-2016/WS/28 (UNESCO 2015) 33 <https://unesdoc.unesco.org/ark:/48223/pf0000245656/Pdf/245656eng.pdf.multi> accessed 12 September 2025.

[6] UNICEF, *A Human Rights-Based Approach to Education for All: A Framework for the Realization of Children's Right to Education and Rights within Education* (UNESCO 2007) 56 <https://unesdoc.unesco.org/ark:/48223/pf0000154861> accessed 14 September 2025. Also International Covenant on Economic, Social and Cultural Rights 1966, Art 13(2)(a); the Universal Declaration of Human Rights 1948 (UDHR), Art 26.

[7] *Copyright and Access to Knowledge: Policy Recommendations on Flexibilities in Copyright Laws* (Consumers International 2006) 2–3 <https://unesdoc.unesco.org/ark:/48223/pf0000147230> accessed 14 September 2025 (a study conducted a comparative price survey of book prices in Indonesia, Thailand, and the US, based on GDP per capita, to illustrate relatively high prices in developing countries).

consumer in the market of knowledge goods.[8] Margaret Chon has looked into this issue in detail:[9]

> Access to textbooks for students varies vastly between developed and developing countries. Textbooks are typically distributed to students 'for free' in the United States as part of the system of public education. Even in the United States, which is one of the most developed among the developed countries, textbooks can be short in supply. In most of the developing countries, however, the state does not provide textbooks; students must purchase them out-of-pocket. The reasons for the lack of state provision include rises in enrollment, economic recession, civil conflict, and pressing economic priorities in public health.

Although it would be challenging to ascertain the expenditure on all learning materials, there are studies available on the cost of textbooks and the budget allocation for textbook purchases in developing countries.[10] Studies reveal that, in developing countries, students do not have access to books at all or they have access to books on a shared basis with other students.[11] In a study of eleven countries, it came out that on average 15%

[8] *World Education Report 2000—The Right to Education: Towards Education for All Throughout Life* (UNESCO 2000) 60 <https://unesdoc.unesco.org/ark:/48223/pf0000119720> accessed 16 September 2025 ('In so far as the "right to lifelong learning" is understood to include a "right" to continuing education, it would seem in practice to amount to little more than the "right" of any citizen to participate, at his or her own expense, in the market for goods and services generally, with more or less encouragement from public funds depending on the situation in individual countries'); see generally Laurence R. Helfer and Graeme W. Austin, *Human Rights and Intellectual Property: Mapping the Global Interface* (CUP 2011) 317.

[9] Margaret Chon, 'Intellectual Property "from Below": Copyright and Capability for Education' [2007] 40 UC Davis L Rev 803, 824.

[10] *Every Child Should Have a Textbook*, Policy Paper 23, Global Education Monitoring Report (UNESCO 2016) <https://unesdoc.unesco.org/ark:/48223/pf0000243321> accessed 16 September 2025.

[11] Phineas Rueckert, '12 barriers to education for Children Living in Poverty' *Global Citizen* (13 August 2019) <www.globalcitizen.org/en/content/12-barriers-to-education-around-the-world> accessed 14 September 2025 (discussing the textbook and student ratio in developing parts of the world, for example, in Tanzania only 3.5% of the sixth grade students had sole use of textbooks, with the rest using books on a sharing basis, while in Cameroon, there is one reading textbook for every eleven students in primary school and thirteen students to each mathematics textbook in second grade); *Accountability in Education: Meeting our Commitments*, Global Education Monitoring Report (UNESCO 2017) 65–67 <www.unesco.org/gem-report/en/publication/accountability-education-meeting-our-commitments> accessed 14 September 2025; *Every Child Should Have a Textbook*, Policy Paper 23, Global Education Monitoring Report (UNESCO 2016) 2 <https://unesdoc.unesco.org/ark:/48223/pf0000243321> accessed 16 September 2025 ('In Togo, in grade 2, there were 3 students for every reading textbook, compared

to 20% of students in the fourth grade do not have textbooks and have to share textbooks with other students.[12] In sub-Saharan Africa, eighteen countries had a low level of textbook availability, with the exception of Botswana, whose student-to-textbooks ratio was 1:1. In Southeast Asian countries, where about one-third of the population lives below the poverty line, the lack of books, libraries, and other learning materials is more acute.[13]

The price of knowledge goods remains the primary barrier to access in developing countries. The scenario worsens in countries where the cost of books is borne by students' families, rather than the government.[14] While discussing affordability, it would be pertinent to note that the prices of books are to be viewed in the context of a country's GDP per capita. The retail prices of books in developing countries are generally lower in absolute terms, but when reckoned in terms of the country's GDP per capita, it comes out that the consumers in developing countries have to pay more

with 8 students for every mathematics textbook'); 'Pupils in poor countries lack textbooks, says UNESCO' *BBC News* (19 January 2016) <www.bbc.com/news/education-35343673> accessed 14 September 2025; *UN Committee on the Rights of the Child, Concluding Observations: India*, UN Doc CRC/C/15/Add.228 (26 February 2004) para 64 (the committee expressed its concern at the lack of relevant learning material); *UN Committee on the Rights of the Child, Concluding Observations: India*, UN Doc CRC/C/15/Add.115 (23 February 2000) para 56 (the committee expressed its concern with respect to 'a drastic shortage of textbooks and other learning materials'); *Education for All 2000-2015: Achievements and Challenges*, UN Doc ED/EFA/MRT/2015/RO/06, Global Monitoring Report (2015) 12 <https://unesdoc.unesco.org/ark:/48223/pf0000232580> accessed 15 September 2025 ('In India, 80% of the primary recurrent budget goes to teacher salaries, while only a small percentage goes to textbooks and other teaching and learning materials').

[12] Argentina, Brazil, Chile, India, Malaysia, Paraguay, Peru, the Philippines, Sri Lanka, Tunisia, and Uruguay (*A View Inside Primary Schools: A World Education Indicators Cross-National Study* (UNESCO Institute for Statistics 2008)); see also W. Mark and H.E. Chew, *Reading in the Mobile Era: A Study of Mobile Reading in Developing Countries* (UNESCO 2014).

[13] A.S. Sadiman, 'Challenges in Education in Southeast Asia', paper presented at the international seminar 'Towards Cross Border Cooperation between South and Southeast Asia: The Importance of India's North East Playing Bridge and Buffer Role' (6 November 2004) <www.seameo.org/VL/library/dlwelcome/publications/paper/india04.htm> accessed 14 September 2025 (a study conducted on ten Southeast Asian countries, namely Brunei Cambodia, Darussalam, Indonesia, Lao PDR, Malaysia, Myanmar, Philippines, Singapore, Thailand, and Vietnam).

[14] *Every Child Should Have a Textbook*, Policy Paper 23, Global Education Monitoring Report (UNESCO 2016) 7 <https://unesdoc.unesco.org/ark:/48223/pf0000243321> accessed 17 September 2025; Borel Foko, Beifith Kouak Tiyab, and Guillaume Husson, *Household Education Spending: An Analytical and Comparative Perspective for 15 African Countries* (UNESCO Pole de Dakar 2012) <https://unesdoc.unesco.org/ark:/48223/pf0000216719/PDF/216719eng.pdf.multi> accessed 17 September 2025 (study showed that school supplies and learning materials made up 34% of total household spending on education).

than the consumers of developed economies for the same book.[15] In some countries, the problem of unaffordability has found its way into the act of procuring illegitimate copies of the books.[16] The high prices, low income, and diffusion through cheap technological copying in the developing world are the most obvious reasons that make piracy unavoidable. Shaver argues pragmatically that 'if the task of access to knowledge is merely to ensure the widest dissemination of an unproblematic, unquestioned good, then surely the library is its highest symbol'.[17] The 'access from below' approach is about struggling to manage the textual diet in a way that satisfies the book hunger, which mostly implicates a tension between the copyright holder's exclusive rights and broader access. If access to knowledge were meant just to ensure access through unauthorized and illegitimate copies, then the access to knowledge movement would have no meaning. The rhetorical framing of the access to knowledge movement is precisely to ensure access to legitimate and unquestionable copies of the work.

2.2. Language Barrier

Another problem that is being faced by developing countries is the non-availability of books in local languages. Because of the shortage of learning materials in local languages, it is possible to attain higher education in developing countries only in a foreign language. Multilingualism in the developing world poses a major challenge to providing knowledge goods in diverse indigenous languages. To realize the linguistic goals in relation to the availability of educational material, it is necessary to have an idea about the existence of hundreds of local languages in the world.

[15] *Copyright and Access to Knowledge: Policy Recommendations on Flexibilities in Copyright Laws* (Consumers International 2006) 41 ('when a student in Indonesia is made to pay US $81.70 for the book, it is equivalent to a student in the US paying US $913.07 for the same Book').

[16] Brett M. Frischmann, 'Evaluating the Demsetzian Trend in Copyright Law' [2007] 3 Rev L & Econ 649, 669 (concludes that social demand for access exceeds private demand, explaining that private demand is the purchaser's or licensee's willingness to pay).

[17] Lea Shaver and Ramesh Subramanian (eds) *Access to Knowledge in India: New Research on Intellectual Property, Innovation and Development* (Bloomsbury 2011) 92 (also discussing that, in India, consumers tend to access illegitimate copies, which has given rise to markets of pirated books).

Studies reveal that about 70% of all the languages of the world are spoken in just twenty countries, which are mostly the poor nations.[18] Asia, home to 4.6 billion people, has more than 2,300 spoken languages. Indonesia has tremendous linguistic diversity with more than 700 spoken languages. India alone has twenty-two official languages, while South Africa has eleven official languages.

Amid the wide linguistic variety, English is accepted as the most successful global language. It is the most widely used language in producing and disseminating knowledge.[19] Some countries, such as Ghana, India, Nigeria, Pakistan, and the Philippines, do not have native speakers of English, yet have adopted English as a second language. Other widely used global languages for publishing information are Chinese, French, German, and Spanish.[20] International publishers aim to publish in international languages to refer to their own market, and it leaves the interests of the consumers in developing countries largely marginalized. This makes the developing nations textually dependent on the countries that publish in major international languages.[21] Clearly, multilingual countries lack books in regional languages because the more languages in which books should be printed and the smaller the readership for any given language, the greater the cost per book, and commercial publishers gain no profits out of books published in 'neglected languages'.[22] It is worth considering that, just like publishers, authors wish to write in those global languages that have the widest readership. Resultantly, there

[18] *Education in a Multilingual World: UNESCO Education Position Paper*, UN doc ED.2003/WS/2 (UNESCO 2003) 12 <https://unesdoc.unesco.org/ark:/48223/pf0000129728> accessed 20 September 2025.

[19] Sergey Lobachev, 'Top Languages in Global Information Production, Partnership' [2008] 3 Canadian J Library and Info Pract and Res 1.

[20] Sergey Lobachev, 'Top Languages in Global Information Production, Partnership' [2008] 3 Canadian J Library and Info Pract and Res 1 (most of the books, scholarly journals, and other learning materials across the world are published in English).

[21] Philip G. Altbach, 'Copyright in the Developing World' in Joseph P. Farrell and Stephen P. Heyneman (eds) *Textbooks in the Developing World: Economic and Educational Choice* (World Bank 1989) 93 ('this dominance places a further strain on limited publishing and other resources').

[22] See generally Philip G. Altbach, 'Copyright in the Developing World' in Joseph P. Farrell and Stephen P. Heyneman (eds) *Textbooks in the Developing World: Economic and Educational Choice* (World Bank 1989) 9 (discussing the reasons responsible for lack of translated versions in developing countries); Lea Shaver, *Ending Book Hunger: Access to Print Across Barriers of Class and Culture* (Yale University Press 2019) 9 (publications in international languages bring huge profits to publishers due to hundreds of millions of potential readers involved).

is a lack of localization of knowledge in the developing world, which holds back the international development goals.

The development goals seem out of reach in low- and middle-income countries, where textbooks carry the weight and imprint of authority throughout the entire nation, and teachers are duty-bound to teach the content cover-to-cover. With no other alternative, students are forced to memorize dense texts with little understanding, which ultimately benefits no one. An evaluation of the education system in rural Kenya reveals that Kenyan students struggle to read and comprehend English textbooks effectively.[23] Another worrying observation is that 70% of students in Malawi and 66% of students in Zambia have a low level of reading in the English language.[24] In India, particularly in rural areas, the incomprehensibility of English learning materials presents an abysmally poor scenario. As long as the material is in English, it should be translated by teachers into their native language.[25] Recognizing the three-language formula, UNESCO has emphasized the need to promote education in a multilingual context.[26]

The purpose of this chapter is not to argue whether books in a foreign language obstruct or facilitate the learning process, but merely to point out the interests of those who have inadequate reading comprehension in foreign languages. To achieve the enhanced learning outcomes in developing countries, it is necessary to align the learning materials with the linguistic needs of the potential readers. There are some provisions that allow the developing countries to adopt the compulsory licence scheme to reproduce or translate books and learning materials, but various conditions and restrictions placed upon the issuance of a licence make the provision unworkable.

[23] Paul Glewwe, Michael Kremer, and Sylvie Moulin, 'Many Children Left Behind? Textbooks and Test Scores in Kenya' [2009] 1(1) American Econ J: Applied Econ 112–35.

[24] Hywel Coleman, 'Dreams and Realities: Developing Countries and the English Language' in Hywel Coleman (ed) *Developing Countries and the English Language: Rhetoric, Risks, Roles and Recommendations* (British Council 2011) 42.

[25] Rama Meganathan, 'Materials Development in English as a Second Language: An Indian Experience' [2008] 8(12) FOLIO.

[26] UNESCO established the term 'multilingual education' in 1999 (cf. General Conference Resolution 30 C/12) to refer to the use of at least three languages in education: the mother tongue, a regional or national language, and an international language; see also *Multilingual Education: Why is it Important? How to implement It?* UN Doc ED.2014/WS/5 (UNESCO 2014) <https://unesdoc.unesco.org/ark:/48223/pf0000226554> accessed 20 September 2025.

The approach 'from below' also implicates the 'knowledge spillovers' flowing in the market, which significantly enhances societal knowledge.[27] Favouring spillovers, Frischman and Lemley provide that spillovers are enormously significant to society and need not be fully internalized through intellectual property (IP) rights.[28] The prospects for poor countries to benefit from knowledge spillovers from rich countries are high, and this can be of global benefit if they produce high-quality knowledge goods in return for the global market.

3. Special Needs of Developing Countries

The international copyright framework has spread from developed to developing countries. In most cases, the copyright laws in developing countries are the outcome of colonization. For example, under the British Raj, the Indian legislature enacted the Indian Copyright Act, 1914, which was completely based on the Imperial Copyright Act of 1911 enacted by the parliament of the United Kingdom. Likewise, in pre-independent Malaysia, the UK enacted the Copyright Act of 1911, which was applied. Colonization has enormously contributed to the evolution of copyright laws in developing countries. After World War II, the developing states started reviewing the laws that were given to them by colonizers. Unfortunately, many states chose to continue with the colonial laws instead of redesigning them in light of their own local needs, interests, conditions, and priorities.[29] Developing countries made some attempts to adjust their educational and development needs within an international framework, but these efforts ultimately failed. Various social and economic factors hinder the creation, production, and dissemination of knowledge in the developing world. The social and economic factors in

[27] See generally Margaret Chon, 'Sticky Knowledge and Copyright' [2011] Wisc L Rev 215, 216 (discussing knowledge's potential for positive spillover that can further the copyright's goal of encouraging learning); Ruth L. Okediji, 'Reframing International Copyright Limitations and Exceptions as Development Policy' in *Copyright Law in an Age of Limitations and Exceptions* (Cambridge University Press 2017) 461 ('Knowledge spillovers are critical for enhancing overall societal knowledge which, in turn, promotes technical change').

[28] Brett M. Frischmann and Mark A. Lemley, 'Spillovers' [2007] 107 Colum L Rev 257, 259 (spillovers are the uncompensated benefits that one person's activity provides to another).

[29] Peter Drahos, 'Developing Countries and International Intellectual Property Standard-Setting' [2005] 5 JWIP 765, 766.

developing countries often do not support a viable publishing industry.[30] Combining with these factors, several other factors also inhibit the indigenous production and distribution of copyrighted educational material, such as low per capita income and multilingual readership. The alternative of importing books from developed countries often gets frustrated by the reason of paying high tariffs and hefty payments to foreign publishers.

For centuries, the developing countries have been in need of bulk access to learning materials at reasonable prices and in local languages. Despite being the most pressing need of developing countries, the bulk access requirements have not galvanized much attention in international copyright literature.[31] It is worth emphasizing that developing states are in specific need of printed books as opposed to e-books.[32] A large chunk of the population in technologically advanced economies may easily possess digital devices like laptops, tablets, and smartphones, but these remain a dream for the majority in developing and least developed economies.

Moreover, many developing countries suffer from energy poverty, which implies a lack of electricity among other inadequate energy resources. If there is no electricity, there can be no access to computers, browsers, the internet, and, hence, e-books.[33] The digital revolution has significantly expanded the way knowledge goods are produced and distributed. While the impact of electronic books can be seen contributing notably in disseminating information, on the other hand, developing countries are not well positioned to adequately benefit from internet-based learning sources due to the higher web costs involved.[34]

[30] Basic social and economic factors impact the productive capacity of the publishing industry. Social factors include the societal attitude towards books, illiteracy rate, and the problem of multiplicity of languages. Economic factors inhibiting book production include an inadequate supply of raw materials. See Charles A. Kennedy, 'Copyright and the Developing Nations' [1969] 13 Patent, Trademark and Copyright J Res and Education 410, 414.

[31] Ruth L. Okediji, 'The International Copyright System: Limitations, Exceptions and Public Interest Considerations for Developing Countries' *UNCTAD–ICTSD Project on IPRs and Sustainable Development* (March 2006) 6.

[32] Susan Isiko Strba, *International Copyright Law and Access to Education in Developing Countries: Exploring Multilateral Legal and Quasi-Legal Solutions* (Martinus Nijhoff Publishers 2012) 38 ('developing countries depend heavily on printed copyrighted works as opposed to electronic versions').

[33] Thomas L. Friedman, *Hot, Flat, and Crowded: Why We Need a Green Revolution—and How It Can Renew America* (Penguin Books 2009) 161.

[34] See generally, Hala Essalmawi, 'Options and Alternatives to Current Copyright Regimes and Practices' in Gaëlle Krikorian and Amy Kapczynski (eds) *Access to Knowledge in the Age*

Evincing the widening digital gap, a report shows that in comparison to 87% of the population being users in developed countries, only 47% of the population are users in developing countries, and 19% in least developed countries.[35] It is essential to note that internet access cannot be measured solely based on affordability. According to the World Economic Forum's Internet for All report, there are four key barriers to internet access: infrastructure; affordability; skills, awareness, and cultural acceptance; and local adoption and use.[36] In many developing countries, such as India and Brazil, poor literacy and a lack of digital skills are the primary factors preventing the population from accessing the internet.[37] The statistics also reveal that, as of April 2025, India ranks 96 out of 155 countries in fixed broadband speed.[38]

Considering these barriers to digital educational resources, the need for printed books in developing and least developed economies becomes imperative. Because the cost of producing print copies is higher than that of digital copies, publishers in the developing world find it risky to invest in printed books. There are numerous hurdles associated with publishing printed learning materials. A corollary to risk in investment is the situation where a particular title may not find sufficient readership to make the expected profits.

Nelson Mandela famously expressed, 'If you talk to a man in a language he understands, that goes to his head. If you talk to him in his own language, that goes to his heart.' In addition to the internet barrier, access

of Intellectual Property (Zone Books 2010) 628 ('The high price of subscriptions to e-resources and printed materials has contributed to higher illiteracy rates in the Global South').

[35] Doreen Bogdan-Martin, 'Measuring Digital Development: Facts and Figures 2019' *ITU* (25 May 2020) <www.itu.int/en/ITU-D/Statistics/Documents/facts/FactsFigures2019.pdf> accessed 20 September 2025.

[36] Among all, infrastructure and affordability remain major problems to many countries, in particular, those with rural and remote populations; *Internet for All: A Framework for Accelerating Internet Access and Adoption*, White Paper prepared in collaboration with the Boston Consulting Group (World Economic Forum 2016) <www3.weforum.org/docs/WEF_Internet_for_All_Framework_Accelerating_Internet_Access_Adoption_report_2016.pdf> accessed 22 September 2025.

[37] *Internet for All: A Framework for Accelerating Internet Access and Adoption*, White Paper prepared in collaboration with the Boston Consulting Group (World Economic Forum 2016) 9 <www3.weforum.org/docs/WEF_Internet_for_All_Framework_Accelerating_Internet_Access_Adoption_report_2016.pdf> accessed 22 September 2025.

[38] 'Median Country Speeds Updated April 2025' *Speedtest* <www.speedtest.net/global-index> accessed 22 September 2025. As of April 2025, India's broadband speed is 62.25 Mbps while Singapore tops the list with 368.50 Mbps.

to reading materials is hugely limited by the non-production of books in the local language to which the reader belongs.[39] As linguistics correspond to diverse communities, developing countries have been lagging in embracing language diversity in the education sector. Access to education cannot be achieved if the supply of books is not in the language of the minority language groups. In other words, to percolate down the benefits of books to the root levels, it is necessary to ensure that the learning contents are translated and adapted even to the speakers of minority languages. In a multilingual context, demand for books remains in hundreds of languages that involve multiple complexities of translation at the publisher's end.[40]

Although many factors impact access to reading material, copyright law is the most significant. Copyright law determines whether translation or abridgement is encouraged and whether reproduction of literary works is allowed for educational purposes. At the time of book publication, most authors assign their rights to translation to the publishing company. In a multilingual context, this places an obligation on publishers to translate books into every language and to ensure an adequate supply for readers. Most of the profits in the publishing industry are generated by publishing in languages with global reach. Publishers show reluctance to publish in indigenous languages on account of 'immediate disadvantage due to the hegemonic domination of foreign languages'.[41]

Drawing upon General Comment 13, Shaver has rightly presented a '4A' framework of access to education, articulating that learning facilities and resources must be (1) available, (2) accessible, (3) acceptable, and (4) adaptable to a diverse population.[42] Though these dimensions are

[39] Lea Shaver, 'Copyright and Inequality' [2014] 92 Washington University L Rev 124.

[40] The translation of children's books is considered to be far more complicated than that for adult learning materials. The translators have to be concerned about linguistics, cultural appropriateness, and standardization. See Viv Edwards and Marriote Ngwaru, 'African Language Publishing for Children in South Africa: Challenges for Translators' [2011] 32 International Journal of Bilingual Education and Bilingualism 435, 450 (noting that publishers are often reluctant 'to expand across all the official languages in terms of their frustrations around the translation process, which was sometimes perceived to be as costly as originating materials in African languages').

[41] Gilbert Motsaathebe, 'Book Publishing in Indigenous Languages in South Africa: Challenges and Opportunities' [2012] 10 INDILINGA—African Journal of Indigenous Knowledge Systems 115 (exploring the major hurdles for book publishing in indigenous languages).

[42] Lea Shaver, 'Right to Read' [2015] 54 Colum J Transnat'l L (2015) 35; *CESCR General Comment No. 13: The Right to Education*, UN Doc E/C.12/1999/10 (1999), reprinted in

significant for both developing and developed countries, the needs of developing countries are more imperative. As an upshot, the access needs of developing countries that are not identical with developed countries can be articulated as: (a) the need for bulk access, (b) to printed reading materials, (c) in indigenous languages, and (d) at affordable pricing.

4. The 1967 Stockholm Protocol Regarding Developing Countries

After discussing the needs of developing nations and their poor institutional capacity to meet these needs in the previous part, it becomes necessary to examine the flexibilities that international copyright law offers to developing countries to realize educational goals.

4.1. Background

In the 1960s, the copyright issues of developing countries sparked debates centred on revising the Berne Convention.[43] A clash of approaches existed between developing and developed countries regarding international copyright law.[44] The difference in attitude was that developed countries were mainly the creators and exporters of copyrighted works, while developing and least developed countries have been in need of such works.[45] Prior to the Stockholm Protocol, there were no provisions for

Compilation of General Comments and General Recommendations Adopted by Human Rights Treaty Bodies, UN Doc HRI/GEN/1/Rev.6, para 6.

[43] Copyright law impeded the dissemination of copyrighted educational material and, hence, contributed to cultural and educational problems in the developing world. *See* Charles A. Kennedy, 'Copyright and the Developing Nations' [1969] 13 Patent, Trademark and Copyright J Res and Education 410, 411.

[44] Stockholm Conference 1967 represented a 'crisis in international copyright', where the developed and developing groups viewed copyright on somewhat different terms. See F. Charles Johnson, 'The Origins of the Stockholm Protocol' [1970] 18 Bulletin Copyright Soc'y USA 91.

[45] The advantageous position of developed nations in the international IP regime was discussed at the Brazzaville meeting: 'International copyright conventions are designed, in their present form, to meet the needs of countries which are exporters of intellectual works; these conventions, if they are to be generally and universally applied, require review and re-examination in the light of the specific needs of the African continent' (from the Preamble to the recommendations adopted by the Brazzaville Conference, 10 August 1963, as quoted in Irwin

the developing countries to ensure access to translations and reprints of learning materials.[46] No technical assistance was provided to developing nations to advance their publishing industries. The 1967 Stockholm Revision of the Berne Convention was the first place where concessions were granted for the benefit of developing countries, and some flexibilities were introduced in the rules.[47] It was an attempt to bring 'an effective economic balance' between developing and developed states regarding copyright protection.[48] The Protocol embodied the theory of 'equitable remuneration'[49] to balance 'the personal and economic interests of the author, on the one hand, and those of the community on the other'.[50] The same idea of balance of interests is also embodied in Article 7 of the UDHR:

> (1) Everyone has the right freely to participate in the cultural life of the community, to enjoy the arts and share in the scientific advancements and its benefits.
> (2) Everyone has the right to the protection of the moral and material interests resulting from any scientific, literary, or artistic production of which he is the author.

The expression 'developing countries' was introduced in copyright literature at the revision of the Berne Convention in 1967.[51] Prior to the Stockholm Conference, the high standards of Berne set difficulties for

A. Olian, 'International Copyright and the Needs of Developing Countries: The Awakening at Stockholm and Paris' [1974] 7 Cornell Int'l LJ 81, 95).

[46] Irwin A. Olian, 'International Copyright and the Needs of Developing Countries: The Awakening at Stockholm and Paris' [1974] 7 Cornell Int'l LJ 81, 95.
[47] Lawrence E. Abelman and Linda L. Berkowitz, 'International Copyright Law' [1977] 22 NY L Sch L Rev 619, 630 (reflecting upon Stockholm as a step to balance the educational needs of developing countries with interests of the authors of developed countries).
[48] H.D. Sacks, 'Crisis in International Copyright: The Protocol Regarding Developing Countries' [1969] 128 J Bus L 26, 27.
[49] Alan H. Lazar, 'Developing Countries and Authors' Rights in International Copyright' [1969] 19 Copyright L Symp 30, 31 (the Protocol embodies a 'theory of copyright which undercut the classic theory of the copyright the author's exclusive right to his works').
[50] Alan H. Lazar, 'Developing Countries and Authors' Rights in International Copyright' [1969] 19 Copyright L Symp 30, 31.
[51] Ndene Ndiaye, 'The Berne Convention and Developing Countries' [1986] 1 Colum JL & Arts 47.

less-developed countries to entertain Berne membership.[52] To accommodate the needs of and to attract a broad membership of less-developed countries, the Berne rules underwent considerable tailoring with an aim to adopt the substantive equality principle. Judge Hesser, in his speech before the Stockholm Conference, rightly expressed that the revision's main exercise was to 'adjust the system of protection under the Berne Convention to the economic, social and cultural needs of these countries'.[53] Drawing attention to the concerns of developing countries, he further pointed out that the high levels of protection deterred the non-European countries from joining the Union.[54]

4.2. Preparatory Work of the Stockholm Conference

Though it is not the aim to delve too deeply into the history of preparatory works of the Protocol, a brief narration is required for an understanding of the derivations.

After the wave of post-World War II decolonization of Africa and Asia, the potency of the Berne Convention was diluted. The original Berne Union had a smaller number of least developed countries, such as Haiti and Tunisia, but decolonization added a significant number of newly independent states, particularly from Africa and Asia.[55] The rise in the number of less-developed countries augmented the problem of high standards of the Convention. After these new memberships to the Union, many lesser-developed members of the Union and those who chose to remain outside the Berne Union thought of re-examining the copyright

[52] Barbara A. Ringer, 'Role of the United States in International Copyright: Past, Present, and Future' [1968] 56 Georgetown LJ 1054 ('The Stockholm revisions, notably the new "Protocol Regarding Developing Countries," mark a substantial departure from the high level of copyright protection that hitherto has been characteristic of the Berne Convention'); F. Charles Johnson, 'The Origins of the Stockholm Protocol' [1970] 18 Bulletin Copyright Soc'y USA 91, 92.

[53] Torwald Hesser, 'Intellectual Property Conference of Stockholm' [1967] 14 Bulletin Copyright Soc'y USA 267, 289–90.

[54] Torwald Hesser, 'Intellectual Property Conference of Stockholm' [1967] 14 Bulletin Copyright Soc'y USA 267, 289–90 (at the previous revisions of the Berne Convention, the European members of the Union could be said to have 'run the show', which was a high protective wall for developing nations).

[55] Peter K. Yu, 'A Tale of Two Development Agendas' [2009] 35 Ohio Northern University L Rev 473.

provisions that were primarily formulated for the developed countries, in light of the specific needs of lesser-developed states.[56]

4.2.1. The Brazzaville Meeting (5–10 August 1963)

Through the efforts of BIRPI and UNESCO, the African Study Conference was convened at Brazaville, Congo, on 5 August 1963. Twenty-three newly independent African countries attended the meeting,[57] along with three non-African countries[58] and six international non-governmental organizations.[59] The meeting aimed to assist African member states and associate members of UNESCO in examining the applicability of principles in their national copyright laws and to consider their adherence to the international convention. Most of these countries, except Ghana, had no national legislation of their own and relied on their mother country's membership in a convention.[60] From the deliberations, it was clear that these countries were not able to work under a copyright scheme similar to those in Western European countries.[61] One Tunisian delegate expressed in relation to international copyright relations: 'Africa should not pay too high a price for the fruits of important knowledge, and African countries should be represented in the preparatory work of the revision of the Berne Convention.'[62]

[56] Peter K. Yu, 'A Tale of Two Development Agendas' [2009] 35 Ohio Northern University L Rev 472 (less developed countries questioned whether those copyright principles would be 'appropriate for them in light of their limited economic development and technological backwardness'); F. Charles Johnson, 'The Origins of the Stockholm Protocol' [1970] 18 Bulletin Copyright Soc'y USA 109.

[57] Algeria, Burundi, Cameroon, Central African Republic, Chad, Congo (Brazzaville), Congo (Leopoldville), Dahomey, Ethiopia, Ghana, Guinea, Ivory Coast, Liberia, Malagasy Republic, Mali, Mauritius, Morocco, Niger, Sierra Leone, Tanganyika, Togo, Tunisia, Uganda.

[58] Non-African countries were Czechoslovakia, Italy, and the United States.

[59] The International organizations represented were the African Society of Culture, the Union of African National Radio and Television Broadcasters (URTNA), the European Broadcasting Union (EBU), the International Literary and Artistic Association (ALAI), the International Confederation of Societies of Authors and Composers (CISAC), and the Internationale Gesellschaft fur Urheberrecht (INTERGU).

[60] Abraham L. Kaminstein, 'Global Copyright: Recent International Copyright Conferences in Africa, Europe, and Asia' [1964] 11 Bulletin Copyright Soc'y USA 225, 226.

[61] Abraham L. Kaminstein, 'Global Copyright: Recent International Copyright Conferences in Africa, Europe, and Asia' [1964] 11 Bulletin Copyright Soc'y USA 226 (discussing the primary concerns of countries attending the meeting, in particular, their need to protect the folklore as a matter of urgency).

[62] F. Charles Johnson, 'The Origins of the Stockholm Protocol' [1970] 18 Bulletin Copyright Soc'y USA 107 (citing 'Report of the African Study Meeting on Copyright' (original document designated RADA/10), contained in (1963) 16(2) UNESCO Copyright Bulletin 171)

Following the deliberations, the Conference appointed a drafting committee which made three specific recommendations:

(1) the reduction of the copyright term stipulated in Article 7 of the Berne Convention;
(2) the modification of article 20 to facilitate the development of bilateral agreements that would allow parties to derogate from their international obligations; and
(3) special provisions for the protection of African folklore and for promoting free educational use of copyrighted works.[63]

The African experts asked UNESCO and BIRPI to assist in drafting a model law that was suitable for their specific needs.

4.2.2. Joint Meeting of the Intergovernmental Copyright Committee and the Permanent Committee of the Berne Union (New Delhi, 2–7 December 1963)

Four months after the Brazzaville meeting, a joint meeting of the Permanent Committee and the Intergovernmental Copyright Committee (the governing bodies of the Berne Union and the Universal Copyright Convention (UCC)) was conducted in New Delhi in December 1963. During the conference, the Indian delegation proposed a study of: (a) introducing into the conventions the right of member countries to grant compulsory licences for the reproduction of copyright works for educational purposes, and (b) introducing into the Berne Convention provisions relating to translation, similar to those in the UCC; and it invited the secretariats to make a study of these questions and report on them to the next joint session of the committees.[64] Mr Chagla, then India's Minister of Education, stressed the need to consider the needs of all countries, in particular the newly independent countries and those in the developing phase.[65] The Indian proposal favouring compulsory

[63] *Records of the Intellectual Property Conference of Stockholm: June 11 to July 14, 1967*, Vol. I, Preparator Documents: S/1, Berne Convention 1967 (WIPO 1971) 67; see also Ndene Ndiaye, 'The Berne Convention and Developing Countries' [1986] 1 Colum JL & Arts 47, 48.
[64] *Records of the Intellectual Property Conference of Stockholm: June 11 to July 14, 1967*, Vol. I, Preparator Documents: S/1, Berne Convention 1967 (WIPO 1971) 67.
[65] F. Charles Johnson, 'The Origins of the Stockholm Protocol' [1970] 18 Bulletin Copyright Soc'y USA 116.

licensing was adopted by both committees, and they recommended the secretariat conduct a study and report to the committees at the following joint session.

Influenced by the recommendations made at the Brazzaville and New Delhi conferences, the following year, a Swedish/BIRPI Study Group consisting of experts recommended the insertion of a new article—Article 25*bis*—that would allow developing countries to provide lower standards of protection.[66] In view of the distressing conditions in the less-developed countries, the Study Group stressed that 'exceptional measures for the benefit of developing countries were in principle justified'.[67] The Study Group deemed it appropriate that the new provisions must operate only for the benefit of developing countries.

The following language of Article 25*bis* was recommended:

> 1) Any country which desires to accede to this Convention but which, with regard to its economic situation and its social needs, does not consider itself immediately in a position to make provision for the protection of all the rights forming the object of this Convention, may, by a notification deposited with .... at the time of accession, declare that it will, for a period of ten years from the accession,
>
> [...]
>
> (d) reserve for itself to determine the regulations for the protection of works covered by this Convention when such works are used for exclusively educational or scholastic purposes;
>
> (e) reserve the right to make arrangements in derogation of Article 20 of this Convention.
>
> [...]
>
> 2) If a country, which has made reservations in accordance with paragraph (1), at the end of the period of ten years prescribed therein, with regard to its economic situation and social needs, still does not consider itself in a position to make provision for the protection of all the rights

[66] Barbara A. Ringer, 'Role of the United States in International Copyright: Past, Present, and Future' [1968] 56 Georgetown LJ 1054, 1066; Peter K. Yu, 'A Tale of Two Development Agendas' [2009] 35 Ohio Northern University L Rev 465, 473.

[67] *Records of the Intellectual Property Conference of Stockholm: June 11 to July 14, 1967*, Vol. I, Preparator Documents: S/1, Berne Convention 1967 (WIPO 1971) 68.

> forming the object of this Convention, such country may, by a notification deposited with the .... before the end of the above-mentioned period, declare that it will maintain for a new period of ten years, one, several or all of the reservations made by the country.[68]

It is essential to analyse the preparatory work of the Stockholm Protocol from two angles: First, what is a developing country? Second, what special provisions were introduced to meet the specific needs of developing countries? The Study Group found it difficult to suggest an objective definition of 'developing countries' due to the difficulty in establishing suitable criteria for the category. As reflected in the above clause (1) of the draft article, the Group recommended leaving the discretion with each country to decide if 'its stage of development allowed it to take advantage of the right of reservation'.[69] However, when a Committee of Governmental Experts considered these recommendations (referred to as the joint proposal) in 1965, six developing countries submitted a new wording on the criterion of beneficiaries. They suggested that:

> Any country of the Union may, having regard to its economic, scientific, social and cultural needs, declare at any time.[70]

But the Study Group's proposal was:

> Any country which desires to accede to this Convention but which, with regard to its economic situation and its social needs, does not consider itself immediately in a position to make provision [for Convention protection] may, . . . at the time of accession, declare. . . .

[68] *Records of the Intellectual Property Conference of Stockholm: June 11 to July 14, 1967*, Vol. I, Preparator Documents: S/1, Berne Convention 1967 (WIPO 1971) 67–68.

[69] *Records of the Intellectual Property Conference of Stockholm: June 11 to July 14, 1967*, Vol. I, Preparator Documents: S/1, Berne Convention 1967 (WIPO 1971) 68; see also Eleanor D. O'Hara, 'Developing Countries – A Definitional Exercise' [1967] 15 Bulletin Copyright Soc'y USA 86.

[70] *Records of the Intellectual Property Conference of Stockholm: June 11 to July 14, 1967*, Vol. I, Preparator Documents: S/1, Berne Convention 1967 (WIPO 1971) 69 (it was stressed that 'it was important not to limit the possibility of making reservations to countries which would accede in the future to the Convention').

There was a proposal by France to start Article 25*bis* with 'Any Developing country', which was accepted by the Permanent Committee,[71] whereas the joint proposal recommended 'economic, social, scientific and cultural needs' and the Study Group used the words 'economic . . . and social needs'. Finally, the following wording became the draft of Article 1 of the Stockholm Protocol:

> Any developing country which ratifies this Convention or accedes to it and which, having regard to its economic situation and its social or cultural needs, does not consider itself immediately in a position to make provision for the protection of all the rights as provided in the Act.[72]

Regarding the nature of reservations, during the meeting of the 1965 Committee of Governmental Experts, each article of the Berne Convention was examined by the participant countries.[73] After having a thorough discussion on the proposal submitted by the Study Group, the committee was presented with a joint proposal by six developing countries. The joint proposal was based on the recommendations submitted by the Study Group, but it differed on some points. Through this proposal, the developing countries made the recommendations to avail themselves of:

> (a) reservations to the right of translation, (b) reservations to the term of protection, (c) right to the protected works for educational or scholastic purposes, and (d) the right to permit reproduction of literary and artistic works for exclusive use in its territory on payment of just

[71] F. Charles Johnson, 'The Origins of the Stockholm Protocol' [1970] 18 Bulletin Copyright Soc'y USA 130.

[72] *Records of the Intellectual Property Conference of Stockholm: June 11 to July 14, 1967*, Vol. I, Preparator Documents: S/1, Berne Convention 1967 (WIPO 1971) 95.

[73] In the meeting, thirty-five countries were represented out of the then fifty-four member states of the Berne Convention: Austria, Belgium, Brazil, Bulgaria, Congo (Leopoldville), Czechoslovakia, Denmark, Finland, France, Germany (Federal Republic), Greece, Hungary, India, Ireland, Israel, Italy, Japan, Lebanon, Luxembourg, Monaco, Morocco, the Netherlands, Norway, Poland, Portugal, Senegal, South Africa, Spain, Sweden, Switzerland, Thailand, Tunisia, Turkey, the United Kingdom, and Yugoslavia; see also F. Charles Johnson, 'The Origins of the Stockholm Protocol' [1970] 18 Bulletin Copyright Soc'y USA 128.

> remuneration to be fixed, failing agreement with the author, by its competent authority.[74]

For the reservation regarding the right of reproduction, the delegations of France and Italy opposed the introduction of such a reservation. The delegation of the Federal Republic of Germany proposed the removal of this reservation from Article 25*bis* and the following words to be added to the provision on restriction of protection:[75]

> . . . including the right to permit this reproduction on payment of just remuneration to be fixed, failing agreement with the author by its competent authority.

Finally, the committee adopted the general formula couched in the following words:[76]

> the right, for exclusively educational, scientific or scholastic purposes, to restrict the protection of literary and artistic works.

The committee made no comments in respect of other provisions of Article 25*bis*, and the text of Article 25*bis* became the culmination of the text presented by the Study Group, the joint proposal, and the proposals made during the meeting.

5. The Provisions of the Protocol

On 14 July 1967, the Stockholm Conference eventually led to the emergence of the 'Protocol Regarding Developing Countries', which was an instrument of six articles appended to the Berne Convention. The Protocol contained the provisions that allowed the lesser-developed countries to

[74] *Records of the Intellectual Property Conference of Stockholm: June 11 to July 14, 1967*, Vol. I, Preparator Documents: S/1, Berne Convention 1967 (WIPO 1971) 70.

[75] F. Charles Johnson, 'The Origins of the Stockholm Protocol' [1970] 18 Bulletin Copyright Soc'y USA 131, 132.

[76] *Records of the Intellectual Property Conference of Stockholm: June 11 to July 14, 1967*, Vol. I, Preparator Documents: S/1, Berne Convention 1967 (WIPO 1971) 71.

make reservations to the Berne Convention in respect of: (i) duration of protection, (ii) broadcasting, (iii) translations, (iv) reproduction for educational and cultural purposes, and (v) use of teaching, study, and research.[77] We shall now examine the substantive provisions of the Protocol that are useful for access to knowledge in the developing countries.

5.1. Translation Reservation

The provision of a translation licence was one of the most beneficial concessions to the developing countries. The provision outlines certain prerequisites for obtaining the licence for translation rights. Any country regarded as a developing country could invoke the following provision contained in Article 1(b)(i) of the Protocol:

> Nevertheless, the exclusive right of translation shall cease to exist if the author shall not have availed himself of it, during a term of ten years from the date of the first publication of the original work, by publishing or causing to be published, in one of the countries of the Union, a translation in the language for which protection is to be claimed.

The above provision restricted the 'exclusive right of translation' of the author. The author's right of translation is made contingent upon the exercise of the right of translation within ten years of the first publication of the original work. The right was required to be exercised 'by publishing or causing to be published, in one of the countries of the Union, a translation in the language for which protection is to be claimed'.[78]

Where a translation had not been published in a country in its national, regional, or official language, after the expiration of three years from the date of first publication of the work, then any national of that country could apply for a non-exclusive licence from the competent authority to translate and publish the translation in a language in which the

[77] Stockholm Revision of the Berne Convention Protocol Regarding Developing Countries 1967, Arts 1(b) (ii)–(ix).

[78] Protocol Regarding Developing Countries 1967, Art 1(b)(i) (reproduced in *Records of the Intellectual Property Conference of Stockholm*, Vol. II, Report of the Work of Main Committee II (1967) 1313).

work was not published. To avoid the grant of a compulsory licence, the owner of the right of translation will have to make or authorize the translation within three years of the first publication. The provision provided for the grant of a 'non-exclusive licence', which meant that the competent authority could grant several licences in respect of the same work. To obtain the licence, the applicant had to prove that he had requested the authorization from the copyright owner and the same had been denied by the owner, or he failed to find the owner of the right, even after 'due diligence' on his part. The 'due diligence' was spelt out in clause (iii) of Article 1(b). However, the licence could be granted on the condition that previous editions in such language are out of print.[79]

If unable to find the owner of the right of translation, the applicant was required to send a notice to the publisher whose name appeared on the work and, where the nationality of the owner was known to the applicant, to the diplomatic or consular representative of the owner's country.[80] Just compensation was required to be paid to the owner, subject to national currency regulations.[81] There was no clarification as to what constitutes 'just' compensation, for what should appear 'just' to the owners in developing countries might not be sufficient as per developed countries' standards.[82] Developing countries were also required to ensure a 'correct translation of the work'.[83]

The licence could not be granted where the author has already withdrawn all the copies from circulation. The rationale for this provision was to protect the moral rights of the author. If, after the publication of the

[79] Protocol Regarding Developing Countries 1967, Art 1(b)(ii) (reproduced in *Records of the Intellectual Property Conference of Stockholm*, Vol. II, Report of the Work of Main Committee II (1967) 1314).

[80] Protocol Regarding Developing Countries 1967, Art 1(b)(iii) (reproduced in *Records of the Intellectual Property Conference of Stockholm*, Vol. II, Report of the Work of Main Committee II (1967) 1314).

[81] Protocol Regarding Developing Countries 1967, Art 1(b)(iv) (reproduced in *Records of the Intellectual Property Conference of Stockholm*, Vol. II, Report of the Work of Main Committee II (1967) 1314).

[82] Dorothy M. Schrader, 'Analysis of the Protocol regarding Developing Countries' [1970] 17 Bulletin Copyright Soc'y USA 160, 187.

[83] Protocol Regarding Developing Countries 1967, Art 1(b)(iv) (reproduced in *Records of the Intellectual Property Conference of Stockholm*, Vol. II, Report of the Work of Main Committee II (1967)); see also Arpad Bogsch, *The Law of Copyright Under the Universal Convention* (3rd edn, A.W. Sijthoff 1968) (while analysing the term 'correct translation', the author expressed: 'A literal translation is not necessarily correct, and a correct translation is not necessarily literal. Probably "correct" is a translation which conveys with the greatest possible fidelity the thoughts expressed in the original').

work, the author has any repentance with respect to his work or feels that the work would damage his reputation in the future, he may withdraw all copies from circulation. However, it would be nearly impossible to establish that all copies of the work have been withdrawn all over the world. The licence granted was valid only for 'publication' in the country where it was applied for.[84] However, copies of a translation made under licence were not realistically restricted to the country where the licence was applied for. They could be exported and sold to other countries if such other countries availed themselves of reservations. Translations could also be exported to the country that has not availed reservations, provided that one of the national, official, or regional languages of such a country is the same as that of the translated work, and such a country's law allows for the act of importation.[85] Each developing country was required to establish a procedure at the national level for processing the applications to determine whether the conditions mentioned in the Protocol are met. The Protocol specified no guidelines for such a procedure to maintain uniformity among countries.

5.2. Reservation for Reproduction of Literary or Artistic Works

As regards the reproduction right, Article 1(c) of the Protocol provided that a beneficiary of the Protocol could apply for a non-exclusive compulsory licence to reproduce and publish a work for educational or cultural purposes.[86] The reservation permitting the reproduction of literary or artistic works is nearly identical in terminology to the translation reservation contained in Article 1 clause (b) of the Protocol. In short, the author was given an exclusive right of reproduction for a period of three years from the date of first publication. If the author failed to publish the

[84] Protocol Regarding Developing Countries 1967, Art 1(b)(v) (reproduced in *Records of the Intellectual Property Conference of Stockholm*, Vol. II, Report of the Work of Main Committee II (1967) 1314).

[85] Protocol Regarding Developing Countries 1967, Art 1(b)(v) (reproduced in *Records of the Intellectual Property Conference of Stockholm*, Vol. II, Report of the Work of Main Committee II (1967) 1314–15).

[86] Protocol Regarding Developing Countries 1967, Art 1(b)(iv) (reproduced in *Records of the Intellectual Property Conference of Stockholm*, Vol. II, Report of the Work of Main Committee II (1967) 1314).

original work, any national of such a country could apply for a compulsory licence to reproduce the work for 'educational or cultural' purposes. It is essential to understand that the reproduction was restricted only to 'educational or cultural' purposes, and it excluded all those works whose educational or cultural purposes were not apparently perceptible, like detective and adventure stories.[87]

5.3. Permitted Restrictions for Educational Uses

The last paragraph of Article 1 of the Protocol provided for the issuance of compulsory licences for uses exclusively for teaching, study, and research in all fields of education, provided that the author was given compensation that conformed to the standards of payment made to the national author. The scope of this reservation concerning 'educational' purposes is more precisely articulated than in paragraph (c). However, this provision was more liberal than the reproduction reservation because it did not apply exclusively to the right of reproduction; hence, a compulsory licence could be issued for any use of literary or artistic works. The ambit of this provision was broadest as it allowed for the issuance of a compulsory licence for any of the rights in literary or artistic works, while the preceding paragraphs of Article 1 permitted restrictions only on specific rights.[88]

6. Assessment of the Stockholm Protocol

The newly independent countries that had become members of the Berne Union approached the Stockholm Conference with great optimism. They had entered the Revision Conference so as to garner a better deal on the duration of copyright, translation, reproduction, and the use of copyrighted material for educational purposes.[89] With the favourable support

[87] Dorothy M. Schrader, 'Analysis of the Protocol regarding Developing Countries' [1970] 17 Bulletin Copyright Soc'y USA 160, 202.

[88] Dorothy M. Schrader, 'Analysis of the Protocol regarding Developing Countries' [1970] 17 Bulletin Copyright Soc'y USA 160, 212.

[89] Peter Drahos with John Braithwaite, *Information Feudalism: Who Owns the Knowledge Economy*? (Earthscan Publications Ltd. 2002) 77.

of BIRPI and UNESCO, the developing countries sensed some hope of a better deal that seemed to suit their special situations. However, when the interests of developing countries culminated in the draft Protocol to the Berne Convention, the foremost publishing and exporting countries emerged as formidable opponents.[90] In particular, the use of the wide expression 'teaching, study and research in all fields of education' created apprehension of confiscation of authors' and publishers' rights. The United Kingdom was the principal opponent of the concessions to developing countries. The UK remarked that:

> The Berne Convention is an instrument primarily designed to meet the needs of countries which have reached a certain stage of development. The United Kingdom can understand the feeling of some developing countries that certain of the obligations of the Convention are too onerous for them to accept. This does not, however, necessarily mean that the Convention should be amended in the way suggested.[91]

Like the UK, France also expressed a similar view that the Protocol would weaken authors' exclusive rights.[92] The Protocol was said to 'steal, or authorize the stealing of other people's property: the intangible but precious property of authors, composers, artists, and publishers'.[93] Much hue and cry was made against taking away IP without any payment to authors to facilitate access to the developing countries. The International Writers Guild prefaced its opposition by calling the reservations 'unfair, unsuitable, and irrational' for it burdened the authors of foreign works.[94]

Apart from the objections raised by highly advanced countries, developing countries also viewed most of the Protocol provisions to be

[90] F. Charles Johnson, 'The Origins of the Stockholm Protocol' [1970] 18 Bulletin Copyright Soc'y USA 180.

[91] *Observations of Governments on the Proposals for Revising the Substantive Copyright Provisions* (Document S/1), BIRPI Doc S/1 (January 1967) 103.

[92] The French government's view was that the Berne system of protection must be higher than that provided under the UCC (for detailed analysis see F. Charles Johnson, 'The Origins of the Stockholm Protocol' [1970] 18 Bulletin Copyright Soc'y USA 144).

[93] Letter, Vice-Chairman of the British Copyright Council, *The Times* (13 April 1967) cited in F. Charles Johnson, 'The Origins of the Stockholm Protocol' [1970] 18 Bulletin Copyright Soc'y USA 180.

[94] F. Charles Johnson, 'The Origins of the Stockholm Protocol' [1970] 18 Bulletin Copyright Soc'y USA 153.

virtually useless.[95] From the viewpoint of the developing countries, the reservation to translation rights did no good, as it provided that the author's exclusive right of translation would expire if not exercised within ten years of first publication. Pragmatically, this provision was unworkable, the reason being 'very few textbooks and technical works would be valuable after such a period'.[96] Furthermore, the procedural formalities to obtain a compulsory licence made the process too expensive, time-consuming, and arduous for developing countries. The Protocol had various flaws; the most glaring one was that it imposed no obligation on the developed countries to facilitate access to their copyrighted educational materials by the developing countries. More importantly, it lacked the provision for access to printed material in developing countries.[97] Additionally, the countries were free to ratify the Convention despite rejecting the substantive provisions.[98] Resultantly, any Berne Member that did not accede to either the substantive provisions or the Protocol was free not to provide any reservations in favour of developing countries. On the whole, the Protocol failed to provide financial and technical support to the developing countries for the growth of their own book publishing industries.[99]

7. The Berne Appendix: A Special Compensated-Use Regime

The first attempt to insert flexibilities in the Berne Convention was through the Stockholm Protocol in 1967. The Protocol could not become

[95] Irwin A. Olian, 'International Copyright and the Needs of Developing Countries: The Awakening at Stockholm and Paris' [1974] 7 Cornell Int'l LJ 81, 101.

[96] Irwin A. Olian, 'International Copyright and the Needs of Developing Countries: The Awakening at Stockholm and Paris' [1974] 7 Cornell Int'l LJ 101.

[97] Susan Isiko Straba, *International Copyright Law and Access to Education in Developing Countries* (Martinus Nijhoff Publishers 2012) 88.

[98] Berne Convention 1886, Art 28 (reproduced in *Records of the Intellectual Property Conference of Stockholm*, Vol. II, Report of the Work of Main Committee II (1967) 1307).

[99] An author expressed that 'in the developing countries there is a lack of qualified translators, editors, compositors, and printers. Paper is scarce or too expensive. Technical facilities are often obsolete. Publishing and bookselling suffer from poor returns. Authors' societies and copyright licensing organizations are only in the course of formation. There is a lack of money and trained specialists. Therefore, the Protocol is no suitable instrument to provide aid for developing countries', cited in Irwin A. Olian, 'International Copyright and the Needs of Developing Countries: The Awakening at Stockholm and Paris' [1974] 7 Cornell Int'l LJ 102.

a legally binding instrument due to the lack of ratification, particularly from developed countries. The second attempt was the Paris Act of the Berne Convention, which replaced the Stockholm Protocol with a new preferential system to the advantage of developing countries. This revision at Paris in 1971 was to overcome the crisis caused by the failure of the Stockholm Protocol. The 1971 revision separated the Act from the Protocol and established a list of special provisions for developing countries, which were incorporated in the Appendix to the Berne Convention. The ability of the copyright owner to refuse to reproduce or translate his or her work and, on the other hand, the developing countries' interest in education for development necessitated a settlement between developed and developing countries.[100] To be precise, the Appendix aims to limit the scope of possible compulsory licences and to grant more protection to copyright owners than was afforded in the Protocol. As Olian spelt out:

> Licenses for translation, available for any purpose under the Protocol, may only be granted under the Paris Appendix 'for the purposes of teaching, scholarship or research'. Reproduction licenses, on the other hand, which had previously been available for any 'educational or cultural purposes' are now restricted to use 'in connection with systematic instructional activities'.[101]

[100] Ruth L. Okediji, 'The International Copyright System: Limitations, Exceptions and Public Interest Considerations for Developing Countries' [2006] UNCTAD–ICTSD Project on IPRs and Sustainable Development 15. Okediji discusses how bulk access issue motivated the adoption of the Appendix:

> Bulk access—that is, access to multiple copies of a copyrighted work at affordable prices—goes directly to the right of an author to control the reproduction of the work. Most developing and least developed countries have the requisite copying technologies to reproduce copyrighted works and supply the local market with cheap copies. In sum, the reproduction right is the legal response to the public goods problem associated with the major categories of intellectual property. There is also a second component to the access problem for developing countries and that is the availability of copies in local languages. The Berne Convention grants authors the exclusive right to translate their works, meaning that even if cheap copies were available for purchase locally, access would nevertheless be meaningless unless those copies were translated. The reproduction and translation rights thus operate in tandem as barriers to access in developing countries.

[101] Irwin A. Olian, 'International Copyright and the Needs of Developing Countries: The Awakening at Stockholm and Paris' [1974] 7 Cornell Int'l LJ 108.

Provisions relating to the author's right to just compensation appear more strengthened in the Appendix. In the Protocol, payment to authors was subject to non-convertible local currency, while the Appendix now required the competent authority to 'make all efforts, by the use of international machinery to ensure transmittal in international convertible currency or its equivalent'.[102]

Among the other peculiar revisions are the 'uses' for which compulsory licences can be obtained. Unlike the Protocol, the Appendix provides for the grant of a compulsory licence for translation only 'for the purposes of teaching, scholarship and research'.[103] The Appendix introduces a system of non-exclusive and non-transferable licences for translation, where a licence can be applied for by any national applicant of a developing country no less than three years after first publication, upon further condition that a translation has not been published in a 'language of general use' in the developing country,[104] or if all the editions are out of print.[105] Where the 'language in general use' in the developing country is not in use in one or more of the developed countries, the waiting period of three years shall be reduced to one year.[106] The concession of this shortened period is available only where the language in question is not English, Spanish, or French. This exclusion of translations from English, Spanish, and French 'must be regarded as a considerable concession in favour of authors and publishers in those languages'.[107]

Though the expression 'general use' has not been defined in the Appendix, the UNESCO/WIPO guidelines on the implementation of the Berne Appendix define 'language in general use' as English, Spanish, and French.[108] With this meaning, translations in colonial languages only

[102] Berne Convention 1886, appendix, Art IV, 6(a)(ii).
[103] Berne Convention 1886, appendix, Art II, para 5.
[104] Berne Convention 1886, appendix, Art II (2)(a).
[105] Berne Convention 1886, appendix, Art II(2)(b).
[106] Berne Convention 1886, appendix, Art II(3)(a).
[107] Saleh Basalamah, 'Compulsory Licensing for Translation: An Instrument of Development?' [2000] 40 IDEA 503.
[108] 'Report of Working Group on the Formulation of Guidelines on the System of Translation and Reproduction Licenses for Developing Countries under the Copyright Conventions' *Copyright: Monthly Review of the World Intellectual Property Organization* (April 1983) 129, para 36 <www.wipo.int/edocs/pubdocs/en/copyright/120/wipo_pub_120_1983_04.pdf> accessed 25 September 2025. (There was much controversy over the expression 'general use'. It was also proposed that this would refer to 'any language officially recognized as one of the national languages of a country'. However, only the English, Spanish, and French language were considered to be the 'languages in general use in one or more developed countries'.)

exempt the issuance of compulsory licence, while keeping mother languages or other native languages outside the ambit of the provisional requirement. It comes as no surprise that in many developing countries, local languages are the medium of instruction.

In India, more than 19,569 mother tongues are spoken by a population of 1.38 billion.[109] Moreover, according to the 2011 Census of India, around 44% of the total population identified Hindi as their mother tongue, while the other top languages, such as Bengali, Marathi, Telugu, and Tamil, are primarily spoken by over a quarter of the population. To apply for the licence to get the books translated into these local languages, one needs to wait for the waiting period, during which various textbooks become redundant and outdated. Clearly, the developing countries, and it goes without saying that the least developed countries, can rarely reap any benefits from these concessions. South Asia, one of the most linguistically diverse areas in the world, is home to more than 650 languages.[110] The language condition formulated in Article II, para 3 makes the provision unworkable because it includes languages in 'general use'.

Another modification is that the applicant must wait six months before the licence is granted, which effectively extends the actual waiting period to three years and six months before the licence can be obtained.[111] If the owner chooses to translate during the six months, the compulsory licence shall not be granted. In essence, the provision works to discourage interested applicants, as very few would be able to take the risk of spending time and money without having any assurance about the issuance of a licence.

About reproduction, a licence which could previously be issued for 'any educational or cultural purpose' is now restricted to use 'in connection with systematic instructional activities', yet this term has not been defined in the Appendix.[112] The duration of the waiting period varies depending on the nature of work. In the case of works of natural and physical sciences, including mathematics and technology, an application

[109] Census (2011) Government of India 4 <http://censusindia.gov.in> accessed 20 September 2025.

[110] 'South Asia Most Diverse with 650 Languages' *The Hindu* (08 January 2018) <www.thehindu.com/news/national/karnataka/south-asia-most-diverse-with-650-languages/article22399276.ece#google_vignette> accessed 24 September 2025.

[111] Berne Convention 1886, appendix, Art II, para 4(a).

[112] Berne Convention 1886, appendix, Art III, para 2(a).

can be made after three years of publication. In respect of works of fiction, poetry, drama, and music, and for art, the waiting period is five years, and for all other works, the waiting period is seven years.[113]

In sum, the Appendix entails the substantive and procedural rules on the issuance of compulsory licences for translations and reproduction. With a view to addressing the bulk access issue in developing countries, the Appendix was also incorporated in the Agreement on Trade-Related Aspects of Intellectual Property Rights (TRIPS).

7.1. Berne Appendix: A Failing Endeavour?

The 1971 Berne Convention Appendix was an attempt to eliminate the 'power inequality' between the corporate copyright owners and the users in poorer countries of the South. It aimed to apply the 'balance' metaphor in international copyright discourse, but it resulted in an insignificant practical benefit to the countries of the South.[114] Even though the Appendix was conceived about the developing countries, it has not been a success in either 'making the application of the Convention easier' or meeting the needs of developing countries regarding education.[115] As Ricketson concluded in 1987, 'it is hard to point to any obvious benefits that have flowed directly to developing countries from the adoption of the Appendix', and it still reveals meagre results even after several decades. Since 1971, 'only a handful of developing countries have so far availed themselves of its provisions'.[116] Certainly, the Appendix's procedural complexity, transaction costs involved in fulfilling the requirements, and the waiting period materially discourage its use by the countries.[117]

[113] Berne Convention 1886, appendix, Art III, para 3.

[114] Alan Story, *Study on Intellectual Property Rights, The Internet, and Copyright*, Study Paper 5 (Commission on Intellectual Property Rights 2002) <www.iprcommission.org/papers/pdfs/study_papers/sp5_story_study.pdf> accessed 26 September 2025 (examining why the 'Appendix model' has failed to overcome the severe information divide in printed materials between rich and poor nations).

[115] Ndene Ndiaye, 'The Berne Convention and Developing Countries' [1986] 1 Colum JL & Arts 47, 55.

[116] Sam Ricketson and Jane C. Ginsburg, *International Copyright and Neighbouring Rights: The Berne Convention and Beyond* (2nd edn, OUP 2006) 957.

[117] Alberto J. Cerda Silva, 'Beyond the Unrealistic Solution for Development Provided by the Appendix of the Berne Convention on Copyright' [2013] 60 J Copyright Soc'y USA 581, 616 (noting the limitations of developing countries' markets and the high transactional costs for publishers operating in small capacities and market sizes).

The lengthy procedure required to obtain licences extensively delays access to educational resources by a significant period of time.[118]

After examining the interlocked provisions of the Appendix, Story has noted three weaknesses in the 'Appendix' model.[119] First, it operates on a 'rights and access model', which means separate contracts, separate permissions, and separate arrangements for each work of translation into each different language. The effect is that each licence has to be applied separately. In the given system, there would be a need for frequent negotiations and correspondence between publishers in the developed countries and the applicants in the poor countries, particularly when they are already deriving good returns from sales in the countries of the North.[120] Second, the Appendix model proceeds on the assumption that there is a harmonious and cooperative negotiation between copyright owners and licensees in the developing countries, and the compulsory licence component remains in the background just as a deterrence in case any unwillingness to cooperate occurs.

Third, the Appendix assumes that the only way to reproduce the educational resources is to transfer the rights to local publishers, as only they would be capable of reproducing copyrighted materials. This assumption does not hold water in the 'photocopying era', where students and teachers get the materials reproduced for themselves on a non-profit basis. The restrictive and expensive 'Appendix model' contains no provision for this as well.[121] Most importantly, the Appendix contains no single provision for unrestricted educational use of the copyrighted works.[122]

Even after years of being in force, the Appendix has not served its intended purpose of ensuring bulk access to copyrighted materials in

[118] Margaret Chon, 'Intellectual Property "from Below": Copyright and Capability for Education' [2007] 40 UC Davis L Rev 803, 829 (outlining the deficiencies of the Appendix to the Paris Act).

[119] Alan Story, *Study on Intellectual Property Rights, The Internet, and Copyright*, Study Paper 5 (Commission on Intellectual Property Rights 2002) 51 <www.iprcommission.org/papers/pdfs/study_papers/sp5_story_study.pdf> accessed 26 September 2025.

[120] Alan Story, *Study on Intellectual Property Rights, The Internet, and Copyright*, Study Paper 5 (Commission on Intellectual Property Rights 2002) 51 <www.iprcommission.org/papers/pdfs/study_papers/sp5_story_study.pdf> accessed 26 September 2025.

[121] Alan Story, *Study on Intellectual Property Rights, The Internet, and Copyright*, Study Paper 5 (Commission on Intellectual Property Rights 2002) 52 <www.iprcommission.org/papers/pdfs/study_papers/sp5_story_study.pdf> accessed 26 September 2025.

[122] Alan Story, *Study on Intellectual Property Rights, The Internet, and Copyright*, Study Paper 5 (Commission on Intellectual Property Rights 2002) 51–52 <www.iprcommission.org/papers/pdfs/study_papers/sp5_story_study.pdf> accessed 26 September 2025.

regional languages. The end result is that the Appendix failed to provide a mechanism that developing countries may use to address the problems associated with their phase of development. As Silva writes, 'the Appendix comes across as an obsolete, inappropriate, bureaucratic, and minimal attempt to provide an air valve for developing countries'.[123] As of 2025, only thirty-two countries have expressed their interest to the Director General of WIPO in availing themselves of the Appendix provisions (see Annexure A).[124] The reason for this is firmly correlated to the complicated and burdensome requirements imposed by the Appendix. The Appendix failed to provide a mechanism that developing countries may use to address the problems associated with their phase of development. As Story writes:

> [A]lthough the Berne Appendix is labelled as a set of 'special provisions regarding developing countries,' it is, in reality, a distraction from the real struggle to win better access rights for the South; it is a mere table scrap, a tactical cul de sac, a legal nightmare. The 'special' situation found across many parts of the South is not addressed and, not surprisingly, its provisions have seldom been used by countries of the South in the 35 years since it came into existence.[125]

Annexure A reflects the total number of member countries that have expressed their interest to the Director General of WIPO. It indicates the notifications that are currently active and those that have become inactive in the past. All the countries availed themselves of Article II and III of the Appendix, except Samoa and Thailand, which relied on only Article II of the Appendix.

Although the declaration does not automatically make access easier, the Appendix provisions must also be adopted and implemented by member states into their domestic laws. Many countries have deposited

[123] Alberto J. Cerda Silva, 'Beyond the Unrealistic Solution for Development Provided by the Appendix of the Berne Convention on Copyright' [2013] 60 J Copyright Soc'y USA 590.

[124] WIPO-Administered Treaties, Notifications on the Berne Convention, WIPO, <www.wipo.int/treaties/en/ShowResults.jsp?country_id=ALL&start_year=ANY&end_year=ANY&search_what=N&treaty_id=15> accessed 27 September 2025.

[125] Alan Story, Colin Darch, and Debora Halbert (eds) *The Copy/South Dossier: Issues in the Economics, Politics, and Ideology of Copyright in the Global South* (The Copy/South Research Group 2006) 139–40.

the declaration, yet have not incorporated the Appendix provision or a similar provision into their national laws. These countries have adopted the compulsory licensing mechanism that varies materially from the Berne mechanism. For instance, Cuba has a mechanism for a compulsory licence to reproduce and translate work, but it does not mention compensation to the owner.[126] Vietnam establishes a licensing mechanism for reproduction, without specifying any royalty or procedural requirements as outlined in the Appendix.[127] As per the mechanism adopted, a licence can be granted in the public interest, namely, 'defense, security, people's livelihood objectives and other interests of the state and society'. Though there is no explicit mention of 'educational purposes' to obtain a compulsory licence, it will be covered under the phrase 'other interests of the state and society' and 'people's livelihood objectives'.

Jordan has adopted a mechanism that is similar to the Appendix mechanism. It provides for a licence to translate foreign works in printed or any other form, provided that three years have elapsed since the first publication.[128] Jordan, being an Arabic-speaking country, could shorten the waiting period to one year, but it chose not to provide the option given under Article II (3)(b) of the Appendix. With respect to reproduction, it provides for the licence of copyrighted material to meet the needs of the public or for school or university education.[129] Bangladesh[130] and Thailand[131] have also adopted a similar language to the Appendix.

To sum up, it can be stated that the member countries have adopted 'idiosyncratic' solutions into their domestic laws to solve the access problem.[132] Some of these solutions even surpass the foresight of the Berne Convention. In other words, many countries have adopted a

[126] Law No. 14 of 28 December 1977, Art 37 (setting forth a provision for a Compulsory Licence for the Use of Works of Great Social Interest and Necessary for Education, Science, Technology and Professional Development).

[127] Intellectual Property Law No. 50/2005/QH11, 29 November 2005, Arts 7, 25, and 42–43.

[128] Copyright Law, Law No. 22 of 1992 (as amended by laws No.14 of 1998, No. 29 of 1999, and No. 52 of 2001), Art 11(a).

[129] Copyright Law 1992 (as amended by laws No. 14 of 1998, No. 29 of 1999, and No. 52 of 2001), Art 11(b)(2) and (c).

[130] Copyright Act 2000, s 52.

[131] Copyright Act, B.E. 2537 (1994), ss 54–55.

[132] Alberto J. Cerda Silva, 'Beyond the Unrealistic Solution for Development Provided by the Appendix of the Berne Convention on Copyright' [2013] 60 J Copyright Soc'y USA 598 (discussing how the developing countries chose not to adopt the bureaucratic and limited mechanism of the Appendix and have adopted their own peculiar solutions to meet the need of wider dissemination of knowledge).

mechanism for compulsory licensing that is much broader than that provided in the Appendix. Several countries appear to have adopted a licensing provision for public interest as opposed to merely for 'systematic instructional activities' or 'teaching, scholarship or research'. Thus, none of the attempts by the Berne Convention effectively met the need for wider dissemination of knowledge in the developing world.

4

Access to Knowledge and Copyright Law in India

A Legal Analysis

1. Introduction

India is the fifth-largest economy in the world, with a GDP of approximately $3.57 trillion in 2023.[1] It is one of the few countries in the world that is experiencing economic growth despite the global economic shift to a lower gear. During the past three decades, India's economy has accelerated gradually and has become globally integrated.[2] Despite having a robust approach towards the economy, India is still lagging in human development. According to the UNDP report, India ranked 134 of 193 countries in the 2024 Human Development Index.[3] The report sets out the systemic inequalities and deprivations that go beyond income. The report lists four essential elements for human development: health, education and knowledge, human security in the face of shocks, and access to new technologies. Access to knowledge is viewed as indispensable for development. It is crucial for the Indian 'knowledge economy' to reach the majority of its population.

According to the 2024 Multidimensional Poverty Index, prepared by UNDP, India is home to 234 million people living in acute

[1] World Development Indicators database, *World Bank* <https://data.worldbank.org/indicator/NY.GDP.MKTP.CD?locations=IN> accessed 29 September 2025.

[2] Junaid Kamal Ahmad, Florian Blum, Poonam Gupta, and Dhruv Jain, 'India's Growth Story', Policy Research Working Paper 8599 (World Bank Group 2018) <http://documents1.worldbank.org/curated/en/941201538406933607/pdf/WPS8599.pdf> accessed 29 September 2025.

[3] *Human Development Report 2023/2024: Breaking the Gridlock* (UNDP 14 March 2024) https://www.undp.org/india/publications/human-development-report-2023-24-0 accessed 2 October 2025.

Access to Knowledge in the Developing World. Vandana Mahalwar, Oxford University Press.
 DOI: 10.1093/9780198986782.003.0004

multidimensional poverty.[4] Although India has been successful in reducing poverty between 2015-16 and 2019-21, it still accounts for a significant proportion of the world's multidimensional poverty.[5] Multidimensional poverty reflects the comprehensive picture of deprivation that poor people experience in various areas, including health, education, and living standards. While urban India has notably profited from economic growth, rural areas are not keeping pace with urban technological developments. More than 850 million Indians, i.e., 60% of the total population, live in villages that lack access to quality education. As per the Economic Survey 2020, rural students spend 10% more money on books as compared to their counterparts in urban areas.[6] The survey indicates that books are the second-largest component of educational expenditure for rural students. Book deprivation is not peculiar to any specific state or section of people. Any population in the low-income bracket comprises the deprived groups, whether in rural or urban areas, or whether they are boys or girls. Hence, book deprivation exists in poor households in rich states, but not among the rich families in poor states. Access to knowledge is considerably influenced by poverty and other social and economic factors, including the affordability of textbooks. It can be said that the persistent socio-economic reality of poverty in India makes reading opportunities impractical for many households. It can be understood that if the literacy rate in India improves, it would significantly alter the global educational landscape. The inverse relationship between education and development is the need to expand the availability of learning materials. In the view of the World Bank:

> Education pays significant dividends in reducing poverty. Good education pays high returns in the contributions to economic growth . . . Educating the poor, women, and the disadvantaged is as good an

[4] *Global Multidimensional Poverty Index 2024: Poverty Amid Conflict* (UNDP 17 October 2024) <https://hdr.undp.org/content/2024-global-multidimensional-poverty-index-mpi#/indicies/MPI> accessed 2 October 2025.

[5] NITI Aayog, *India National Multidimensional Poverty Index: A Progress Review 2023* (UNDP and OPHI 18 July 2023) <www.undp.org/india/publications/national-multidimensional-poverty-index-progress-review-2023> accessed 2 October 2025.

[6] 'Economic Survey 2019-20', Volume II, Ministry of Finance, Government of India (January 2020) 278 <https://www.indiabudget.gov.in/budget2020-21/economicsurvey/doc/echapter_vol2.pdf> accessed 4 October 2025.

investment as any India can make. India faces many educational challenges and particularly those of narrowing or closing the gaps between rich and poor, boys and girls, privileged groups and under castes.[7]

2. Barriers of the Indian Textual Diet

'I can't buy my Class 12 books until I sell my old Class 11 books', says Nazia on her first day of school.[8]

As per the last Census, despite tremendous strides in literacy rate, increasing from 64.8% in 2001 to 74% in 2011,[9] millions of Indian children are still living under the condition of extreme poverty, which has a direct impact on their educational lives. Even with several years of funding under the Sarva Shiksha Abhiyan,[10] Samagra Shiksha Abhiyan,[11] and Padhe Bharat Badhe Bharat,[12] books are still short for all classes in most primary schools. As per the Annual Status of Education Report (Rural) 2022, 'the availability of reading material other than textbooks has gone down from 6.6% to 5.2% households'.[13] The problem is not limited to textbooks; there is a visible scarcity of all kinds of learning

[7] 'Reducing Poverty in India: Options for More Effective Public Services', Report No. 17881-IN (World Bank 1998) <http://documents.worldbank.org/curated/en/793451468752712746/India-Reducing-poverty-in-India-options-for-more-effective-public-services> accessed 4 October 2025.

[8] Aman Sethi and A. Mariyam Alavi, 'Students are Fighting to Stay in the Education Arms Race, Class of 2018 Project' *The Hindustan Times* <www.hindustantimes.com/class-of-2018/in-textbook-struggle-students-fight-to-stay-in-Indias-education-arms-race.html> accessed 4 October 2025.

[9] Figures taken from the Census of India 2011, see <https://censusindia.gov.in/census.website/> accessed 13 October 2025.

[10] Sarva Shiksha Abhiyan is an initiative by India's government for universalization of elementary education for children aged six to fourteen years. It seeks to provide quality education by strengthening school infrastructure and by providing teaching–learning materials to children at no cost.

[11] In 2018, the Government of India launched a programme 'Samagra Shiksha Abhiyan' for the students from pre-school to class 12. Under the programme, government schools across the country are granted library funds to strengthen their libraries. It has been extended further for a period of five years, from 1 April 2021 to 31 March 2026. 'Samagra Siksha Abhiyan for school education' *Ministry of Education* (02 February 2022) <https://pib.gov.in/PressReleasePage.aspx?PRID=1794742> accessed 12 October 2025.

[12] 'Library Grant for Promoting Reading Habits' *Ministry of Education* <https://samagra.education.gov.in/library.html> accessed 12 October 2025 (to foster the habit of reading and to strengthen school libraries, the provision for a separate annual library grant was initiated under the Padhe Bharat Badhe Bharat Scheme).

[13] *Annual Status of Education Report (Rural) 2022* (ASER Centre 18 January 2025).

materials, whether due to excessive cost, fewer volumes in neglected languages, or format. There is a combination of factors, including copyright, that leads to severe access issues related to reading materials. Although reports reveal a significant increase in access to learning materials over the past few years, India is one of the developing countries that is still unable to provide textbooks to every student.

2.1. Price of the Learning Material

As featured in *The Tribune*, Sumit Sangwan, an engineering student in Sirsa, found himself in a quandary as to how to access his engineering course book when the two copies in the college library were already issued and, at Rupees 2,500, the cost of a new book was nearly unaffordable for him.[14] Like many others, Sumit faced book hunger first-hand as a college student.

Generally, it is believed that the cost of books in India is low and, hence, affordable. The concept of affordability needs consideration from two different angles. First, consider only the price of a book in India, which may be lower than the price in any developed country, such as the USA. Second, how much this price comprises of the percentage of per capita income in that particular country. When we rely on empirical evidence and surveys of comparative costs as they currently exist, it suggests that buyers in the US are paying a significantly smaller portion of their incomes than their counterparts in India. Buyers in India have to spend a significant proportion of their incomes to buy books. For families with meagre disposable income, books are too expensive to buy. In other words, these families have to pay a relatively higher price for a book as a percentage of their per capita income.

If we compare the prices of books in absolute terms, the prices of books in India are lower than in the US. Nevertheless, lower prices of books do not mean more affordable books. When the list price of a book is viewed in terms of a country's average individual income, it becomes visible

[14] Geetu Vaid, 'Books of Hope' *The Tribune* (01 November 2015) <www.tribuneindia.com/news/archive/features/school-heads-to-seek-parents-views-151596> accessed 12 October 2025.

that Indian buyers will have to spend extra portions of their income on books as compared to buyers in the US. It is important to note that the remainder of the household income, after fulfilling basic needs like food, clothing, and shelter, determines the affordability of books.

There is a slew of reasons that contribute toward higher prices relative to per capita income. Chon discusses the reasons for excessive prices:

> The price of textbooks can be very high relative to per capita income for a number of reasons. In the case of state owned or assisted publishing, these reasons include inefficient manufacturing methods, state monopolies, and favoritism. In the case of market-based textbook publishing, these reasons may include industry consolidation and lack of competition. Higher prices may be caused by the failure of multinational publishers to engage in differential pricing, so that a student in a developing country may pay a relatively high price for a book as a percentage of per capita GDP compared to a student in a developed country.[15]

Nielsen's India Book Market Report finds that, with more than 9,000 publishers and 21,000 book retailers, India is the sixth-largest book market in the world and the second-largest for English-language books.[16] The report says that even though there are a variety of government initiatives, 'the Indian book industry receives no direct investment from the government—a serious roadblock for publishers'. The other challenges to the publishing sector include a complex distribution system, lengthy credit cycles, rising direct costs, and widespread piracy.

India is not the only developing country to suffer due to the rising cost of academic literature.[17] When applying Chon's analysis to the higher education context, a crucial aspect to consider is that the top academic

[15] Margaret Chon, 'Intellectual Property "from Below": Copyright and Capability for Education' [2007] 40 UC Davis L Rev 825; see also Andrew Rens, Achal Prabhala, and Dick Kawooya, *Intellectual Property, Education and Access to Knowledge in Southern Africa* (ICTSD, UNCTAD, and TRALAC 2006) 13 <https://unctad.org/system/files/official-document/ictsd-tralac2006d1_en.pdf> accessed 5 October 2025 (analysing how the lack of competition in the publishing industry enables the publisher to control the market for given educational materials).

[16] *Nielsen India Book Market Report 2015: Understanding the India Book Market* (Nielsen 2015).

[17] Jacob P. Koshy, 'Rising Cost of Science Journals Worries Top Science Officials' *Mint* (25 Oct 2012) <www.livemint.com/Politics/trpj70vM3TaZW8j64orqMJ/Rising-cost-of-science-journals-worries-top-science-official.html> accessed 5 October 2025.

research journals are dominated by a few international publishers. Averse to promoting Indian journals, it encourages foreign players to create a publishing monopoly in the market, resulting in prohibitive prices for academic literature. Moreover, a remarkable gap exists between budget allocation and price escalation in journal subscriptions. Libraries are constantly struggling to pay the exorbitant prices of academic research resources within their existing budgetary constraints. Studies have shown that due to the rising cost of journals, many libraries are compelled to reduce the number of journal subscriptions.[18] Due to the high pricing, the majority of journal articles are behind paywalls and inaccessible to most universities in India.

Expensive books have exponentially contributed to a pernicious but expected form of resistance—'piracy'. According to the Study on Copyright Piracy in India, conducted by the Ministry of Human Resource Development (MHRD), two primary reasons lead to book piracy: the high price of the book and its popularity.[19] Identifying another pervasive form of piracy, the MHRD report provides that:

> Piracy in the form of mass photocopying of books is largely prevalent in India, especially in and around educational institutions. Students borrow books from libraries and then get these photocopied from the photocopier kept at the institution where from the books are borrowed. While copyright law permits photocopying of literary works for limited private uses such as research, review or criticism what happens, many a time is that the entire book is photocopied including the cover pages.[20]

It was around the 1970s when book pirates emerged. Today, pirate publishing is flourishing apace in India. With the use of the latest reproduction and printing technologies, a book's format, cover, colour, and

[18] Jiban K. Pal and Prabir Kumar Das, 'Progress Through Partnership: Consortia Based e-Resource Subscription Initiatives in India', Workshop on Consortia Based Subscription of Online Resources (Indian Statistical Institute 2008).

[19] 'Study On Copyright Piracy In India' *MHRD, Government of India* <https://copyright.gov.in/documents/study%20on%20copyright%20piracy%20in%20india.pdf> accessed 7 October 2025.

[20] 'Study On Copyright Piracy In India' *MHRD, Government of India* <https://copyright.gov.in/documents/study%20on%20copyright%20piracy%20in%20india.pdf> accessed 7 October 2025.

barcode, as well as the text, are copied by pirates to make the illegal copies indistinguishable from the original ones. This phenomenon, however, is limited to a narrow segment of bestselling authors because of the small scale on which distribution is typically organized.[21] The pirate book trade is typically carried out by vendors on the streets and at traffic signals, who hawk inexpensive and illegal versions at a margin of profit that no regular bookseller can compete with.[22] Unsurprisingly, students prefer to buy their expensive course books from the street seller at less than half the book cover price. Interestingly, pirate book publishing is not confined only to expensive books. Despite low prices, school textbooks are also pirated at an alarmingly high rate. The delayed availability of textbooks at the time of the reopening of schools triggers the pirates to capitalize on it.[23] It is clear that book piracy satiates the appetite for books of those who need them, but, in contrast, it massively undermines the lucrative markets of publishers. As Nilanjana Roy puts it, '[t]he romantic view of piracy is that it keeps books and authors in circulation; in practice, only a handful of authors are gainers'.[24]

2.2. Digital Divide

In the absence of printed books, the promise of education remains a distant dream, as reading materials are available only in digital format, and the majority of readers lack access to proper gadgets and proficiency. While the digitized readings prove to be an easy means of learning for the privileged class, it does not serve the textual diet of the underprivileged class. In internet access, the stark divide in rural and urban areas also remains significant. The word 'divide' signifies barriers in connectivity, capacity, and technical infrastructure issues. Access to digital books

[21] Lawrence Liang, 'India: The Knowledge Thief' in Joe Karaganis (ed) *Shadow Libraries: Access to Educational Materials in Global Higher Education* (MIT Press 2018) 201.

[22] Sonia Faleiro, 'The Book Boys of Mumbai' *The New York Times* (04 January 2013) <www.nytimes.com/2013/01/06/books/review/the-book-boys-of-mumbai.html?auth=login-google> accessed 7 October 2025.

[23] Eric Falt, 'Riding Rough Seas of Book Piracy' *The Pioneer* (04 May 2019) <www.dailypioneer.com/2019/columnists/riding-rough-seas-of-book-piracy.html> accessed 9 October 2025.

[24] Nilanjana S Roy, 'The pirate wars' *Business Standard* (17 March 2014) https://www.business-standard.com/article/opinion/nilanjana-s-roy-the-pirate-wars-114031700592_1.html accessed 9 October 2025.

requires reliable internet capabilities. There has been a significant rise in the number of internet users over the last decade; however, the population in rural areas and low-income households still lacks access to the internet. The inequality in access to digital learning materials ranges from devices like mobile phones or computers to internet services and electricity. Smartphones can help with attending online classes, but they are not ideal for reading lengthy materials, such as books. Most importantly, communities need to have access to electricity resources to charge their devices and to connect them to the internet. Though India has seen a significant rise in access to the internet, there is still a lack of devices like laptops and mobiles. A large number of users in rural India use the internet on shared devices. In rural India, around 67% of the population is dependent on shared devices.[25] According to a survey conducted by NSSO, the percentage of households possessing a computer or laptop is 4.2% in rural India and 21.6% in urban areas.[26] All of this takes a long time to build the digital capabilities to encourage literacy through e-books.

2.3. Language Barrier

Another important reason for access impediments is the language barrier. India is one of the four countries, along with Nigeria, Indonesia, and Papua New Guinea, that have the most 'living' indigenous languages.[27] There are more than 19,500 spoken languages and dialects in India. There is a desperate shortage of books in local languages, as most of the books are published in Hindi and English. This causes book hunger because readers do not get access to books in their own languages. This linguistic diversity creates a significant gap in linguistic equality and access to learning resources. This gap puts those readers at an extreme

[25] *Internet in India 2024* (Internet and Mobile Association of India (IAMAI) 2024) <www.iamai.in/sites/default/files/research/Kantar_%20IAMAI%20report_2024_.pdf> accessed 9 October 2025.

[26] 'Comprehensive Annual Modular Survey 2022-23' 79th Round (National Sample Survey Office 2024) <www.mospi.gov.in/sites/default/files/publication_reports/CAMS%20Report_October_N.pdf> accessed 9 October 2025.

[27] 'Education in Mother Languages Improves Student Learning and Sustains Heterogeneous Traditions' *Economic & Political Weekly* (21 February 2020) <www.epw.in/engage/article/education-mother-languages-tradition#> accessed 10 October 2025

disadvantage who are forced to read a textbook written in a language that is too advanced for them. As Mirchandani rightly said, 'textbooks are usually written by elites and only benefit the best students'.[28]

English medium textbooks can be suitable for the majority of students in urban area schools, but they are not suitable for students and many teachers in rural area schools.[29] In other words, they must confront language difficulties in comprehending basic concepts. Children fail to learn because they have to read the book in a language that they do not understand. This adds an extra step to learning, namely the translation of the book's content into one's own language. When students are unable to comprehend the content, it converts the act of learning into an act of memorization.[30] Linguistic barriers may potentially negatively impact students' motivation to learn through reading books.

3. Academic Libraries in India

In a community marked by 'book scarcity', one can easily expect readers to depend heavily on public institutions for reading and learning materials. As an alternative channel of education, reading materials can be found in libraries, which serve to expand literacy and public opinion within the community. Public libraries, as an embodiment of a variety of informational resources, are considered 'stimulative centres for national awakening and public spirit'.[31] The libraries of renowned ancient universities, such as Takshila and Nalanda, were the repositories of India's vast knowledge. Though libraries in India have existed since ancient times, the development of public libraries accelerated in the post-independence era with a focus on building a knowledge society. The Madras Public

[28] Rajesh Mirchandani, 'Why Kids Are Dropping Out of School and What Works in Education—Podcast with Karthik Muralidharan' *Centre for Global Development* (18 August 2015) <www.cgdev.org/blog/why-kids-are-dropping-out-school-and-what-works-education-podcast-karthik-muralidharan> accessed 10 October 2025.

[29] M. Shuheb Khan, 'For Schools in Rural India, the Appropriate Language of Instruction Remains a Conundrum' *The Wire* (17 July 2017) <https://thewire.in/education/appropriate-language-rural-areas-english-hindi-conundrum> accessed 10 October 2025.

[30] Andy Smart and Shanti Jagannathan, *Textbook Policies in Asia: Development, Publishing, Printing, Distribution, and Future Implications* (Asian Development Bank 2018).

[31] 'Library Movement in Madras—20th May 1920' in N. Ravi (ed) *The Hindu Speaks on Libraries* (Kasturi & sons 1992) 3.

Library Act, 1948, was the first library legislation that provided for the establishment of public libraries in the State of Madras.[32] Dr S.R. Ranganathan, a mathematician turned librarian, was one of the library pioneers who made efforts for this legislation and inspired the vision of public libraries across the country. His 'Five Laws of Library Science' was one of the earliest formulations that furthered the objectives of the Access to Knowledge movement. The laws that served as guidelines to the librarian's mission are:

1. Books are for use.
2. Books are for all.
3. To every book its reader.
4. Save the time of the reader.
5. The library is a growing organism.

Due to the influence of Ranganathan's five laws of library science, the libraries at that time underwent myriad positive changes to maximize access to readers.[33]

After independence in 1947, over the next half-century, ten states in India enacted library legislation based on the Madras Public Libraries Act.[34] India wanted to feed its population with some amount of literacy. That created the need to expand library services as an aid to literacy education.[35] To date, nineteen out of twenty-nine states have enacted library

[32] Prashant Iyengar, 'Public Libraries and Access to Knowledge (A2K): A History of Open Access (OA) and the Internet in India in the Nineteenth and Twentieth Centuries' in Ramesh Subramanian and Lea Shaver (eds) *Access to Knowledge in India: New Research on Intellectual Property, Innovation & Development* (Bloomsbury Academic 2011) 46.

[33] Tom Kwanya, Christine Stilwell, and Peter G. Underwood, 'Library 2.0 Principles and Ranganathan's Fifth Law' [2010] 28 Mousaion 2.

[34] (i) Madras (Tamil Nadu) Public Libraries Act 1948, (ii) Andhra Pradesh Public Libraries Act 1960, (iii) Mysore (Karnataka) Public Libraries Act 1965, (iv) Maharashtra Public Libraries Act 1967, (v) West Bengal Public Libraries Act 1979, (vi) Manipur Public Libraries Act 1988, (vii) Kerala Public Libraries Act 1989, (viii) Haryana Public Libraries Act 1989, (ix) Mizoram Public Libraries Act 1993, and (x) Goa Public Libraries Act 1993. For more details, see Prashant Iyengar, 'Public Libraries and Access to Knowledge (A2K): A History of Open Access (OA) and the Internet in India in the Nineteenth and Twentieth Centuries' in Ramesh Subramanian and Lea Shaver (eds) *Access to Knowledge in India: New Research on Intellectual Property, Innovation & Development* (Bloomsbury Academic 2011) 48.

[35] R.K. Sandhu and H.S. Sandhu, 'Villages with and without Libraries in India' [1979] 11 Int'l Libr Rev 269.

legislation, of which only five have a library excess or tax levy provision, while sixteen states continue with no library legislation at all. Despite these legislative efforts, some scholars have observed that, contrary to Great Britain and the United States, India is 'a century behind in matters of library legislation.'[36]

Balaji and Vinay expressed that 'the legislative process and legal issues involved in policy making, combined with the lack of political consensus and goodwill, have severely constrained the growth, coverage and development of public libraries for people in India.'[37] India is facing challenges in automating and integrating library resources and services,[38] due to 'acute shortage in infrastructure, funds and lack of local policies.'[39] There have been several government initiatives, such as the National Mission on Public Libraries launched in 2014, that aimed to modernize and digitize the collections of 9,000 public libraries across India, facilitating readers with access to information. Despite such efforts, reports on the quality of these libraries cast a shadow over their capacity to meet the access demands of readers. Because of the acute shortage of funds, the majority of public libraries have been languishing and are on the verge of closure. For example, in Bihar, only 51 out of 540 libraries have survived over the last six decades. Most of the rural libraries in Bihar lack even basic reading materials. It is difficult to imagine books, periodicals, and journals in such libraries as they are not even able to subscribe to daily newspapers.[40] Libraries in other states, too, are not high on the priority list. By most accounts, public libraries in India have dwindled to provide access to educational resources and that makes piracy unavoidable to many readers.

[36] James Heitzman and A.Y. Asundi, 'Evaluation of Public Libraries in India: The Case of Karnataka' [2000] 16 Information Development 142, 154.

[37] B. Preedip Balaji, M.S. Vinay, and J.S. Mohan Raju, 'A Policy Review of Public Libraries in India', working paper (Indian Institute for Human Settlements 2018) 5.

[38] R.K. Matoria, P.K. Upadhyay, and M. Moni, 'Automation and Networking of Public Libraries in India using the e-Granthalaya Software from the National Informatics Centre' [2007] 41 Program: Electronic Libr and Info Systems 47, 58.

[39] Rupinder Singh, 'Status and Challenges of Public Libraries' Automation in Punjab' [2012] 2 IJIDT (2012) 146, 152.

[40] B.K. Mishra, 'Libraries in Bihar on Verge of Closure Due to Shortage of Funds' *The Times of India* (29 December 2020) <https://timesofindia.indiatimes.com/city/patna/libraries-in-bihar-on-verge-of-closure-due-to-shortage-of-funds/articleshow/79997615.cms> accessed 10 October 2025.

4. The Right to Education: A Fundamental Right

India made education a fundamental right in 2002 through an amendment to the Constitution of India. The Constitution (86th Amendment) Act, 2002, inserted a new Article 21A under Part III of the Constitution, which states: 'The State shall provide free and compulsory education to all children of the age of six to fourteen years in such manner as the State may, by law, determine'. Unfortunately, Article 21A is couched in restrictive language that limits the rights available only up to the age of 14 years, thereby restricting them to elementary education. The right is also enshrined under Article 45 of the Directive Principles of State Policy under the Constitution of India that corresponds to Article 13(1) of the International Covenant on Economic, Social and Cultural Rights, which provides that '[t]he State shall endeavor to provide, within a period of ten years from the commencement of this Constitution, for free and compulsory education for all children until they complete the age of fourteen years'. The newly introduced Article 51A(k) imposes a fundamental duty on parents or guardians to provide opportunities to educate their children between the ages of six and fourteen years.

As the Supreme Court laid down in *Avinash Mehrotra v Union of India*,[41] the Constitution of India mandates that compulsory education of children be achieved, which is free from the fetters of cost, parental obstruction, or State inaction. To achieve this goal, Articles 21A and 51A(k) balance the relative burden of education on the parent and the state.

The Supreme Court of India has affirmed the fundamental right to education in many cases. Taking a broader view of the right to life, the Supreme Court of India expressed in *Francis Coralie Mullin v The Administrator, Union Territory of Delhi and Ors*[42] that 'the right to life includes the right to live with human dignity and all that goes along with it, namely, the bare necessaries of life such as adequate nutrition, clothing and shelter and facilities for reading, writing and expressing oneself in diverse forms'. The right to education does not find an explicit mention in the court's expression; however, it is implicated as an integral part of a dignified life under Article 21.

[41] 6 SCC 398 (2009).
[42] [1981] AIR 746.

A decade later, in 1992, the Supreme Court of India drew upon its precedent in *Mohini Jain v State of Karnataka & Ors* by contending that the 'right to education is the essence of the right to life and directly flows and is interlinked with it, and life living with dignity can only be assured when there is a significant role of education'.[43] The Supreme Court then re-examined the *Mohini* decision in *J.P. Unnikrishnan v State of Andhra Pradesh*[44] and held that the right to education is a fundamental right under Article 21 of the Constitution, as 'it directly flows' from the right to life.

Pursuant to Article 21A, the parliament of India enacted a rights-based law, known as the Right of Children to Free and Compulsory Education Act, in 2009, which guarantees free and compulsory education to all children between the ages of six and fourteen years. The Act examines education through the lens of the 'minimum legal entitlements' of children attending schools. One of the entitlements of children is to get free textbooks, which stems from the concept of 'free' education. The meaning of 'free education' is at variance with how it is conceptualized on the international stage. The Committee on Economic, Social and Cultural Rights defines the term 'free' as the availability of primary education without charge to the child, parents, or guardians.[45] It covers all the direct costs of schooling as the sole obligation of the governments, while the indirect costs, which are generally not included in free education, may be allowed on a case-by-case basis.[46] The direct cost of education covers textbooks, which are provided free of cost by many countries, namely, Austria, Bulgaria, Denmark, Finland, Germany, Iceland, Italy, Sri Lanka, and Sweden. Countries like Nepal and Russia provide textbooks at subsidized rates, while Armenia loans books to students against payment of an annual fee, or the parents have to contribute to the cost of textbooks.[47] In

[43] 1992 AIR 1858.

[44] 1993 AIR 2178.

[45] *CESCR General Comment No. 11: Plans of Action for Primary Education (Art. 14 of the Covenant)*, UN Doc E/1992/23 (1999) para 7 <www.refworld.org/legal/general/cescr/1999/en/8359> accessed 10 October 2025.

[46] *CESCR General Comment No. 11: Plans of Action for Primary Education (Art. 14 of the Covenant)*, UN Doc E/1992/23 (1999) para 7 <www.refworld.org/legal/general/cescr/1999/en/8359> accessed 10 October 2025.

[47] *The '4 As' Framework, Progress Report*, UN Doc E/CN.4/2000/6 (UNHRC 2000) 20, para 54 <www.ohchr.org/en/issues/education/sreducation/pages/annualreports.aspx> accessed 10 October 2025.

India, the Right to Education (RTE) Act has a provision for the distribution of free textbooks by the government to children attending school.[48] However, experiences in the field indicate a persistent struggle to effectively implement free textbooks. Non-supply, inadequate supply, and late supply of textbooks are the major challenges before authorities trying to make access equitable. Despite significant steps taken by the government post-RTE Act era, access to books is still not universal in its coverage.

4.1. Pratham—'A Book in Every Child's Hand'

While poverty-stricken families feel unable to bear the expense of textbooks, Pratham, India's largest non-governmental organization, endeavours to provide free books. Established in 1995, Pratham started providing pre-school education to children in slums in Mumbai. Today, Pratham has expanded its non-profit services of providing quality education to underprivileged youth and children to more than twenty states in the country. Recognizing the need for affordable books for children in Indian languages, Pratham Books, a not-for-profit children's book publisher, has adopted a three-pronged approach towards access to reading materials: 'the creation of books, the enablement of access to these books, and, finally, the resources to use these books to help children read.'[49] With a mission of 'a book in every child's hand', Pratham Books has published more than 5,000 print books. In 2015, it also launched Story Weaver, a digital platform that provides access to over 20,000 books in more than 233 languages, including 56 Indian languages and 177 foreign languages, such as mainstream, vulnerable, indigenous, and classical languages.[50] It contains a tool that allows readers to save e-books, which can be read offline later. The platform has open-sourced books from both Indian and international publishers, and most importantly, it allows users to translate the books into neglected indigenous languages, such as Gondi, Kora,

[48] The Right of Children to Free and Compulsory Education Rules 2010, rule 9.

[49] 'Towards Book Security for Every Child' *Annual Report 2019-20* (Pratham Books 2020) <https://prathambooks.org/wp-content/uploads/2020/12/Annual-Report_19-20_FINAL.pdf> accessed 10 October 2025.

[50] Aruna Chandaraju, 'Ample Fodder for Young Intellect' *The Hindu* (10 April 2020).

Pawari, Korku, Santali, Surjapuri, and many others.[51] Furthermore, by designing the library-in-a-classroom, Pratham Books creates a library-like atmosphere for children. A library-in-a-classroom is a hanging library on classroom walls that provides children with physical proximity to books, in addition to their course textbooks. Mission Million Books is a joint initiative by the Ratna Nidhi Charitable Trust and the Alibaba Group, aiming to distribute one million free books to 10,000 schools and colleges in India.

5. Access to Knowledge and Copyright Law in India

Like most other developing countries, India faces the fundamental challenge of promoting public access to information and knowledge. For many decades, the Indian copyright policymakers have been attempting to balance the copyright law with local educational needs. One of the early attempts can be traced back to 1914 when the Government of India enacted the Copyright Act 1914 by modifying the 1911 British Imperial Act to accommodate its specific linguistic, cultural, and educational needs.[52] To promote equitable access in the education sphere, any domestic copyright law must contain strong limitations and exceptions to copyright. To this end, India has taken legislative efforts to include exceptions and limitations for educational purposes. However, the ambiguities surrounding the essential terms used in the Copyright Act 1957, e.g. 'educational purpose', 'organised educational activity', and 'teaching', make it a case for broader interpretations of the exceptions and limitations to copyright.[53] The Delhi High Court set a precedent by liberally interpreting 'fair dealing' by allowing for the reproduction of copyrighted materials for educational purposes without any quantitative or

[51] Suzanne Singh, 'First Person: How Pratham Books Has Used the Lockdown to Expand the Reach of Its e-Books for Children' *Scroll.in* (3 June 2020) <https://scroll.in/article/963623/first-person-how-pratham-books-has-used-the-lockdown-to-expand-the-reach-of-its-ebooks-for-children> accessed 5 October 2025.

[52] Lionel Bently, 'Copyright, Translations, and Relations between Britain and India in the Nineteenth and Early Twentieth Centuries' [2007] 82 Chicago-Kent L Rev 1181.

[53] Lawrence Liang, 'India: The Knowledge Thief' in Joe Karaganis (ed) *Shadow Libraries: Access to Educational Materials in Global Higher Education* (MIT Press 2018) 215.

qualitative restrictions.[54] To broaden our understanding of the Copyright Act 1957, it would be essential to delve into the legislative history of the provisions that aim to balance the interests of the owner with the educational requirements of users.

5.1. Historical Evolution of Copyright Law in India

Like other British colonies, imperial legislation was extended to British India as well. Since the time of British India, legal transplantation has been the primary means through which the copyright regime has been established. But the challenge in transplanting a law from other jurisdictions is that it presumes the existence of a certain structure and legal consciousness.[55] Legal transplantations are intended to benefit the recipient country, but in the absence of careful evaluation and proper implementation, they can be ineffective in a foreign soil. The process of incorporating imperial legislation into Indian law through organic transplantation dates back to the Literary Copyright Act of 1842.[56] The imperial reach of the Literary Copyright Act of 1842 extended to all the colonies, settlements, and possessions of the Crown at that time.[57] The Act protected the copyright for the life of the author and a further term of seven years commencing from the author's death, or a term of forty-two years, whichever was longer.[58] 'Copyright' was defined as 'the sole and exclusive liberty of printing or otherwise multiplying copies of any subject to which the said word is herein applied'.[59] Under this Act, if any book[60] were first

[54] *The Chancellor, Masters & Scholars of The University of Oxford & Ors v Rameshwari Photocopy Services & Anr.* 2017 (69) PTC 123 (Del).

[55] Peter K. Yu, 'The Transplant and Transformation of Intellectual Property Laws in China' in Nari Lee, Niklas Bruun, and Li Mingde (eds) *Governance of Intellectual Property Rights in China and Europe* (Edward Elgar 2016) 20, 42.

[56] Arul George Scaria, *Piracy in the Indian Film Industry: Copyright and Cultural Consonance* (CUP 2014) 48.

[57] The legislation was titled as the Copyright Act 1842 (5 & 6 Vict. c.45); Lionel Bently, 'The "Extraordinary Multiplicity" of Intellectual Property Laws in the British Colonies in the Nineteenth Century' [2011] 12 Theoretical Inq L 161, 173 (explaining that the Act of 1842 reaffirmed the imperial scope of copyright law).

[58] The Literary Copyright Act 1842, s 3.

[59] The Literary Copyright Act 1842, s 2.

[60] The term 'book' was defined to 'mean and include every volume, part or division of a volume, pamphlet, sheet of letter-press, sheet of music, map, chart, or plan separately published'. See the Literary Copyright Act 1842, s 2.

published in the United Kingdom by an author who was a resident in one of the British possessions, the book would benefit from copyright protection in the British dominions. The Act defined the British dominions as 'all parts of the United Kingdom of Great Britain and Ireland, the islands of Jersey and Guernsey, all parts of the East and West Indies, and all the colonies, settlements and possessions of the Crown which are now or hereafter may be acquired'.[61] To ensure the prevention of book piracy, section 15 of the Act provided that:

> if any person shall, in any Part of the British Dominions, after the passing of this Act, print or cause to be printed, either for Sale or Exportation, any Book in which there shall be subsisting Copyright, without the Consent in Writing of the Proprietor thereof, or shall import for Sale or Hire any such Book so having been unlawfully printed from Parts beyond the Sea, or, knowing such Book to have been so unlawfully printed or imported, shall sell, publish, or expose to Sale or Hire, or shall have in his Possession for Sale or Hire, any such Book so unlawfully printed or imported, without such Consent as aforesaid, such Offender shall be liable to a special Action on the Case at the Suit of the Proprietor of such Copyright, to be brought in any Court of Record in that Part of the British Dominions in which the Offence shall be committed.

Even with the application of imperial legislation, there was considerable room left for the colonies to develop their own laws. There existed two reasons for the colonial variation. First, the 1842 Act applied only to books first published in the United Kingdom. Consequently, colonies were free to establish their own laws for the protection of books first published in their jurisdiction.[62] Second, the Act applied only in relation to books and musical works, leaving colonies free to pass their own legislation for the protection of artistic works, dramatic works, and related rights.

[61] The Literary Copyright Act 1842, s 2.

[62] Lionel Bently, 'The "Extraordinary Multiplicity" of Intellectual Property Laws in the British Colonies in the Nineteenth Century' [2001] 12 Theoretical Inq L 174, 176 (discussing the local laws passed by India, Lower Canada, New Zealand, Nova Scotia, and the Cape of Good Hope).

During the East India Company's regime in 1947, the first statute on copyright law was passed by the Governor General in Council, which was modelled on the Literary Copyright Act of 1842. This law was enacted to confer copyright protection on the books first published in the territory of India.[63] The Act mandated the registration of copyright with the Home Office for the enforcement of rights. The term of protection was as in the Literary Copyright Act of 1842, that is, life of the author plus seven years post mortem, but in no case was the term to exceed more than forty-two years.

5.2. The Indian Copyright Act 1914

The Act of 1847 was followed by the Indian Copyright Act of 1914, enacted by the Government of India. The 1914 Indian Copyright Act was a small piece of legislation consisting of fifteen sections, and the entire Imperial Copyright Act 1911 was annexed in its first schedule. This Act aimed to extend the provisions of the Imperial Copyright Act of 1911 to British India. Section 27 of the 1911 Imperial Act granted British possessions some flexibility to modify the operation of the Act in light of differences in matters relating to legal procedure and remedies. Section 27 of the Imperial Act 1911 provided that 'the legislature of any British possession to which this Act extends may modify or add to any of the provisions of this Act in its application to the possession, but, except so far as such modifications and additions relate to procedure and remedies, they shall apply only to works the authors whereof were, at the time of the making of the work, resident in the possession, and to works first published in the possession'. The scope of leeway provided was limited, but the Government of India decided to take advantage of the limited

[63] An Act for the encouragement of learning in the territories subject to the government of the East India Company, Act XX of 1847. The preamble to the Act explained that:

> it is doubtful whether the [1842 Imperial] Act . . . has made appropriate and sufficient protection for the enforcement in every part of the said territories subject to the Government of the East India Company of the said right by proprietors thereof, and whether the said Act of Parliament has made provision for the enforcement of the said right by or against any persons not being subject to the jurisdiction of the courts established by Her Majesty's Charter.

flexibilities by determining its own course of action in relation to copyright.[64] As pointed out by Baxi, the 1914 Act brought about two major changes. The first was the introduction of criminal sanctions for copyright infringement, and the second was the restriction of the term of protection for translation rights.[65] By the Act of 1914, the term of translation rights was set at ten years from the date of publication for works first published in India.[66] However, authors retained their 'sole rights' if they published or authorized publication of their work's translation in any language, for a period of ten years from the date of publication. In short, a book first published in the English language in India can now be translated into Hindi by anyone if it has not been translated into Hindi within the past ten years. Before this legislation, a book authored in the English language could be translated into any other language without any authorization from the copyright owner of the English-language version.[67] Scholars like Bently observed that restricting the scope of translation rights in respect of Indian works was intended to facilitate the diffusion of works into regional languages and to promote the publishing industries in various indigenous languages. Baxi pointed out that the authors could not experience any benefit from limited translation rights because only publishers were making a good income from the translation, and authors were not receiving any proceeds from the sale.[68] The enactment of the 1914 Act was a symbolic attempt by the Government of India to balance copyright law with the educational requirements of the nation. It encouraged the owners of copyright to publish or authorize the publication of translations of their works within a ten-year period, which further confers a separate copyright in the translated version for a period of fifty years.[69]

[64] Lionel Bently, 'Copyright, Translations, and Relations between Britain and India in the Nineteenth and Early Twentieth Centuries' [2007] 82 Chicago-Kent L Rev 1181, 1224.

[65] Upendra Baxi, 'Copyright Law and Justice in India' [1986] 28 JILI 500.

[66] The Indian Copyright Act 1914, s 4.

[67] Prashant Reddy Thikkavarapu, 'The DU Photocopy Judgement—A Chronicle of the Missed Arguments' [2018] 2 Indian L Rev 231.

[68] Upendra Baxi, 'Copyright Law and Justice in India' [1986] 28 JILI 500.

[69] Prashant Reddy Thikkavarapu, 'The DU Photocopy Judgement – A Chronicle of the Missed Arguments' [2018] 2 Indian L Rev 231.

5.3. The Copyright Act 1957

The 1914 Act continued till the Copyright Act 1957 was brought into force on 24 January 1958. After India got independence from the British Raj in 1947, the Constituent Assembly adopted its own Constitution in 1949, which conferred legislative powers on the parliament in copyright-related matters. After the 1955 Copyright Bill was introduced before parliament, it was referred to the Joint Parliamentary Committee (JPC). The JPC, having fifteen members from the Rajya Sabha and thirty members from the Lok Sabha, suggested substantial modifications in the bill[70] after thoroughly analysing it, though these modifications were not binding on the government. After holding thirteen meetings, the JPC submitted its final report, which contained drastic changes to the bill. While considering the bill clause by clause, the committee heard the evidence tendered before them by representatives of various organizations.[71] Some of the radical modifications contained in the report included the copyright term to be life of author plus fifty years as prescribed under the Berne Convention, not to make copyright registration compulsory as it would be 'an undue restriction on the owner of the copyright to exercise his rights', and the definitions of 'government work', 'infringing copy', 'photograph', 'pseudonymous work', and 'exclusive licence' were recast.[72] An important recommendation was made regarding the term of translation rights. Acknowledging the multilingual attribute of India, the committee expressed that 'there should be as few restrictions on translation of works as possible'. The committee favoured retaining the translation provision of the 1914 Act that provided for production, reproduction, performance, or publication of a translation in any Indian language of an Indian work after the expiry of a period of ten years from the date of the first publication of the work, provided that no translation has been produced within the period of ten years.[73]

[70] Report of the Joint Committee of the Houses on the Copyright Bill 1955 (Rajya Sabha Secretariat 1956) 905–06.

[71] Report of the Joint Committee of the Houses on the Copyright Bill 1955 (Rajya Sabha Secretariat 1956) 907.

[72] Report of the Joint Committee of the Houses on the Copyright Bill 1955 (Rajya Sabha Secretariat 1956) 909.

[73] Report of the Joint Committee of the Houses on the Copyright Bill 1955 (Rajya Sabha Secretariat 1956) 952.

When the JPC returned the bill to the Rajya Sabha, most of the modifications made to the bill by the JPC were accepted by the Rajya Sabha. Several crucial points of debate arose among members of parliament, including the term of copyright protection, translation rights, and the nature of property rights in creative works. When the bill was initially placed before the Rajya Sabha on 1 October 1955, it had a provision for a copyright term of the life of the author and twenty-five years. However, the government accepted the JPC's recommendation to extend the period to fifty years. On 15 May 1957, Dr K.L. Shrimali, the Minister of State in the Ministry of Education and Scientific Research, said that, by restoring the term of protection to life of author plus fifty years, 'we have gone in line with most of the countries in the world who are signatories to the Berne Convention'.[74] In his speech, he enumerated three factors that must be considered while defining the scope of protection for property. First, authors must be incentivized through direct or indirect pecuniary return, and they must also have control over the marketing of their property. Authors can enjoy the fruits of their labour for their whole lives. But it is equally vital to consider the families of authors who are dependent on their income. Post mortem fifty years is the period during which a surviving family can enjoy the pecuniary return of the creation.[75] Then, the publisher's interest is also to be considered as it is the publisher who ultimately gives birth to the work of the author. In other words, authors depend upon the publishers, and publishers continue to receive a pecuniary return for their investments in authors' work.[76]

Many members of parliament eloquently spoke in favour of fifty years of protection after the author's death. Ramdhari Singh Dinkar, a renowned Hindi poet and freedom fighter, was also a member of parliament. He informed the House that the reduction of the copyright term in the Copyright Bill of 1955, from post-mortem protection of fifty years to twenty-five years, had sparked a revolt among authors and their organizations, and they had requested the government not to proceed with this change.[77] Dinkar described that there was a huge protest among PEN, a prestigious organization of authors and the Sahitya Academy against

[74] Rajya Sabha, Debate on the Copyright Bill 1955 (15 May 1957) 221.
[75] Rajya Sabha, Debate on the Copyright Bill 1955 (15 May 1957) 221.
[76] Rajya Sabha, Debate on the Copyright Bill 1955 (15 May 1957) 222.
[77] Rajya Sabha, Debate on the Copyright Bill 1955 (14 May 1957) 120.

the Copyright Bill. After having a discussion in the Sahitya Academy, the author members of the Academy, along with some members of the parliament, met Maulana Azad. In the words of Dinkar, Maulana suggested forming a committee of authors who submitted their recommendations to the government.

Dinkar believed that the democracy in a nation is closely tied to its author's freedom of expression, hence, to give freedom to authors should be the top priority of the government's agenda. While stressing the need for independence of authors in a democratic country, he said:

> If we really want to have democratic India, then the government's first agenda should be to give maximum freedom to authors and newspapers so that they may criticize anybody legitimately. Only then the democracy can be strengthened. (*Translated version*)

While advocating for fifty years of post-mortem protection, he drew attention towards the economic condition of authors in India. Unlike very few authors like Pandit Jawaharlal Nehru and Dr Radhakrishnan, many authors were earning a scanty livelihood from their writings, and they left nothing behind after their deaths. In the context of translation rights, he presented two prevalent views. One was that there would be no free flow of literature in India if they failed to make translation free. The other view was that there is no harm if an author earns money from the translations of his or her work.[78] He also gave an example of the Copyright Act 1914, which allows translation of a work after the expiration of ten years from the date of first publication of the work. Consequently, authors had no translation rights after the first ten years of publication. This provision favoured the publishers because they could translate and publish the works of renowned authors, such as Sharat Chandra Chatterjee and Gurudev.[79] Such authors never received a penny out of the translations of

[78] Rajya Sabha, Debate on the Copyright Bill 1955 (14 May 1957) 127.

[79] Rajya Sabha, Debate on the Copyright Bill 1955 (14 May 1957) 127. While explaining the condition of Indian authors, Shri Ramdhari Singh Dinkar stated:

> When Sharat Chandra gained fame as an author in India, the Hindi publishers exploited his famous works by getting his books translated in Hindi. Fifty thousand copies of each of his book were sold, but Sharat Chandra did not get a single penny because the law was in the favour of publishers. The same happened with Gurudev.

their own works. Putting the monetary factor aside, he argued, authors' sentiments must be respected by not translating their works during their lifetime against their wishes.

Next, Dinkar drew the attention of the House towards the then-existing provision on the use of passages in textbooks. The said provision was section 2(1) of the 1911 Act, incorporated into the first schedule of the Copyright Act 1914, which read as:

> Copyright in a work shall be deemed to be infringed by any person who, without the consent of the owner of the copyright, does anything the sole right to do which is by this Act conferred on the owner of the copyright. Provided that the following acts shall not constitute an infringement of copyright: -
>
> ...
>
> (iv) The publication in a collection, mainly composed of non-copyright matter, *bona fide* intended for the use of schools, and so described in the title and in any advertisements issued by the publisher, of short passages from published literary works not themselves published for the use of schools in which copyright subsists. Provided that not more than two of such passages from works by the same author are published by the same publisher within five years, and that the source from which such passages are taken is acknowledged.

This provision provided that there was no copyright infringement if only two passages were used in a textbook. The size of the passages was not defined in the provision, which means there could be one passage of twenty-five pages and a second passage of ten pages, that is, a total of thirty-five pages, and still it would not amount to infringement. Dinkar emphasized that the ambiguity in the 'two passage rule' must be removed by clearly defining it in terms of the maximum number of sentences that

> During Gurudev's lifetime, his books were translated into Hindi. You know, Hindi publishing is a huge market. Gurudev's books were widely sold in Hindi and there could be no restriction. *(translated version)*

MP Nihar Ranjan Ray also agreed with Dinkar that translation rights must be co-extensive with the original authorship.

could be used in textbooks.[80] The amendments proposed by Dinkar were accepted by most of the members, including R.C. Gupta, P.N. Sapru, Nihar Ranjan Ray, and Rajendra Pratap Sinha. At the end of the meeting, Shrimali expressed that India, being a welfare state, had the responsibility to consider the interests of society as well.[81] In addition to restoring the interests of authors, he highlighted that:

> At the same time, continuously we do keep in mind the interests of the society and I think the type of measure that has emerged is a very happy compromise between an individualistic society and totalitarian society. The individual has been given his due rights. At the same time, his rights are not unrestricted. The individual and the society are both interdependent.[82]

When the bill was placed before the Lok Sabha, Shrimali described the government's take on restoring the term of copyright protection, namely, post-mortem fifty years of protection. He reasoned that the family of the author had been the main consideration in extending the term from twenty-five years to fifty years, so that the author's family may get financial support from the author's works. In response, the Speaker raised a pragmatic point:

MR SPEAKER: What if the copyright is sold away?

DR K.L. SHRIMALI: For the life of the author the copyright will be that of the author.

MR SPEAKER: If it is sold away, all this argument disappears-whether his children have to be provided for, etc.

DR K.L. SHRIMALI: It won't go into the public domain automatically.

MR SPEAKER: But it will go away to the publishers.

DR K.L. SHRIMALI: The author is free to give it away to the publisher.

MR SPEAKER: Therefore, all this argument that this is *parampara*, that the children will be protected, etc., all this disappears.

80 Rajya Sabha, Debate on the Copyright Bill 1955 (14 May 1957) 131.
81 Rajya Sabha, Debate on the Copyright Bill 1955 (15 May 1957) 314.
82 Rajya Sabha, Debate on the Copyright Bill 1955 (15 May 1957) 315.

DR K.L. SHRIMALI: But the point is that the author must determine whether he wants to part with his work or wants to keep the copyright to himself.

MR SPEAKER: Most of the authors sell away.[83]

The point raised by the Speaker had a practical dimension in the copyright amendment. However, this perspective was not attended by Rajya Sabha members and the entire debate took place with a presumption that it is always the author who owns the copyright, which in reality is not true in most cases. While advocating the extension of post-mortem protection to fifty years, Rajya Sabha members placed the entire focus on authors and overlooked the fact that, in practice, most authors sell their copyright to publishers.

Another member of the Lok Sabha, D.C. Sharma, talked about reducing the duration of protection because of the low incidence of literacy in India:

> We have to take into account the social context of our country and it is this. So far as literacy is concerned, ours is a backward country. . . . But taking into account the low incidence of literacy in this country and also the slow progress of free and universal education in this country as well as the fact that the cultural resources of our country are not available to the people at large, I would have thought that the period for which an author could enjoy the copyright after his death should have been equal to the average expectation of life of an individual. This means that you will give this copyright business to an author for about generations. It may be possible in other countries. It may be done in some of the countries of the West. . .. But I think it should be done only up to the average expectation of life of an Indian citizen, that is, 30 years or 35 years.

It can be said that Sharma gave a figure of thirty-five years precisely because, in the proposed bill, the duration of protection could be measured not as a fixed number of years but through the age of the author. This was extensively explained by Pandit Thakur Das Bhargava. Bhargava said that, as per the proposed author-centric bill, the duration of protection

[83] Lok Sabha, Debate on the Copyright Bill 1955 (27 May 1957) 2168.

could reach even 100 years, which is unreasonably extensive to be monopolized.[84] According to him, twenty-five years of post-mortem protection was also a lengthy period, particularly when an author writes at an early age and dies old. If an author lives 100 years, the public will hardly have any copyright left.[85]

However, the majority of the members agreed to maintain a post-mortem protection period of fifty years, aligning with the majority of member states that are signatories to the Berne Convention and the Universal Copyright Convention (UCC). Maintaining twenty-five years of protection would have led to discrimination against Indian authors, as India, being a signatory to the Berne Convention, was obligated to provide fifty years of protection to foreign authors, but its own authors' works would be protected for only twenty-five years. As far as translation rights were concerned, the JPC had suggested creating an exception under section 5, under which a translation could be produced by any person if the owner did not translate the work within ten years of its original publication. But the members of the Houses championed the stronger translation rights. Thereupon, section 32 was created in the Act of 1957, under which one could apply for a compulsory licence to translate any literary or dramatic works, provided that the translation of such work had not been published within seven years in India.

In the words of Baxi, the enactment of the Copyright Act of 1957 was propelled by many reasons. First, the Act of 1914 was not appropriate in the face of the changed constitutional status of India. Second, a need was felt to bring the changes in the law into conformity with the 1948 Brussels Act of the Berne Convention and the UCC of 1952. Third, 'the new and advanced method of communication' demanded the upgradation of the law. Fourth, the experiences of the working of the Imperial Law of 1911 and 'the growing public consciousness of the rights and obligations of the authors' actuated the need for 'an independent self-contained law'.[86]

The 1957 Act emerged truly as independent Indian legislation, as it was not a replica of an English legislative proposal. The Act contained fifteen chapters, which were divided into seventy sections. The term of

[84] Lok Sabha, Debate on the Copyright Bill 1955 (27 May 1957) 2195–96.
[85] Lok Sabha, Debate on the Copyright Bill 1955 (27 May 1957) 2197.
[86] Upendra Baxi, 'Copyright Law and Justice In India' [1986] JILI 502.

copyright protection remained the life of the author plus fifty years. The registration of copyright was made optional, implying that it would not be required for either acquiring or enforcing the copyright. Chapter II of the new legislation established new institutions, such as a Registrar of Copyrights,[87] the Copyright Office,[88] and Copyright Board.[89] The Copyright Board's essential function was to adjudicate and determine the rival claims related to licences and assignments.

The Copyright Act of 1957 remains in effect to govern copyright in India to date. However, the Act has undergone various substantial changes as a result of amendments made in 1983, 1984, 1992, 1994, 1999, and 2012. For educational purposes, the 1983 amendment brought the most substantial changes.

5.3.1. The Copyright (Amendment) Act 1983

In the seventies, Justice M.C. Chagla discussed two grave problems in his autobiography, *Roses in December*. These problems continue to exist to date, though the extent of the problem has shrunk. One was the wastage in adult education in India. He called it 'wastage' because students had no further interest in education after completion of their schooling. As per Chagla, the only solution to this problem was 'to supply them with the type of reading material that would excite their interest and curiosity'. Non-access to books was the pivotal problem. Another problem was the textbook trade. Referring to the Berne Convention and the UCC, he observed that 'the stumbling-block in our way was the law and conventions relating to copyright'.[90] At a joint session of the Berne Convention and the UCC at New Delhi in 1963, he emphasized the significance of amending the Conventions to make books more affordable in developing countries, while safeguarding the authors' rights. Despite huge opposition from developed countries, particularly the UK, developing nations succeeded in 1971 at the Paris Revision Conference in incorporating the compulsory

[87] The Copyright Act 1957, s 10.

[88] The Copyright Act 1957, s 9.

[89] The Copyright Act 1957, s 11.

[90] M.C. Chagla, *Roses in December: An Autobiography* (Bharatiya Vidya Bhavan 1975) 365 (the author mentioned that 'our proposal was that the copyright of a book should vest in Government after seven years, after which period the Government concerned should have the right to reproduce and translate particular books').

licensing system into the copyright regime.[91] Through the amendment in 1983, the compulsory licensing provisions were inserted in sections 32, 32A, and 32B of the Copyright Act 1957.

The Copyright (Amendment) Act of 1983 introduced various substantial changes relating to compulsory licensing, piracy, author's rights, and corporate copyright. The publishers heartily welcomed the long-awaited provisions on compulsory licence.[92] The amendment empowered the Copyright Board to grant a compulsory licence, upon fulfilment of certain conditions, to the applicant for the reproduction of copyright works without the copyright owner's consent. The 1983 amendment aimed to comply with the 1971 Paris revisions of the Berne Convention and the UCC, which enabled developing member states to grant compulsory licences for the translation and reproduction of works of foreign origin required for the purposes of teaching, scholarship, or research.[93] The amended provision provided that:

> Notwithstanding anything contained in sub-section (1), any person may apply to the Appellate Board[94] for a licence to produce and publish a translation, in printed or analogous forms of reproduction, of a literary or dramatic work; other than an Indian work, in any language in general use in India after a period of three years from the first publication of such work, if such translation is required for the purposes of teaching, scholarship or research:
>
> Provided that where such translation is in a language not in general use in any developed country, such application may be made after a period of one year from such publication.[95]

The Explanation to Section 32 provided that:

> For the purposes of this section, —

[91] Prashant Reddy T. and Sumathi Chandrashekaran, *Create, Copy and Disrupt* (OUP 2017) 145.

[92] Samuel Israel, 'Copyright in India: National and International: The 1983 Amendment of the Indian Copyright Act, 1957' [1983] 18 Economic and Political Weekly 1984.

[93] P. Narayanan, *Law of Copyright and Industrial Designs* (4th edn, Eastern Law House 2007).

[94] Substituted for 'Copyright Board' by Act 7 of 2017 (w.e.f. 26 May 2017).

[95] The Copyright Act 1957, s 32(IA).

(c) 'purposes of research' does not include purposes of industrial research, or purposes of research by bodies corporate (not being bodies corporate owned or controlled by Government) or other associations or body of persons for commercial purposes;

(d) 'purposes of teaching, research or scholarship' includes—
  (i) purposes of instructional activity at all levels in educational, institutions, including Schools, Colleges, Universities and tutorial institutions; and
  (ii) purposes of all other types of organised educational activity.

Another important change brought by the Copyright Amendment Act 1983 was the insertion of section 31A, under which any person could apply to the Copyright Board (now Appellate Board) for a compulsory licence to publish or translate any unpublished work, or any work published but withheld from the public in India, or work whose author is dead or unknown or cannot be found, or work the copyright owner of which cannot be found.

The other material addition to the Act was section 32A, which was designed to ensure that the copyright works that have once been published are not unduly withheld from the public later by the proprietor. The amendment is noteworthy for its approach of making the withheld editions of literary, scientific, or artistic works available to the public for *systematic instructional activities.*[96] This section also contained a

[96] The Indian Copyright Act 1957, s 32A, reads as follows:

(1) Where, after the expiration of the relevant period from the date of the first publication of an edition of a literary, scientific or artistic work,—
  (a) the copies of such edition are not made available in India; or
  (b) such copies have not been put on sale in India for a period of six months, to the general public, or in connection with systematic instructional activities at a price reasonably related to that normally charged in India for comparable works by the owner of the right of reproduction or by any person authorised by him in this behalf, any person may apply to the Appellate Board for a licence to reproduce and publish such work in printed or analogous forms of reproduction at the price at which such edition is sold or at a lower price for the purposes of systematic instructional activities.

...

Explanation.—For the purposes of this section, 'relevant period', in relation to any work, means a period of—
  (a) seven years from the date of the first publication of that work, where the application is for the reproduction and publication of any work of, or relating to, fiction, poetry, drama, music or art;

provision for the translation of said works into a language in general use in India.[97]

Scholars, like Israel, have pointed out that the provisions on compulsory licensing that allowed the reprinting and translation of works originally published in developed countries led to a substantial departure from reciprocity, as the provisions allowed India to publish the copyrighted materials of developed countries in its own land even against their will and on such terms that might not be acceptable to the proprietor of the copyright.[98] However, works published in India and other developed countries continued to enjoy international protection for their works. There is no doubt that publishers in developed countries would have always preferred to licence Indian publishers to reproduce and translate their titles on their own terms, instead of involuntarily dealing with the Indian publishers licensed by the Copyright Board.[99]

In consonance with the Berne Appendix, section 32B was also added in 1983, which provides for the termination of licences if, after the issuance of a licence, the owner of the work publishes a translation of such work in the same language.

5.3.2. The Amendment of 2012

The next significant transformation for educational purposes was brought about by the Amendment Act of 2012. The amendment made an attempt to simplify the procedure for the grant of a licence. Prior to the amendment, section 30 required licences to be in writing and signed by the owner of the copyright or by his or her duly authorized agent. Through the amendment, the term 'signed' was deleted from section 30, requiring licences to be in writing only.[100] Moreover, before the 2012

(b) three years from the date of the first publication of that work, where the application is for the reproduction and publication of any work of, or relating to, natural science, physical science, mathematics or technology; and

(c) five years from the date of the first publication of that work, in any other case.

[97] The Copyright Act 1957, s 32A (5).

[98] Samuel Israel, 'Copyright in India: National and International: The 1983 Amendment of the Indian Copyright Act, 1957' [1983] 18 Economic and Political Weekly 1985.

[99] Samuel Israel, 'Copyright in India: National and International: The 1983 Amendment of the Indian Copyright Act, 1957' [1983] 18 Economic and Political Weekly 1985.

[100] The Copyright Act 1957, s 30; see also S. Sivakumar and Lisa P. Lukose, 'Copyright Amendment Act, 2012: A Revisit' [2013] 55 JILI 162.

amendment, section 31 provided that if the copyright proprietor of any 'Indian work' refused to republish the work and had withheld the work from the public, then on receipt of a complaint, the Copyright Board may direct the Registrar of Copyrights to issue a licence to the complainants. To extend the scope of compulsory licences to foreign works, the 2012 amendment omitted the term 'Indian work' from section 31 and the term 'complainant' has been replaced with the words 'such person or persons who, in the opinion of the Copyright Board, are qualified to do so'. As a consequence of the amendment, a compulsory licence can now be issued in respect of any work that is withheld from the public, not only Indian works. The 2012 amendment has also amplified the ambit of section 31A, which, before the amendment, provided for a compulsory licence in case of both published and unpublished works that are withheld from the public in India.[101]

Another remarkable change is through the expansion of the 'fair dealing' clause given in section 52(1)(a). While the previous enactment allowed the use of 'literary, dramatic, musical or artistic works only', the new amendment has broadened the ambit of fair dealing by allowing it with any work except computer programs. This means that sound recordings and cinematographic works can also be used for fair dealing purposes. The purposes of fair dealings have also been enlarged. Earlier, fair dealings with works were limited to the purposes of private use, including research, while the new amendment has also added 'personal use'.

5.4. Limitations and Exceptions for Educational Purposes

This section will examine how India has addressed the education-related limitations and exceptions in its copyright law. The Copyright Act 1957 provides compensated and uncompensated limitations and exceptions for educational purposes. Limitations and exceptions can be found in the form of statutory or compulsory licences, as well as in fair dealing provisions.

[101] The Copyright Act 1957, s 31A; see also Zakir Thomas, 'Overview of Changes to the Indian Copyright Law' [2012] 17 JIPR 328.

5.4.1. Licensing Provisions

Initially, the Copyright Act 1957 had only two sections on compulsory licensing, i.e. sections 31 and 32. Taking the benefit of the Berne Appendix, the Indian parliament expanded the limitations on copyright by inserting sections 31A, 32(IA), 32A, and 32B.

The Act provides for compulsory licensing in works withheld from the public and in the case of unpublished or published works. Section 31 deals with the general provisions of compulsory licensing. Section 31 covers the situation where the owner of copyrighted work has refused to republish or allow the republication of the work, due to which the work is withheld from the public. Section 31A, incorporated on the lines of Berne Appendix, provides for the issuance of compulsory licensing where any work is withheld from the public because the author is dead or unknown or cannot be traced or the copyright owner cannot be found.

Apart from the compulsory licensing provisions, the Act contains two additional licensing provisions that aim to serve educational purposes. Section 32 allows any person to apply for a licence to produce and publish a translation of a literary and dramatic work in any language after a period of seven years from the first publication of the work. In case of foreign works, section 32(IA) allows any person to apply for a licence to produce and publish a translation for the purposes of teaching, scholarship or research,[102] in any language in general use in India after a period of three years. An application for a licence can be made for the translation of work into one language only.[103]

The waiting period to apply for a licence is one year if the language is not in general use in any developed country. The Act does not define the term 'general use'. However, the guidelines issued jointly by UNESCO and WIPO can be referred to, which define 'language in general use' as English, Spanish, and French. The explanation to Section 32 defines the phrase 'purposes of teaching, research or scholarship' to include '(i) purposes of instructional activity at all levels in educational institutions,

[102] The Copyright Act 1957, explanation to s 32 provides that 'purposes of research' does not include purposes of industrial research, or purposes of research by bodies corporate (not being bodies corporate owned or controlled by government) or other associations or body of persons for commercial purposes.

[103] The Copyright Rules 2013, rule 32(2).

including Schools, Colleges, Universities and tutorial institutions; and (ii) purposes of all other types of organised educational activity'.

Based on the Berne Appendix, section 32A is another licensing provision that allows an application for a reproduction licence to be made for any literary, scientific, or artistic work that is unavailable in the country or if the copies have not been put on sale for a period of six months. In case of works to be used in systematic instructional activities, 'non-availability at a reasonable price' is the ground to apply for a licence. The copyright owner will have to ensure that copies are available at prices reasonably comparable with those of similar works in India, failing which the applicant can seek a licence to reproduce and publish such edition at a lower price.[104]

Section 32B has placed the owners of copyright in a better position by granting them the ultimate autonomy to publish the translation after the licence has been issued. However, the reproduction or translation licence shall stand terminated if the owner publishes the reproduction or translation of such work in the same language at prices reasonably related to the price generally charged in India for comparable works. This can be said to perform two functions: first, it guards the owners from being subjected to compulsory licence; second, it demotivates applicants from putting in their time, effort, and money for a licence that can be terminated at any time.

5.4.2. Fair Dealing Doctrine: Delimiting the Copyright Monopoly

Like other copyright legislation worldwide, the Indian Copyright Act 1957 grants the owner of a copyright an exclusive right over the copyrighted work. To strike a balance between the exclusive rights granted to the copyright owner and the competing interest of the public, an exception known as the 'fair dealing doctrine' is recognized. Before proceeding towards the fair dealing doctrine, it is important to reflect upon the fundamental differences that exist between the American fair use doctrine and the English fair dealing doctrine. The largest presumed difference between the two is that 'fair use' is considered an American concept while the doctrine of 'fair dealing' is supposed to have ossified

[104] The Copyright Act 1957, s 32A (1).

under the UK law. However, the historical account documented by various scholars[105] proves this conventional dichotomy to be flawed.[106] If we look into the historical development of the doctrine of fair use, it tells us that the concept of fair use originated as a judge-made law, which was first evolved by English judges and then by American judges, who mutually influenced and cross-referenced each other.[107] It was Lord Ellenborough's statement in *Cary v Kearsley* in 1802 that established a definitive defence of 'fair use', as he referred to the concept of 'fair use' and not 'fair dealing'. He wrote:

> That part of the work of one author is found in another, is not of itself piracy, or sufficient to support an action; a man may *fairly adopt* part of the work of another: he may so make use of another's labours for the promotion of science, and the benefit of the public: but having done so, the question will be, Was the matter so taken *used fairly* with that view, and without what I may term the *animus furandi*?[108]

It was only with the codification of the UK 1911 Copyright enactment that the 'fair dealing' terminology was adopted, and its application was restricted to five enumerated purposes only. Section 2(1) of the UK Copyright Act 1911 provides that:

> [T]he following acts shall not constitute an infringement of copyright:
> (i) any fair dealing with any work for the purpose of private study, research, criticism, review or newspaper summary.

In view of Bradshaw, the reason behind the UK parliament's decision to use the expression 'fair dealing' as opposed to 'fair use' seems to be

[105] Matthew Sag, 'The Pre-History of Fair Use' [2011] 76 Brooklyn L Rev 1371; Alexandra Sims, 'Appellations of Piracy: Fair Dealing's Prehistory' [2011] 3 Intell Prop Q.

[106] Ariel Katz, 'Debunking the Fair Use vs. Fair Dealing Myth: Have We Had Fair Use All Along?' in S. Balganesh, N. Wee Loon, and H. Sun (eds) *The Cambridge Handbook of Copyright Limitations and Exceptions* (CUP 2021) 111.

[107] Ariel Katz, 'Debunking the Fair Use vs. Fair Dealing Myth: Have We Had Fair Use All Along?' in S. Balganesh, N. Wee Loon, and H. Sun (eds) *The Cambridge Handbook of Copyright Limitations and Exceptions* (CUP 2021) 113.

[108] *Cary v Kearsley* (1802) 170 Eng Rep 679.

a mystery.[109] However, while codifying the doctrine, the UK parliament did not bring any substantial changes to the nature and scope of the doctrine.[110] On the rationale of separate codification of the fair dealing clause, J.M. Easton questioned the need to have an explicit provision for enumerated purposes as 'fair dealing for other purposes has always been ... permitted and, presumably, it was not intended to cut down the rights of fair use previously enjoyed under the old law'.[111]

The expression 'fair use' in use in American copyright law these days is an open-ended and flexible exception that requires judicial interpretation on a case-by-case basis. Unlike the four-factor concept of 'fair use' that involves (i) the purpose and character of the use, (ii) the nature of the copyrighted work, (iii) the amount and substantiality of the portion used, and (iv) the effect of the use upon the potential market, the 'fair dealing doctrine' is similar to the close-ended concept of fair dealing that is restricted to limited uses of copyrighted works *viz.* (i) private or personal use, including research, (ii) criticism or review, and (iii) the reporting of current events and current affairs, including the reporting of a lecture delivered in public. Though the term fair dealing is not defined anywhere in the Copyright Act 1957, the defence of fair dealing is dealt with under section 52 of the Act. It can be described as 'a privilege in others than the owner of a copyright to use the copyrighted material in a reasonable manner without his consent, notwithstanding the monopoly granted to the owner by the copyright'.[112]

Section 52(1)(a) of the Copyright Act provides:

> [F]air dealing with any work, not being a computer programme, for the purposes of—
> (i) private or personal use, including research;
> (ii) criticism or review, whether of that work or of any other work;

[109] David Bradshaw, 'Fair Dealing as a Defence to Copyright Infringement in UK Law: An Historical Excursion from 1802 to the Clockwork Orange Case 1993' [1995] 10 Denning LJ 67, 71. (The exact origins of the label 'fair dealing' may, therefore, have to remain a mystery.)

[110] Ariel Katz, 'Debunking the Fair Use vs. Fair Dealing Myth: Have We Had Fair Use All Along?' in S. Balganesh, N. Wee Loon, and H. Sun (eds) *The Cambridge Handbook of Copyright Limitations and Exceptions* (CUP 2021) 113.

[111] J.M. Easton, *The Law of Copyright in Works in Literature, Art, Architecture, Photography, Music and the Drama by the Late Walter Arthur Copinger* (5th edn, Stevens & Haynes 1915) 144.

[112] Horace G. Ball, *The Law of Copyright and Literary Property* (Banks & Co. 1944) 260.

(iii) the reporting of current events and current affairs, including the reporting of a lecture delivered in public.

This exception permits a person to fairly deal with any copyrighted material for any of the abovementioned purposes. The first clause, in particular, that is 'private or personal use including research', is envisaged to promote research and learning by disseminating educational materials. This exception plays a critically important role in facilitating learning by providing access to knowledge. In the absence of a proper definition of 'personal use', there remains uncertainty as to what makes a personal use lawful or infringing. Litman has attempted to define personal use on the assumption that a subset of personal use will be lawful and the other subset will be infringing.[113] She defines personal use as 'a use that an individual makes for herself, her family, or her close friends'.[114] Tussey gives a broader definition of 'personal use'; he writes that personal use means 'consumption or adaptation of intellectual properties by individual users for their own purposes, including uncompensated sharing of works with others'.[115] To put it simply, 'personal use' implies the use of a copyrighted work for an individual's own private purposes that are non-commercial in nature. A common example is an individual reading a book and copying its contents. The Madras High Court in *Blackwood v Parasuraman* gave a structured view that '[p]rivate study only covers the case of a student copying out a book for his own use, but not the circulation of copies among other students'.[116] Photocopying of a book for private purposes also falls within the ambit of personal use, as Justice Endlaw in the DU Photocopy case rightly pointed out:

> [R]eproduction by the students for the purposes of their private or personal use, whether by way of photocopying or by way of copying the same by way of hand, would indeed make the action of the student a fair dealing therewith and not constitute infringement of copyright.[117]

[113] Jessica D. Litman, 'Lawful Personal Use' [2007] 85 Tex L Rev 1871.
[114] Jessica D. Litman, 'Lawful Personal Use' [2007] 85 Tex L Rev 1894.
[115] Deborah Tussey, 'From Fan Sites to Filesharing: Personal Use in Cyberspace' [2001] 35 Georgia L Rev 1129, 1134.
[116] AIR I959 Mad. 4l0.
[117] *The Chancellor, Masters & Scholars of the University of Oxford & Ors. v Rameshwari Photocopy Services & Anr.* CS(OS) 2439/2012.

In *Blackwood & Sons Ltd. v A.N. Parasuraman*, Justice Rajgopala Ayyangar explained the implication of 'fair' in 'fair dealing':

> Two points have been urged in connection with the meaning of the expression 'fair' in 'fair dealing' (1) that in order to constitute unfairness there must be an intention to compete and to derive profit from such competition and (2) that unless the motive of the infringer were unfair in the sense of being improper or oblique the dealing would be fair.[118]

It is plausible to know the grammatical meaning of the term 'fair', but to define 'fair dealing' is paradoxical. As Lord Denning eloquently explained in *Hubbard v Vosper*:

> It is impossible to define what is 'fair dealing'. It must be a question of degree. You must consider first the number and extent of the quotations and extracts. Are they altogether too many and too long to be fair? Then you must consider the use made of them. If they are used as a basis for comment, criticism or review, that may be fair dealing. If they are used to convey the same information as the author, for a rival purpose, that may be unfair. Next, you must consider the proportions. To take long extracts and attach short comments may be unfair. But short extracts and long comments may be fair. Other considerations may come to mind also. But, after all is said and done, it must be a matter of impression. As with fair comment in the law of libel, so with fair dealing in the law of copyright. The tribunal of fact must decide.[119]

It is worth noting that most of the cases of infringement are against intermediaries who facilitate the provision of literary materials to others for reading and not against the personal user.[120] In India, most books are photocopied at shops, unlike in the US, where self-service photocopying is facilitated in universities and libraries. When any learning materials

[118] AIR 1959 Mad. 410.
[119] (1972) 2 QB 84.
[120] Arpan Banerjee, 'Copyright Violation or Access to Education: Navigating Legal Dichotomies' [2017] 12 NALSAR Student L Rev 102 ('the target users of these course packs, are not the target consumers of worldwide publishing houses'); see also Aaron Perzanowski and Jason Schultz, 'Copyright Exhaustion and the Personal Use Dilemma' [2012] 96 Minnesota L Rev 2067, 2073 ('facilitators, unlike everyday consumers, are attractive targets for litigation').

are photocopied by photocopying shops as intermediaries, such materials are eventually read by students for personal use. The Delhi University photocopy case[121] is the most notable one, wherein the plaintiff publisher took action against intermediaries who facilitated reading without a licence. In this case, three leading publishing houses—Oxford University Press, Cambridge University Press, and Taylor & Francis—brought an action against the University of Delhi and its authorized Rameshwari Photocopy Service for copyright infringement of their publications. The plaintiffs accused the defendants of photocopying, reproducing, and distributing the compilations of their publications in the form of 'course packs'.[122] The course packs were compiled on the basis of readings prescribed by the university, and the university had authorized the photocopy shop to run its enterprise. On the basis of these facts, the plaintiffs impleaded the University of Delhi in the matter. The university later argued that it had 'nothing to do' with the impugned acts, but it took up the matter 'in the interest of the students'.[123] The university pleaded that it licensed the Rameshwari photocopy shop within its premises to facilitate photocopying by students for educational and research purposes.[124] One of the contentions made by the plaintiffs was that copying by hand was recognized by the Act, but not photocopying, and that too on a mass scale. Single photocopying is permitted by law for personal use, but not mass-scale photocopying.[125] Following the elaborate interpretation of various provisions, namely, sections 52(1)(a), 52(1)(h), and 52(1)(i), the matter was eventually resolved in favour of the defendants.

In short, personal uses of copyrighted works are non-infringing and create no liability. The personal use exception seems to have been carved out to enhance public access, enjoyment, and preservation of works, which are copyright's constitutional purposes.

[121] *The Chancellor, Masters and Scholars of the University of Oxford & Others v Rameshwari Photocopy Services and Others*, CS(OS) 2439/2012.

[122] *The Chancellor, Masters and Scholars of the University of Oxford & Others v Rameshwari Photocopy Services and Others*, CS(OS) 2439/2012, para 1.

[123] *The Chancellor, Masters and Scholars of the University of Oxford & Others v Rameshwari Photocopy Services and Others*, CS(OS) 2439/2012, para 18.

[124] *The Chancellor, Masters & Scholars of the University Of Oxford & Ors. v. Rameshwari Photocopy Services & Anr.*, RFA(OS) 81/2016, para 5.

[125] *The Chancellor, Masters & Scholars of the University Of Oxford & Ors. v. Rameshwari Photocopy Services & Anr.*, RFA(OS) 81/2016, para 27.

Research is explicitly mentioned as an exception under section 52(1)(a)(i). The Copyright (Amendment) Act 1994 replaced the term 'research or private study' with 'private or personal use, including research'. The 'research' exception plays a crucial role for researchers in almost every field, as academic research is a must to fill gaps in existing knowledge and, also, to produce new literary materials like books and journal articles. The rationale behind the exception is to maximize the production of works.

In 1966, the High Court of Delhi opined that 'Article 21 may also be said to recognise . . . right to acquire useful knowledge, . . . as necessary to the orderly pursuit of happiness by free man'. In *Francis Coralie Mullin v The Administrator, Union Territory of Delhi*, the Supreme Court of India expressed that 'the right to life includes the right to live with human dignity and all that goes along with it, namely, the bare necessaries of life such as adequate nutrition, clothing and shelter and facilities for reading, writing and expressing oneself in diverse forms'.[126]

Moreover, the High Court of Delhi stated that 'the basic purpose of Section 52 is to protect the freedom of expression under Article 19(1) of the Constitution of India so that research, private study, criticism, review or reporting of current events could be protected'.[127]

Hence, it can be said that the right to research has a constitutional basis, besides a statutory recognition in section 52(1)(a)(i).[128]

Review and criticism are other exceptions available to reproduce the copyrighted work. In other words, for the purpose of exemplifying the review or criticism, one can quote from a copyrighted work. In *Civic Chandran v Ammini Amma*, the court held that even if portions are taken for the purpose of criticism, it will only amount to fair dealing and not an infringement of copyright. The court observed:

> The term fair dealing has not been defined as such in the Act, but Section 52 (1), (a) and (b) specifically refers to 'fair dealing' of the work and not to reproduction of the work. Accordingly, it may be reasonable

[126] *Francis Coralie Mullin v The Administrator, Union Territory of Delhi* 1981 AIR 746.
[127] *Wiley Eastern Ltd. And Ors. v Indian Institute of Management* 1995 (35) DRJ 522.
[128] M.P. Ram Mohan and Aditya Gupta, 'Right to Research and Copyright Law: From Photocopying to Shadow Libraries' [2022] 11 JIPEL 216.

> to hold that the reproduction of the whole work or a substantial portion of it as such will not normally be permitted and only extracts or quotations from the work will alone be permitted even as fair dealing. In the circumstances, the quantum of extracts or quotations permissible will depend upon the circumstances of each case. It may not be proper to lay down any hard and fast rules to cover all cases where infringement of copyright is alleged on the basis of extracts or quotations from the copyrighted work. The court will have to take into consideration the quantum and value of the matter taken in relation to the comments or criticism.[129]

In *Academy of General Education, Manipal v B Manini Mallya*, the court reasoned that 'when a fair dealing is made, inter alia, of a literary or dramatic work for the purpose of private use including research and criticism or review, whether of that work or of any other work, the right in terms of the provisions of the said Act cannot be claimed'.[130]

Section 52(1)(h) is another relevant provision for the use of copyrighted works for educational purposes. It allows for:

> [T]he publication in a collection, mainly composed of non-copyright matter, bona fide intended for instructional use, and so described in the title and in any advertisement issued by or on behalf of the publisher, of short passages from published literary or dramatic works, not themselves published for such use in which copyright subsists:
>
> Provided that not more than two such passages from works by the same author are published by the same publisher during any period of five years.

Before the amendment of 2012, the provision allowed 'for the use of educational institutions'. Through the amendment, the phrase 'for instructional use' was used in place of 'for the use of educational institutions'. This provision permits the publication of small passages from published literary works for educational use. If any student or teacher publishes small passages of a literary work that consists mainly of non-copyrighted

[129] 16 PTC 329 (Kerala).
[130] *Academy of General Education v B. Malini Mallya* ILR 2008 KAR 1074.

material, for the purpose of instructional use in any educational institution, it would not amount to infringement.

Section 52(1)(i) is another provision that allows for reproduction of literary work by a teacher or student in the course of instruction. The provision reads as:

> [T]he reproduction of any work—
> (i) by a teacher or a pupil in the course of instruction; or
> (ii) as part of the question to be answered in an examination; or
> (iii) in answers to such questions.

Before the amendment of 2012, the provision contained the phrase 'a literary, dramatic, musical or artistic work'. The amendment broadened the scope of the provision by the use of the new term 'any work' that includes cinematographic work and sound recordings. The use of the term 'reproduction' in the provision seems to have blinkered the scope of the exception crafted for learning purposes. Mere reproduction, without communication, cannot be said to serve the purpose of learning in a teacher–pupil setup.

5.4.3. The Rameshwari Photocopy Case: An Analysis

The judgment in the Rameshwari photocopy case is one of the radical mandates and also a victory of the principle of equitable access to knowledge. The decision aimed to strike a balance between the monopolies granted to proprietors and the access available to users. In August 2012, a suit was filed by three international publishers and their Indian counterparts, namely Oxford University Press, Cambridge University Press, and Taylor & Francis, against the University of Delhi and Rameshwari Photocopy Services, a local photocopy shop located on the University's premises. The suit involved the issue of unauthorized photocopying of copyrighted books published by the petitioners. The suit was filed to obtain a permanent injunction restraining the defendants from infringing the plaintiffs' copyrights in various books. The Association of Students for Equitable Access to Knowledge (ASEAK) and the Society for Promoting Educational Access and Knowledge (SPEAK) also filed the intervention to address the public interest issues in the case.

As per the plaintiffs, the defendants reproduced publications of the plaintiffs and stocked large quantities of these course packs for immediate sale to students.[131] The reproduction of chapters ranged from 5% to 33.25% of the total book text, that is, from six to sixty-five pages of copyrighted books. The books were procured from the library, and the photocopier charged 40 paise per page for photocopying. The Rameshwari photocopier shop was required to provide 3,000 photocopies per month to the Delhi School of Economics, free of cost.[132] The action in this case was not an author's claim versus the photocopier shop but a publisher's claim versus the photocopier shop and the university.[133] Nobel Laureate Amartya Sen, in a letter to Professor Nivedita Menon, lamented the attitude of the publishers on the use of photocopied course packs. He also expressed his concern to have 'some academic arrangements' for the education of students that are less difficult and more sensible.[134] The purpose of this litigation was not merely to prevent the practice of unauthorized reproduction and sale by the defendants, but also to make some revenue through a legitimate stream by issuing licences to the defendants.[135] The plaintiffs are members of the Indian Reprographic Rights Organisation (IRRO), which is a registered copyright society for reprographic works, registered under section 33 of the Copyright Act 1957. Established in the year 2000, the IRRO issues licences to users and collects licence fees on behalf of authors and publishers. Plaintiffs have submitted that the defendant's actions are depriving the plaintiffs of a revenue stream that they were otherwise entitled to.[136] They also claimed that such infringing activities disincentivized authors, as authors receive a percentage of the revenues from book sales.[137] Conversely, many authors endorsed the right of students to photocopy and also acknowledged that authors do

[131] Plaint in *The Chancellor, Masters & Scholars of The University of Oxford & Ors v Rameshwari Photocopy Services & Anr.* 2016 (68) PTC 386 (Del) [16].

[132] Written Statement filed by Rameshwari Photocopy Shop in *The Chancellor, Masters & Scholars of The University of Oxford & Ors v Rameshwari Photocopy Services & Anr* 2016 (68) PTC 386 (Del) [a].

[133] Eashan Ghosh, 'Fundamental Errors in Fundamental Places: A Case for Setting aside the Delhi University Photocopying Judgment' [2016] 9 NUJS L Rev 1, 3.

[134] Amlan Mohanty, 'Authors, Academics and Students Protest Publishers' Move in Delhi University Copyright Case' *Spicy IP* (19 September 2012) <https://spicyip.com/2012/09/authors-academics-and-students-protest.html> accessed 12 August 2025.

[135] Plaint in *The Chancellor, Masters & Scholars of The University of Oxford & Ors v Rameshwari Photocopy Services & Anr.* 2016 (68) PTC 386 (Del) [16].

[136] Plaint in *The Chancellor, Masters & Scholars of The University of Oxford & Ors v Rameshwari Photocopy Services & Anr.* 2016 (68) PTC 386 (Del) [17].

[137] Plaint in *The Chancellor, Masters & Scholars of The University of Oxford & Ors v Rameshwari Photocopy Services & Anr.* 2016 (68) PTC 386 (Del) [17].

not rely solely on royalties, as many of them are employed as teachers in colleges and universities.[138]

As per the Managing Director of Cambridge University Press India, the IRRO offered a reprographic licence to the defendants at a fee of 50 paise per page. But the defendants did not seem willing to obtain the licence as it increased the cost of the course pack. That is, the 200-page course pack, which cost Rupees 200, would cost Rupees 300 after obtaining a licence from the IRRO.[139] While this was the best solution from the publisher's angle, students were reluctant to pay extra for the same course pack which they were buying at a lower price.[140] The litigation culminated in a determinative case as it unveiled the future of 'fair access' in India, with clarity on educational institutions' requirement to obtain a licence from copyright societies.[141]

The legal issue in the case revolved around the interpretation of an educational exception given under section 52(1)(i) of the Copyright Act 1957 that permits the unauthorized reproduction of copyrighted works 'by a teacher or pupil in the course of instruction'. When the case was before the trial court judge, Justice Rajiv Sahai Endlaw gave a textual interpretation to the term 'teacher or pupil', by not restricting the meaning to include only an individual teacher or pupil, but by extending it to include the institution and its students as well.[142] The court placed reliance upon Explanation (d) to section 32, which provides that 'purposes of teaching, research or scholarship' includes 'purposes of instructional activity at all levels in educational institutions, including schools, colleges, universities and tutorial institutions'. Justice Endlaw opined that section 52(1)(i) uses only 'teacher or a pupil' and not 'educational institution' because of the

[138] Shubashree Desikan, 'Delhi University Students Impleaded on Copyright Row' *The Hindu* (09 June 2013) <www.thehindu.com/features/education/delhi-university-students-impleaded-on-copyright-row/article4794919.ece> accessed 12 August 2025.

[139] Prashant Reddy, 'Is This a "Fair" Solution to the OUP/CUP-DU Copyright Infringement Lawsuit?' *SpicyIP* (11 September 2012) <https://spicyip.com/2012/09/is-this-fair-solution-to-oupcup-du.html> accessed 12 August 2025.

[140] Shubashree Desikan, 'Delhi University Students Impleaded on Copyright Row' *The Hindu* (09 June 2013) <www.thehindu.com/features/education/delhi-university-students-impleaded-on-copyright-row/article4794919.ece> accessed 12 August 2025.

[141] Lawrence Liang, 'Paternal and Defiant Access: Copyright and the Politics of Access to Knowledge in the Delhi University Photocopy Case' [2017] 1 Indian L Rev 36, 55.

[142] Prashant Reddy Thikkavarapu, 'The DU Photocopy Judgement – A Chronicle of the Missed Arguments' [2018] 2(3) Indian L Rev 224,242.

fact that education had always been institutionalized in India. Hence, the application of section 52(1)(i) would not be limited to reproduction by an individual teacher or pupil, but would 'apply to reproduction by educational institutions in the course of instructions as well'.[143] On appeal, the Division Bench largely upheld the trial court's findings, but based its decision on slightly divergent reasoning.

Rameshwari Photocopy Services took the defence under section 52(1)(a) and 52(1)(h), but not under section 52(1)(i), which was the subsection most central to the decision of the single judge, Justice Endlaw. The defendant also pleaded that students could not afford to buy all these expensive books and that it was making these reading materials available at a nominal rate to the students. The University of Delhi, and its written statement, pleaded the defence under section 52(1)(i), which allows students and educational institutions to reproduce any work for educational purposes. The university also pleaded that section 52(1)(i) does not provide any capping on the quantum of permissible reproduction, hence unlimited photocopying is permitted under the said provision.[144]

Referring to Article 13 of the Agreement on Trade-Related Aspects of Intellectual Property Rights (TRIPS) and Article 9 of the Berne Convention, the publishers contended that section 52(1)(i) must be interpreted in consonance with India's international obligations, which clearly express that reproduction must not be in conflict with the normal exploitation of the work and does not unreasonably prejudice the legitimate interest of the author. The Division Bench rejected this argument by observing that 'nothing much turns on Article 13 of the TRIPS Agreement and Article 9 of the Berne Convention for the reason that the contents thereof are merely directory and have enough leeway for the signatory countries to enact the copyright law in their municipal jurisdiction concerning use of copyrighted works for purposes of dissemination of knowledge'.[145]

[143] *The Chancellor, Masters & Scholars of The University of Oxford & Ors v Rameshwari Photocopy Services & Anr* 2016 (68) PTC 386 (Del).

[144] *The Chancellor, Masters & Scholars of The University of Oxford & Ors v Rameshwari Photocopy Services & Anr.* 2017 (69) PTC 123 (Del) para 5.

[145] *The Chancellor, Masters & Scholars of The University of Oxford & Ors v Rameshwari Photocopy Services & Anr.* 2017 (69) PTC 123 (Del) para 63.

The next major issue involved in this case was whether the requirement of 'fairness' has to be read into all the exceptions under section 52 or if it applies only to section 52(1)(a), wherein it is expressly mentioned. Section 52(1)(i) simply provides for unauthorized reproduction of copyrighted works by 'a teacher or pupil in the course of instruction', without any mention of fair dealing or fair use. The plaintiffs urged that fair use must be read into the provision 52(1)(i). It is very much imaginable why the publishers chose the interpretation under the four-factor fair use principle. As Liang claimed, the third and fourth factors, i.e., the amount of work taken and its impact upon the potential market, would have benefited the publishers.[146] Justice Endlaw reasoned that the general principles of fair dealing are envisaged in section 52(1)(a), which includes all personal uses and research, while other provisions under section 52 deal with specific uses, like section 52(1)(i), which is a specific provision for education.[147] Elucidating the difference between a general provision and a special clause, he stated that 'the extent of Section 52(1)(i) . . . cannot be widened or restricted by applying the parameters of Section 52(1)(a)'.[148]

The Division Bench also rejected the four-step interpretation of section 52(1)(i) and reasoned that 'there has to be fairness in every action, and, irrespective of a statute expressly incorporating fair use, unless the legislative intent expressly excludes fair use, and especially when a person's result of labour is being utilized by somebody else, fair use must be read into the statute'.[149] As to what constitutes 'fair use', the court deviated from the universal construct of the four-factor test and offered a new parameter to gauge fairness in the context of teaching, that is, the use would be legal to the extent justified by the purpose of use. The court explained that:

> [I]t would have no concern with the extent of the material used, both qualitative or quantitative. The reason being, 'to utilize' means to make

[146] Lawrence Liang, 'Paternal and Defiant Access: Copyright and the Politics of Access to Knowledge in the Delhi University Photocopy Case' [2017] 1 Indian L Rev 36, 46.

[147] *The Chancellor, Masters & Scholars of The University of Oxford & Ors v. Rameshwari Photocopy Services & Anr.* 2016 (68) PTC 386 (Del), para 43.

[148] *The Chancellor, Masters & Scholars of The University of Oxford & Ors v. Rameshwari Photocopy Services & Anr.* 2016 (68) PTC 386 (Del), para 43.

[149] *The Chancellor, Masters & Scholars of The University of Oxford & Ors v. Rameshwari Photocopy Services & Anr.* 2016 (68) PTC 386 (Del), para 31.

> or render useful. To put it differently, so much of the copyrighted work can be fairly used that is necessary to effectuate the purpose of the use i.e. make the learner understand what is intended to be understood.[150]

Without formulating any principles, the court established that fairness in section 52(1)(i) has to be determined on the touchstone of 'purpose of use'.[151] One of the contentions raised by the plaintiffs was that Section 52(1)(i) does not contemplate the institution's intervention in the reproduction of works, and there must exist a direct connection between the teacher and the pupil to say, under clause (i), the reproduction can be made by a teacher or pupil, but not by any intermediary like the Rameshwari photocopier in the present case. The court rejected the argument and observed that 'common sense tells us that neither the teacher nor the pupils are expected to purchase photocopiers and photocopy the literary work to be used during the course of instruction in the classroom'.[152] The court also reasoned that no profits were being made from the photocopying of the course packs in question.

In the same manner, the phrase 'in the course of instruction' was also given a broad interpretation. The university pleaded that the term 'in the course of instruction' must be interpreted expansively.[153] ASEAK also argued that the term 'in the course of instruction' must be broadly interpreted and must not be limited to classroom teaching.[154] It also relied upon a significant judgment delivered in *Longman Group Ltd.*, wherein the High Court of New Zealand interpreted the phrase 'in the phrase of instruction' to include 'anything in the process of instruction with the process commencing at a time earlier than the time of instruction, at least for a student. So long as the copying forms part of and arises out of the course of instruction, it would normally be in the course of instruction.'[155]

Justice Endlaw examined the question: when can the instruction be said to begin, and when does it end? He delved into the meaning of the phrase 'in the course of' and followed the decision of the Apex court in

[150] 2017 (69) PTC 123 (Del) para 33.
[151] 2017 (69) PTC 123 (Del) para 33.
[152] 2017 (69) PTC 123 (Del) para 60.
[153] 2017 (69) PTC 123 (Del) para 5.
[154] 2017 (69) PTC 123 (Del) para 7.
[155] (1991) 2 NZLR 574.

Md. Serajuddin v The State of Orissa,[156] wherein the constitutional bench held that the expression 'in the course' connotes 'not only a period of time during which the movement is in progress but postulates a connected relation'.[157] After applying different interpretations made by the courts, Justice Endlaw concluded that the phrase 'in the course of instruction' in the context of teaching would mean reproduction of any work while the process of imparting instruction by the teacher and receiving instruction by the pupil continues, that is, during the entire academic session for which the pupil is under the tutelage of the teacher. The process of instruction begins when the teacher starts reading for delivering lectures and includes setting question papers, prescribing textbooks, and taking questions from students after class.[158] On appeal, the Division Bench of the High Court of Delhi also held that the phrase 'in the course of instruction' is of wide import. The court acknowledged that regardless of whether the term 'course' is considered as a verb or a noun, it would embrace the entire process of education as in a semester.[159] The Division Bench disposed of the appeal by refusing the interim injunction to the publishers and ruled that the reproduction and distribution of academic course packs to pupils did not constitute infringement, provided that the purpose of instructional use justified reproduction. Three months later, the publishers withdrew the case and preferred not to appeal to the Supreme Court of India.

5.4.4. The case of Sci-Hub in India

One more copyright infringement suit is pending before the High Court of Delhi, involving the question of free access to educational materials. On 21 December 2020, three global academic publishers filed a copyright infringement suit against free-access online repositories, Sci-Hub and Libgen, in the Delhi High Court. The three top-tier publishing houses publish scientific and academic journals and titles, including The Lancet, The Cell, Grey's Anatomy, and Journal of Applied Polymer Science. In the petition, the plaintiff publishers sought a dynamic injunction, directing

156 (1975) 2 SCC 47.
157 2016 (68) PTC 386 (Del) para 65.
158 2016 (68) PTC 386 (Del) para 72.
159 2017 (69) PTC 123 (Del) para 39.

Indian service providers to block the Sci-Hub and Libgen sites, which provided free access to the plaintiff's paywalled journals. Considering it as 'a matter of public importance', the court refused to order the immediate blocking of sites, but the final verdict is yet to come. The publishers have asserted that they have the exclusive right to reproduce, distribute, issue copies, make available to the public, and/or communicate to the public their original literary work. As claimed by the publishers, Sci-Hub and Libgen's act of providing free access to their copyrighted journals and articles constitutes infringement of copyright.

As the final outcome of the case is yet to come, the court has ordered a ban on the Sci-Hub website as an interim relief.[160] While passing the interim order, the court explicitly relied upon the orders passed by multiple foreign jurisdictions, wherein Sci-Hub was found to 'infringe copyrights by using unauthorized means to access and download literary works belonging to several copyright owners including the plaintiffs'. In the present case, the judicial duty involves addressing the poignant challenges of access to knowledge goods in a developing country, while relying upon the decisions of foreign jurisdictions. The stark contrast between economic private rights and public interests is not peculiar to India; however, the court in this case has the responsibility to rule decisively in India's socio-economic context. In so doing, the most daunting task is to allocate the private and public interests in knowledge goods, given that the goods, as information, perform a twin role of both 'input' and 'output' in an innovation process. One shudders to think of an outcome that affects the interests of researchers and academics across the country, as the consequences may significantly increase the cost of research. This whole issue contextualizes the tensions between copyright and free access to educational materials.

The fundamental rationale for copyright protection is the promotion of creativity through sufficient protection, and all at once, it also aims for the dissemination of knowledge and access to copyrighted literary materials through the doctrine of fair dealing. Copyright provides the owner of copyright with the exclusive right to control the use of his work for a limited period of time, while fair dealing is a doctrine enshrined in the Copyright Act 1957, which allows the reproduction or use of a

[160] *Elsevier Ltd. & Ors. v Alexandra Elbakyan & Ors.* 2025 SCC OnLine Del 5678.

copyrighted work that would otherwise amount to an infringement of the copyright of the content owner. It permits the use of copyrighted materials for private purposes, including research, criticism, or review. The doctrine places the onus on the defendant to prove that the dealing (1) fits within one of the permitted purposes and (2) is 'fair'. Fair dealing is a question of fact, degree, and interpretation. It is non-viable to carve out a straitjacket formula for fair dealing; what is 'fair' would depend individually upon the facts and circumstances of a given case.

The function of copyright exceptions is particularly crucial for developing countries, as they are considered 'doctrinal tools to facilitate economic development by providing citizens with the basic means to engage in intellectual endeavours and to participate in the global knowledge economy '.[161] The court, while deciding the question of infringement, would need to determine the applicability of the research exception and whether the research exception can be interpreted to include 'facilitation of research'.

Apart from recalling positivist Bentham's principle of utility, which says that law should aim at the 'greatest happiness of the greatest number of people', it seems pertinent to engage in analysis of Article 19 of the Universal Declaration of Human Rights, adopted in 1948, providing that '[e]veryone has the right to freedom of opinion and expression; this right includes freedom to hold opinions without interference and to seek, receive and impart information and ideas through any media and regardless of frontiers'. To say the least, the exchange of ideas and knowledge fuels the production of further knowledge by the scientific community.

Noticeably, the impacts of private rights in knowledge goods are not evenly distributed across countries. In developing economies, the effect of prohibitive prices of global knowledge goods is deleterious compared to the relative impact on a developed nation.

It is no surprise that in India the most significant barrier to access is 'affordability'. The construction of affordability is relative to the average per capita income in a country. A researcher in a developing country may pay a relatively high price for research literature as a percentage of per capita

[161] Ruth L. Okediji, 'The International Copyright System: Limitations, Exceptions and Public Interest Considerations for Developing Countries' *UNCTAD—ICTSD Project on IPRs and Sustainable Development* (March 2006) 35.

GDP compared to a researcher in a developed country. Speaking of institutions, libraries are constantly grappling with the exorbitant prices of academic research resources, given existing budgetary constraints. Studies have shown that, due to the rising cost of journals, many libraries are compelled to reduce the number of journal subscriptions they hold. Due to high pricing, the majority of journal articles remain behind paywalls and are inaccessible to most universities in India.

Hence, the debate about rights would be meaningless without examining the social context in which such rights are established. While handling the dispute of copyright infringement, the court must protect the special interests of a developing economy. One can only hope that a 'trial and error' experimentation does not ensue.

5

Access to Knowledge through Human Rights Framework

1. Introduction

The access to learning materials, as an essential aspect of access to knowledge, is a prerequisite for the realization of the human right to education. It is an empowering right that further enables the fulfilment of other various rights. The argument to promote access to knowledge emanates not merely from the intellectual property (IP) discourse, but also from the human rights perspective. This argument can also be framed in terms of the normative aspects of distributive justice, economic development, and democratic participation in an information society.[1] The phrase 'access to knowledge' in exact terms cannot be traced in international human rights instruments. However, the concept of A2K is deeply rooted in the human rights regime, especially social and economic rights, such as the right to education,[2] freedom of expression,[3] right to health,[4] and 'the right to take part in cultural life and to enjoy the benefits of scientific progress and its application'.[5] The proliferation of IP rights (IPR) has run afoul of the human rights regime by restricting access to a few privileged classes.

[1] Laura DeNardis, 'The Global Politics of Interoperability' in Gaëlle Krikorian and Amy Kapczynski (eds) *Access to Knowledge in the Age of Intellectual Property* (Zone Books 2010) 513.
[2] International Covenant on Economic, Social and Cultural Rights 1966 (ICESCR), Art 13.
[3] ICESCR, Art 19.
[4] ICESCR, Art 12.
[5] ICESCR, Arts 15(a) and (b).

Access to Knowledge in the Developing World. Vandana Mahalwar, Oxford University Press.
 DOI: 10.1093/9780198986782.003.0005

2. The Human Rights Approach to Access to Knowledge in International Instruments

For decades, most legal scholars and public interest advocates have argued that copyright accounts for access to information and freedom of speech. The scholars have phrased these arguments in terms of creativity, public interest, and economic development. If access to knowledge is a human right, then it would be considered as an interaction between equals, but if it is not, then access to knowledge should be given priority as a higher norm.

The human rights approach to A2K can be seen through the lens of the right to education and freedom of expression. The rights-based A2K approach finds strong support in the international human rights regime. The right to access learning materials need not be introduced as a 'new' human right. It can be found at the intersection of other rights guaranteed in human rights documents. There exists a normative support to A2K through the already established right to education and freedom of expression, among other human rights.

'Access' can be viewed as a universal human right. The right to access educational texts means everyone's accessibility to educational materials at affordable prices. It also implies that everyone must have access to an adequate supply of the material. It also means the availability of learning material in indigenous languages. Conceptualizing 'access to educational material' would primarily demand the reorientation of copyright law. The right to education is fulfilled when every individual has ample access to learning texts in their own language.

At present, there is no international human rights instrument that uses the phrase 'right to access educational texts'. At the same time, this discussion does not mean that the right to access must be added to the list of rights that are recognized in the Universal Declaration of Human Rights (UDHR). Instead, it can be justified as an underlying component of already established human rights.

According to the UN Human Rights Office, states have a duty to protect and facilitate the enjoyment of basic human rights. These rights include the right to education,[6] the right to science and culture, the right

[6] UDHR, Art 26(1). ('Everyone has the right to education. Education shall be free, at least in the elementary and fundamental stages. Elementary education shall be compulsory. Technical

to freedom of expression, and the right to development.[7] From these basic rights, some essential rights are derived, such as the right to access learning materials, the right to research, and the right to freedom of opinion and expression.[8] Hence, the right to access learning materials is a derivative of a basic human right. The right to access can be understood as an implicit specification of human rights recognized in the UDHR and other binding covenants. As a specific right, the right to access is a subset of the generic right, the right to education, which was recognized at the international level in the UDHR in 1948. Numerous interpretations of the human rights documents refer to the role of the right to education. The UDHR makes references to the overall development of human personality. Article 26(2) of the UDHR proclaims that 'education shall be directed to the full development of the human personality and to the strengthening of respect for human rights and fundamental freedoms'. The language of the Declaration steers to an expansive concept of education by prioritizing 'the full development of the human personality' as an essential aim of education.[9] Article 26 of the UDHR was further expanded by Article 13 of the International Covenant on Economic, Social and Cultural Rights (ICESCR), another international instrument that legally binds states to fulfil the right of everyone to education.[10]

Furthermore, Article 8 of the Declaration on the Right to Development[11] provides that:

> (1) States should undertake, at the national level, all necessary measures for the realization of the right to development and shall ensure, inter alia, equality of opportunity for all in their access to basic resources, education, health services, food, housing, employment and the fair distribution of income. Effective measures should be undertaken to ensure that women have an active role

and professional education shall be made generally available and higher education shall be equally accessible to all on the basis of merit.')

[7] Declaration on the Right to Development 1986, Art 8.
[8] UDHR, Art 19.
[9] Lea Shaver, 'The Right to Read' [2015] 54 Colum J Transnat'l L 1, 15.
[10] Adopted by the United Nations General Assembly on 16 December 1966.
[11] Adopted by General Assembly resolution 41/128 on 4 December 1986.

in the development process. Appropriate economic and social reforms should be carried out with a view to eradicating all social injustices.

(2) States should encourage popular participation in all spheres as an important factor in development and in the full realization of all human rights.

The right to education places an obligation on all states, developed or underdeveloped, to achieve the universal goal of free and primary education for all. The right to education is described as an empowering right that facilitates participation in political, economic, social, and cultural life.[12] It is also an essential enabler for the exercise of other human rights. The UN Committee on Economic, Social and Cultural Rights has interpreted the right to education by emphasizing its dual nature as having both intrinsic and utilitarian values:

> Education is both a human right in itself and an indispensable means of realising other human rights. As an empowerment right, education is the primary vehicle by which economically and socially marginalised adults and children can lift themselves out of poverty and obtain the means to participate fully in their communities. Education has a vital role in empowering women, safeguarding children from exploitative and hazardous labour and sexual exploitation, promoting human rights and democracy, protecting the environment, and controlling population growth. Increasingly, education is recognised as one of the best financial investments States can make. But the importance of education is not just practical: a well-educated, enlightened and active mind, able to wander freely and widely, is one of the joys and rewards of human existence.[13]

[12] J. Donnelly and R. Howard, 'Assessing National Human Rights Performance: A Theoretical Framework' [1988] 10 Human Rights Quarterly 214, 248. Donnelly and Howard categorized rights as 'survival rights', 'membership rights', 'protection rights', and 'empowering rights'. Empowering rights are defined to be those that 'provide the individual with control over the course of his or her life, and in particular, control over (not merely protection against) the state'. These rights include the right to a free press, freedom of association, and the right to education.

[13] *CESCR General Comment No. 13: The Right to Education*, UN Doc E/C.12/1999/10 (1999), reprinted in *Compilation of General Comments and General Recommendations Adopted by Human Rights Treaty Bodies*, UN Doc HRI/GEN/1/Rev.6, para 6.

There has been a debate among scholars about whether all human needs need to be translated into the language of human rights. The defenders of human rights expansion emphasize that the human rights language empowers states to address violations of human rights through social action and litigation. For example, the right to education must in some way regulate the free market in the sector of educational services.[14] However, the minimalist approach of human rights provides that the recognition of new rights undermines the endeavours to protect the more fundamental and urgent individual rights. Correspondingly, the recognition of 'right to access' might dilute the efforts to protect the existing human rights, which are more fundamental, such as the right to education and the right to freedom of expression.

Milan Kundera has highlighted the tendency to convert every human need into a human right:

> The world has become man's right and everything has to become a right: the desire for love the right to love; the desire for rest the right to rest; the desire for friendship the right to friendship; the desire to exceed the speed limit the right to exceed the speed limit; the desire for happiness the right to happiness; the desire to publish a book a right to publish a book; the desire to shout in the street in the middle of night a right to shout in the middle of the night.[15]

On the usefulness of attaching the label 'human rights', Alston states that the proliferation of new rights would lead to the decline of human rights currency.[16] To elevate the 'access' need to the status of a human right would be a costly affair. Theorists argue that the status of human rights must be accorded sparingly, so that its effectiveness does not get diluted.[17] Scholars have viewed the human rights expansion as a problem of 'rights proliferation', 'overproduction of human rights', or 'rights inflation'.

[14] Upendra Baxi, 'Too Many, Or Too Few, Human Rights?' [2001] 1 Human Rights L Rev 1, 6.

[15] Milan Kundera, *Immortality*, translated by Peter Kussi (Faber and Faber 1992) 153.

[16] Philip Alston, 'Conjuring Up New Human Rights: A Proposal for Quality Control' [1984] 78 American J Int'l L 607, 614 (proposing a list of criteria that must be fulfilled in order to qualify as a human right).

[17] Lea Shaver, 'The Right to Read' [2015] 54 Colum J Transnat'l L 1, 44; Upendra Baxi, 'Too Many, or Too Few, Human Rights?' [2001] 1 Human Rights L Rev 1 (arguing that the production of contemporary human rights raises new and difficult issues, as does the notion of quality).

Amidst this debate of minimalist versus expansive approaches to human rights, some scholars have suggested a solution: to recognize a hierarchy of human rights.[18] But the primary question would be, can there be any hierarchy of rights, and if so, what would that hierarchy be?

Discussing the 'hierarchy' of human rights implies prioritizing some rights over others. As per the OHCHR, the official status is that all human rights are equal and no hierarchy of human rights exists.[19] Despite this claim, scholars have argued that there exists an implied hierarchy of human rights.[20] Müller emphasizes that 'a transcendental foundation of rights always presupposes a hierarchy because it appeals to principles and higher rights serving as a basis for other, more specific rights'. In *A Theory of Justice*, John Rawls circumvents the word 'hierarchy' and discusses 'lexical order', which means the ranking of rights based on lexical priorities.[21]

If there is any possibility of admitting the hierarchy of human rights, the right to access would be assigned a secondary priority as compared to other rights. If one has to choose between the right to freedom from servitude and the right to access, the primary importance will be assigned to the right to freedom from servitude. However, both rights must be realized. This chapter does not aim, though, to discuss the hierarchies of rights in the international copyright regime. It is a must to acknowledge

[18] Lea Shaver, 'The Right to Read' [2015] 54 Colum J Transnat'l L 1, 47; see also Tom Farer 'The Hierarchy of Human Rights' [1992] 8 American University Int'l L Rev 115, 119.

[19] 'Frequently Asked Questions on a Human Rights-Based Approach to Development Cooperation', UN Doc HR/PUB/06/8 (UN 2006) <www.ohchr.org/Documents/Publications/FAQen.pdf> accessed 10 October 2025:

> Is there any hierarchy among human rights?
>
> No, all human rights are equally important. The 1948 Universal Declaration of Human Rights makes it clear that human rights of all kinds—economic, political, civil, cultural and social—are of equal validity and importance. This fact has been reaffirmed repeatedly by the international community, for example in the 1986 Declaration on the Right to Development, the 1993 Vienna Declaration and Programme of Action, and the near-universally ratified Convention the Rights of the Child.
>
> Human rights are also indivisible and interdependent. The principle of their indivisibility recognizes that no human right is inherently inferior to any other. Economic, social and cultural rights must be respected, protected and realized on an equal footing with civil and political rights.

[20] Fernando Suárez Müller, 'The Hierarchy of Human Rights and the Transcendental System of Right [2019] 20 Human Rights Rev 47, 66 (explaining human rights as part of a system that is structured hierarchically); see also Vittorio Hösle, *Moral und Politik* (CH Beck 1997) (stressing the need to grasp the idea of the hierarchy of human rights).

[21] John Rawls, *A Theory of Justice* (HUP 1971).

that the hierarchies in international copyright law exist at different levels. Hierarchy in copyright law has taken place not only among rights but also between exceptions. International copyright law has set up various hierarchies among rights and exceptions. They exist between (a) exclusive economic and moral rights, (b) rights of national and foreign authors, and (c) exceptions to copyrights.

3. Copyright and Right to Education: A Conflict?

Copyright and human rights, the two counterparts, have an intriguing intersection and engagement with each other. There can be two approaches to the copyright–human rights interface, premised on different normative foundations. The first approach is based on the conflict model and views copyright as being fundamentally in conflict with human rights. This approach views the stronger copyright protection as incompatible with and impeding human rights, especially the economic, social, and cultural rights. This model resolves the conflict through recognizing the normative primacy of human rights over copyright in areas where the conflict arises.[22]

The second approach sees copyright law and human rights law as compatible with each other. As per this approach, both areas of law, human rights law and copyright law, strive to balance public and private rights, that is to provide incentives on one hand and access on the other. This approach aims to define the 'appropriate scope of private monopoly power that gives authors and inventors a sufficient incentive to create and innovate, while ensuring that the consuming public has adequate access to the fruits of their efforts'.[23]

The tensions between these two legal regimes present 'external' and 'internal' conflicts. It is significant to identify the areas of 'external' and 'internal' conflicts between human rights and copyright in the international

[22] *Intellectual Property Rights and Human Rights*, Res. 2000/7, UN Sub-Comm'n on the Promotion and Protection of Human Rights, UN Doc E/CN.4/Sub.2/RES/2000/7 (17 August 2000); see also Laurence R. Helfer, 'Human Rights and Intellectual Property: Conflict or Coexistence?' [2003] 5 Minnesota Intell Prop Rev 47, 48.

[23] *Intellectual Property Rights and Human Rights*, Res. 2000/7, UN Sub-Comm'n on the Promotion and Protection of Human Rights, UN Doc E/CN.4/Sub.2/RES/2000/7 (17 August 2000).

framework. The internal conflicts are the conflicts between the rights within the same document, be it a human rights document or an international copyright document. External conflicts occur at the intersection of two regimes, where these regimes confront each other.[24]

3.1. In-Built Limits on Access

There is no clear way to resolve the clash of competing rights that co-exist within human rights system. The principle of human rights primacy would not be helpful to resolve the conflicts that exist within the human rights document. The universal, indivisible, and interdependent nature make the resolution to internal conflicts even more arduous.[25]

In UDHR, Article 26[26] and 27[27] create room for conflict between the right to compulsory and accessible education, on one hand, and the

[24] Peter K. Yu, 'Intellectual Property, Human Rights, and Methodological Reflections' in Irene Calboli and Maria Lillà Montagnani (eds) *Handbook on Intellectual Property Research* (Oxford University Press 2021); see also Peter K. Yu, 'Reconceptualizing Intellectual Property Interests in a Human Rights Framework' [2007] 40 UC Davis L Rev 1039, 1047 (discussing how, in case of external conflicts, it's necessary to distinguish between the human rights and non-human rights aspects of IP protection; in case of external conflict, the non-human rights need to be subordinated to human rights); see also Michael D. Birnhack, 'Acknowledging the Conflict Between Copyright Law and Freedom of Expression Under the Human Rights Act' [2008] Tel Aviv University Law Faculty Papers, paper 55.

[25] *Vienna Declaration and Programme of Action*, UN Doc A/CONF.157/23 (UN General Assembly 12 July 1993) para 5 <www.refworld.org/legal/resolution/unga/1993/en/14730> accessed 12 October 2025 (all human rights are universal, indivisible, and interdependent and interrelated).

[26] UDHR, Art 26 reads as:

(1) Everyone has the right to education. Education shall be free, at least in the elementary and fundamental stages. Elementary education shall be compulsory. Technical and professional education shall be made generally available and higher education shall be equally accessible to all on the basis of merit.
(2) Education shall be directed to the full development of the human personality and to the strengthening of respect for human rights and fundamental freedoms. It shall promote understanding, tolerance and friendship among all nations, racial or religious groups, and shall further the activities of the United Nations for the maintenance of peace.
(3) Parents have a prior right to choose the kind of education that shall be given to their children.

[27] UDHR, Art 27 reads as:

(1) Everyone has the right freely to participate in the cultural life of the community, to enjoy the arts and to share in scientific advancement and its benefits.
(2) Everyone has the right to the protection of the moral and material interests resulting from any scientific, literary or artistic production of which he is the author.

moral and material interests of authors, on the other. Article 27, as a human right, is of a universal nature and vested in every human being. Moreover, the human rights that are embodied in UDHR are to exist independently of such rights' recognition in the legal systems, customs, or enforcement in individual countries.

Article 27 of the UDHR and Article 15(1) of the ICESCR give rise to a paradoxical juxtaposition of a public right of access to scientific advancements and their benefits and a private right to protection of moral and material interests resulting from any scientific, literary, and artistic production. The dichotomy of rights in Article 27 presents a divide between access to the benefits of arts and scientific advancements and moral and material interests.[28] Likewise, in ICESCR, Articles 13[29] and 14[30] confront

[28] James W. Nickel, *Making Sense of Human Rights: Philosophical Reflections on the Universal Declaration of Human Rights* (University of California Press 1987) 3.

[29] ICESCR, Art 13, reads as:

1. The States Parties to the present Covenant recognize the right of everyone to education. They agree that education shall be directed to the full development of the human personality and the sense of its dignity, and shall strengthen the respect for human rights and fundamental freedoms.
   They further agree that education shall enable all persons to participate effectively in a free society, promote understanding, tolerance and friendship among all nations and all racial, ethnic or religious groups, and further the activities of the United Nations for the maintenance of peace.
2. The States Parties to the present Covenant recognize that, with a view to achieving the full realization of this right:
   (a) Primary education shall be compulsory and available free to all;
   (b) Secondary education in its different forms, including technical and vocational secondary education, shall be made generally available and accessible to all by every appropriate means, and in particular by the progressive introduction of free education;
   (c) Higher education shall be made equally accessible to all, on the basis of capacity, by every appropriate means, and in particular by the progressive introduction of free education;
   (d) Fundamental education shall be encouraged or intensified as far as possible for those persons who have not received or completed the whole period of their primary education;
   (e) The development of a system of schools at all levels shall be actively pursued, an adequate fellowship system shall be established, and the material conditions of teaching staff shall be continuously improved

[30] 'Each State Party to the present Covenant which, at the time of becoming a Party, has not been able to secure in its metropolitan territory or other territories under its jurisdiction compulsory primary education, free of charge, undertakes, within two years, to work out and adopt a detailed plan of action for the progressive implementation, within a reasonable number of years, to be fixed in the plan, of the principle of compulsory education free of charge for all.'

Article 15(1)(c).[31] Articles 13 and 14 aim to make secondary-level education accessible to all, while Article 15(1)(c) embraces the concerns for the protection of moral and material interests stemming from the personal link maintained between the creator and the creation. The conflict stems from the fact that everyone's right to free education at the primary level provided in Articles 13 and 14 gets confronted by the moral and material interests of authors and inventors given in Article 15(1)(c).

Article 27 of the UDHR and Article 15(1)(c) of the ICESCR give the right to protection of interests in IP creations. These rights exist independently and irrespective of the protection provided by existing IP instruments. It covers two kinds of interests: moral interests and material interests.[32] The protection of moral interests covers the human dignity and respect of authors as it 'safeguards the personal link between authors and their creations'.[33] It would be pertinent to discuss the protection of material interests, as it stands in direct conflict with the right to education. The protection of material interests includes the economic rights of the creators to enjoy an adequate standard of living. For a proper understanding of 'material interests' given under Article 27(2), it is necessary to revisit the drafting history of the provision. The drafting history reveals that the phrase 'material interests' covers 'just remuneration' for one's intellectual labour. The current IP regime offers the required protection to the material interests of creators in their intellectual creations.

[31] ICESCR, Art 15(1) (c) reads as:

The States Parties to the present Covenant recognize the right of everyone:

(c) To benefit from the protection of the moral and material interests resulting from any scientific, literary or artistic production of which he is the author.

[32] Alain Strowel and François Thikens, 'Freedom of Expression and Copyright Under Civil Law: Of Balance, Adaptation and Access', in Jonathan Griffiths and Uma Suthersanen (eds) *Copyright and Free Speech: Comparative and International Analyses* (OUP 2005) 292 (clause 1 and 2 of Article 27 of UDHR are complementary; the first clause gives a passive right to culture that is a right of enjoyment, while the second clause is an active right, that is the right to become an author).

[33] *CESCR General Comment No. 13: The Right to Education*, UN Doc E/C.12/1999/10 (1999), reprinted in *Compilation of General Comments and General Recommendations Adopted by Human Rights Treaty Bodies*, UN Doc HRI/GEN/1/Rev.6, para 6. *CESCR General Comment No. 17: The Right of Everyone to Benefit from the Protection of the Moral and Material Interests Resulting from Any Scientific, Literary or Artistic Production of Which He Is the Author (Article 15 (1)(c) of the Covenant)*, UN Doc E/C.12/GC/17 (2006) para 2 <www.refworld.org/docid/441543594.html> accessed 12 October 2025 (covering the right of paternity, right of integrity, and right of disclosure among others).

However, Article 27(2) and Article 15(1)(c) nowhere mention what the level of protection should be. As Torremans stated, 'a lot of freedom is left to contracting states in relation to the exact legal format of that protection.'[34] Yu also writes that states are free to decide for themselves the kind of protection that will meet the requirement and would suit their local conditions.[35] In copyright law, the life-span protection to the author is not the only acceptable mode that is needed to realize the protection of the material interests of authors.[36] The human rights instruments do not dictate the level and mode of protection. Therefore, states are free to adopt their own model of protection.

Although the right to economic exploitation of the work is reserved with the creator, this right is not absolute and unlimited. The German Constitutional Court has held very clearly in the context of copyright that although the protection of property rights 'implies that the economic exploitation of the work in principle vests with the author, the constitutional protection of property rights does not extend to all such exploitations. It is a matter for the legislature to determine the limits of copyright by imposing appropriate criteria, taking into account the nature and social function of copyright and ensuring that the author participates fairly in the exploitation of his work.'[37]

3.2. Articulating Human Rights in TRIPS

The Agreement on Trade-Related Aspects of Intellectual Property Rights (TRIPS) is another instrument that provides an intersection of human rights, such as the right to education and copyright, through the articulation of minimum standards of IP protection. There are numerous points

[34] Paul L.C. Torremans, 'Is Copyright A Human Right?' [2007] Michigan State L Rev 271, 279.

[35] Peter Yu, 'The Anatomy of the Human Rights Framework for Intellectual Property' [2016] 69 Southern Methodist University L Rev 61.

[36] *CESCR General Comment No. 17: The Right of Everyone to Benefit from the Protection of the Moral and Material Interests Resulting from Any Scientific, Literary or Artistic Production of Which He Is the Author (Article 15 (1)(c) of the Covenant)*, UN Doc E/C.12/GC/17 (2006) para 16 <www.refworld.org/docid/441543594.html> accessed 12 October 2025.

[37] Alain Strowel and François Thikens, 'Freedom of Expression and Copyright Under Civil Law: Of Balance, Adaptation and Access' in Jonathan Griffiths and Uma Suthersanen (eds) *Copyright and Free Speech: Comparative and International Analyses* (OUP 2005) 287, 293.

of intersection between human rights and the TRIPS Agreement but TRIPS aims to protect only the material interests of the authors, leaving the moral interests approach totally unaddressed and unidentified.

As the Preamble to the TRIPS Agreement clearly states, it aims to promote effective and adequate protection of IPR. However, it primarily concerns itself with private economic rights over public human rights, including the right to education, thereby expanding the sphere of conflict between the two.[38] Moreover, Article 9 of TRIPS sets the minimum standards to be maintained by states to protect the copyright of owners, while Article 7 emphasizes the adoption of a balanced approach while doing so. Article 7 of TRIPS, *Objectives*, provides that:

> The protection and enforcement of intellectual property rights should contribute to the promotion of technological innovation and to the transfer and dissemination of technology, to the mutual advantage of producers and users of technological knowledge and *in a manner conducive to social and economic welfare*, and *to a balance of rights and obligations.*

The expression 'in a manner conducive to social and economic welfare' demonstrates that the recognition and enforcement of IPR are subject to the public interest. Hence, Article 7 seeks a balanced approach that focuses on the mutual advantages of both owners and users rather than prioritizing users only. But the question is, can the rights ever be balanced? Article 7 of TRIPS aims to strike a balance between the private economic rights and public interests, like human rights, by achieving the goal of advancing development as well as social welfare.[39]

Similarly, Article 8 of the TRIPS Agreement lays down the normative principle, by providing that:

> 1. Members may, in formulating or amending their laws and regulations, adopt measures necessary to protect public health and

[38] Vandana Mahalwar, 'Copyright and Human Rights: The Quest for a Fair Balance' in Manoj K. Sinha and Vandana Mahalwar (eds) *Copyright Law in the Digital World: Challenges and Opportunities* (Springer Nature 2017) 161.

[39] Christophe Geige, Daniel J. Gervais, and Martin Senftleben, 'The Three-Step Test Revisited: How to Use the Test's Flexibility in National Copyright Law' [2014] 29 American University Int'l L Rev 598.

nutrition, and to promote the public interest in sectors of vital importance to their socioeconomic and technological development, provided that such measures are consistent with the provisions of this Agreement.

2. Appropriate measures, provided that they are consistent with the provisions of this Agreement, may be needed to prevent the abuse of intellectual property rights by right holders or the resort to practices which unreasonably restrain trade or adversely affect the international transfer of technology.

Article 8 resonates with the Preamble of the TRIPS Agreement by recognizing the public interest of least developed countries in areas of vital importance to socio-economic and technological development. In other words, Article 8 can be interpreted to promote the development goals of less-developed countries. Moreover, the Preamble to the TRIPS Agreement not only concentrates on the aim of fostering adequate protection mechanisms but also addresses the 'underlying public policy objectives of national systems' and, concerning least developed countries, the need 'in respect of maximum flexibility in the domestic implementation'.[40] Both Articles 7 and 8.1 ask members to implement the obligations given under the Agreement in a way coherent with public policy encouraging social and economic welfare.

4. Balancing Interests

The human rights approach to access to knowledge involves an implicit balance between the rights of authors and larger societal interests. Referring to Article 15 of the ICESCR, Audrey Chapman elaborated that:

> To be consistent with the full provisions of Article 15 of the International Covenant on Economic, Social and Cultural Rights, the type and level of protection afforded under any intellectual property regime must facilitate and promote cultural participation and scientific progress and

[40] Paul Torremans, 'Is Copyright a Human Right?' [2007] Michigan State L Rev 271, 280.

> do so in a manner that will broadly benefit members of society both on an individual and collective level.[41]

Thus, any degree of copyright protection will further confer the rights upon the individual right holders. Achieving a balance between these interests is imperative and has also been internalized to some extent by copyright law. Copyright law is familiar with the balance of interests. The private interests of the copyright holder and broader public interests are introduced in the copyright law for the sake of balance. Stringent copyright protection threatens the human right to education. Proliferation of authors' rights need not entail restrictions on access interests. The negative impact of copyright laws can be mitigated by imposing certain limits on owner rights. The international copyright regime attempts to strike a balance in various ways. First, the TRIPS Agreement states clearly that the copyright protection extends only to expressions and not to ideas, procedures, methods of operation, or mathematical concepts as such.[42] Second, Article 13 of the TRIPS Agreement is a step towards striking a balance between copyright and public interests by laying down the three-step test on the limitations to copyright. Article 13 asks the states to confine the limitations or exceptions:

(i) to certain special cases;
(ii) which do not conflict with a normal exploitation of the work; and
(iii) do not unreasonably prejudice the legitimate interests of the right holder.

Article 13 would apply where a compulsory licence is granted on the ground of unreasonably high prices charged by the copyright owner that prevented a person from accessing the educational material.[43] The three-step test fulfils two purposes: first, it specifies the areas for which copyright owners do not require rights to maximize their income; second, it puts forth a compensation mechanism for the limitations that are in

[41] Audrey R. Chapman, 'Approaching Intellectual Property as a Human Right: Obligations Related to Article 15(J)(c)' [2001] Copyright Bulletin 14.
[42] TRIPS Agreement 1994, Art 9.2.
[43] Carlos M. Correa, *Trade Related Aspects of Intellectual Property Rights: A Commentary on TRIPS Agreement* (OUP 2007) 146.

the public interest but can significantly impact the material interests of copyright holders.[44] The limitations are founded on the defence of basic human rights, such as the right to education and the right to freedom of expression. Mostly, the limitations and exceptions conflict with the copyright holders' interests in maximizing the possible profits from their investments, though in certain circumstances, the limitations and exceptions are inclined towards the interests of the owner. Hence, the three-step test needs to be interpreted in a manner that does not jeopardize the appropriate and ample solution for the conflict of interests. The solution has to be in such a manner that the monopolistic rights leave *enough and as good in common* for others. Locke's labour theory, which allows the creators to use and enjoy the fruits of their labour, leaving enough and as good in common for others, introduces the concept of intergenerational equity in the copyright regime. In the context of the three-step test, the limitations have to be viewed through the lens of intergenerational equity. The postulate of intergenerational equity favours the limitations in support of educational purposes and exceptions that support uses of copyrighted material for personal use. The idea of intergenerational equity seems to be founded on utilitarian considerations, that is, today's readers are tomorrow's authors.

In this regard, the Max Planck Institute for Intellectual Property and a group of experts proposed a declaration that confirmed the balanced interpretation of the three-step test in copyright law. The signatories to the declaration declare that:

> The Three-Step Test should be interpreted in a manner that respects the legitimate interests of third parties, including
> - interests deriving from human rights and fundamental freedoms;
> - interests in competition, notably on secondary markets; and
> - other public interests, notably in scientific progress and cultural, social, or economic development.[45]

[44] Daniel J Gervais, 'How Intellectual Property and Human Rights Can Live Together: An Updated Perspective' in P. Torremans (ed) *Intellectual Property Law and Human Rights* (3rd edn, Wolters Kluwer 2015) 347.

[45] Christophe Geiger, Reto Hilty, Jonathan Griffiths, and Uma Suthersanen, 'Declaration: A Balanced Interpretation of the "Three-Step Test" In Copyright Law' [2010] 1 JIPITEC 119, 122.

The current international copyright regime fails to recognize and protect the 'public interests' adequately. While the TRIPS Agreement primarily stresses that states must grant and protect private rights, it defines the exceptions and limitations too narrowly so that the member states may provide safeguards to safeguard the public interest. Many scholars have argued that Articles 7 and 8 of the TRIPS Agreement are reasonably ambiguous in their objectives. From the standpoint of the less-developed countries, the public interest safeguards are more favourable to the developed countries. However, scholars have argued that there are many provisions that least developed countries could use to their benefit.[46] The TRIPS Agreement needs to be interpreted through a 'pro-development lens' that interprets the provisions to the least developed countries' local advantage.[47] While the Preamble to the agreement recognizes public policy objectives, including developmental objectives, human rights, such as the right to education, do not appear explicitly anywhere in the Agreement. To benefit the Global South, in terms of development and access needs, human rights are to be used as a tool to interpret the provisions of the TRIPS Agreement.

5. Conceptualizing the Proportionality Test in Copyright Law

The standard of proportionality carries special relevance in balancing access needs with copyright. Against the background of conflicting interests, the principle of proportionality can be seen as a standard for scrutinizing the limitations and exceptions in copyright law. The proportionality test, as a legal historical tool, is used for balancing the rights. As per the proportionality principle, in case of conflict between copyright and human rights, the solution should be developed in such a way that it does not impinge upon other rights. Property rights should be granted to a person, keeping in mind that they do not cause disproportionate

[46] Peter K. Yu, 'TRIPS and its Discontents' [2006] 10 Marquette Intell Prop L Rev 369, 391.

[47] Jade Kouletakis, 'Decolonising Copyright: Reconsidering Copyright Exclusivity and the Role of the Public Interest in International Intellectual Property Frameworks' [2002] 71 GRUR International 30.

harm to the basic rights of others. Hence, the principle demands that the least destructive measures be adopted for protecting the interests of right holders. The application of the proportionality test requires that copyright should not be conferred on its holder in such a manner that is grossly disproportionate to what is deserved in that situation.[48] In this context, it would be imperative that the judiciary pay attention while weighing the basic human right against copyright in order to adhere to the obligations resulting from the international human rights regime.

The fair use defence as a limitation on copyright gives too much discretion to the courts to determine the contours of copyright. While applying the four-factor fair use test, the court must interpret the law in a manner that allows a fair balance to be struck between fundamental rights. Judges are expected to interpret domestic copyright laws and their exceptions in light of the fundamental rights. In other words, the courts need to draw on fundamental rights as the legal basis while adjudicating the validity of the limitation on copyright. The judges must determine whether the fundamental right-limiting measure is in proportion to the right. Nonetheless, the proportionality test would be of relevance only in cases where the issue of fundamental rights is involved. In the present case, proportionality would act as an important safeguard to determine the fairness of the act done for educational purposes. With regard to a conflict between copyright and the unauthorized use of work for educational purposes, courts can keep the broad copyright protection within reasonable limits and prevent the exclusive right from violating the fundamental rights. In national systems having a closed list of exceptions to an open-ended fair use test, an appropriate balancing tool becomes imperative. In contrast to the narrowly defined limitations, the advantage of the fair use test is its flexible nature that enables the courts to broaden the limitations as per the new circumstances. Conferring discretion upon the courts involves the risk of legal uncertainty. However, having established case law generating educational benefits would enhance the foreseeability of forthcoming decisions and that, in turn, would ensure a sufficient amount of legal certainty. Hence, the courts can adopt the appropriate

[48] Justine Pila, 'Pluralism, Principles and Proportionality in Intellectual Property' [2014] 34 Oxford J Leg Stud 192.

balancing tools to enable limitations and enhance the flexibilities in the copyright regime.

It is pertinent to note that the Supreme Court of Canada has rendered a number of significant decisions on the balance between copyright and user rights. In *Théberge v Galerie d'Art du Petit Champlain*, Justice Binnie reflected on the balancing of interests by holding that:

> [T]he Copyright Act is usually presented as a balance between promoting the public interest in the encouragement and dissemination of works of the arts and intellect and obtaining a just reward for the creator . . . The proper balance among these and other public policy objectives lies not only in recognizing the creator's rights but in giving due weight to their limited nature . . . Excessive control by holders of copyrights and other forms of intellectual property may unduly limit the ability of the public domain to incorporate and embellish creative innovation in the long-term interests of society as a whole, or create practical obstacles to proper utilization.[49]

The Court in *Théberge* emphasized the limited nature of the creator's right but did not expressly articulate about the user's rights. A few years later, the Supreme Court of Canada delivered a seminal judgment in *CCH Canadian Ltd. v Law Society of Upper Canada* by holding that the fair dealing exception is a user's right.[50] Through this seminal pronouncement, the Supreme Court placed the user's right on the same footing as the creator's rights. In *CCH*, the court employed fair dealing as a tool to achieve a balance between copyright protection and a user's right to access the copyrighted works. The importance of these decisions lies not only in widening the scope of fair dealing but also in the name of 'balance'.

[49] *Théberge v Galerie d'Art du Petit Champlain Inc* [2002] SCC 34, paras 30–31.
[50] *CCH Canadian Ltd. v Law Society of Upper Canada* [2004] 1 SCR 339, para 48.

6

Rhetoric for Access

A Review

Philip Altbach remarked on the responsibility towards the availability and accessibility of print learning materials that:

> [T]he time has come to recognize that the production of books and journals is more than a business, and that trade in knowledge and knowledge products is somehow different than commerce in automobiles or coconuts. Those who control knowledge distribution have a responsibility to ensure that knowledge is available throughout the world at a price that can be afforded by the Third World.[1]

The relationship between copyright and the encouragement of education and learning has been more critical in developing countries. In developing nations, the impact of high prices of copyrighted knowledge goods is more deteriorating than in developed countries. The top-down approach of the international copyright regime seems to have failed to address the priorities and special needs of the developing countries. By contrast, the bottom-up approach highlights the interests and needs of the developing world for print learning resources that are available, affordable, and accessible. There can be many ways to estimate the social costs, benefits, and costs of copyright protection. However, the primary focus here is on the development dilemma that the high levels of copyright protection have posed for the developing world.

The copyright regime, like other intellectual property (IP) systems, is based upon the maximalist rights culture. It assumes stronger copyright protection to be better as it promotes creation, and hence, more rights

[1] Philip G. Altbach, 'The Subtle Inequalities of Copyright' [1996] 8 The Acquisitions Librarian 17, 26.

Access to Knowledge in the Developing World. Vandana Mahalwar, Oxford University Press.
 DOI: 10.1093/9780198986782.003.0006

are considered to be better. Copyright protection indeed promotes creation; however, access to knowledge is one of the areas that is not better served by copyright protection. Lord Camden in *Donaldson v Becket*,[2] while speaking against the common law right of copyright, declared that knowledge and science are not things to be bound in such cobweb chains. Comparing access with slavery, he warned that if there is a perpetual right, 'all our learning will be locked up in the hands of the Tonsons and the Lintots of the age'. He criticized copyright as an instrument of incentivizing the creativity and dissemination of works. Hence, copyright needs to be protected judiciously. For example, stricter copyright protection in the case of musical works would help in accelerating the economy of a country, while the same level of protection in literary works would make access to books and learning materials unaffordable. The nations, as welfare states, are under a moral obligation to provide basic amenities like education to their people. At the same time, copyright acts as an impediment to acquiring educational materials. The degree of the impact of these impediments is the cost of higher levels of IP protection. The maximalist approach of 'more rights the better' and the lack of balance between IP protection and development priorities have caused significant losses. The cost of this loss is as daunting as the cost of underdevelopment in the world. Boyle claims that it is not good even for the developed world, as it represents narrow interests and does not include much democratic scrutiny. There is limited participation by civil society in the formulation of IP policy.[3] It is no surprise that the least developed countries have been upset due to the stringent levels of protection mandated by the Agreement on Trade-Related Aspects of Intellectual Property Rights (TRIPS) and its direct impact on access to knowledge.

Given the pressing needs of developing countries and the inequitable nature of the international copyright system, scholars have suggested a reassessment of the current copyright regime. Alan Story concluded that it is in the interest of the countries of the South that Berne be repealed and a new framework be established on radically different grounds.[4] It has been argued that the balance of rights in the copyright system is a

[2] [1774] 2 Bro PC 129.

[3] James Boyle, 'A Manifesto on WIPO and the Future of Intellectual Property' [2004] 3 Duke L & Tech Rev 1, 13.

[4] Alan Story, 'Burn Berne: Why the Leading International Copyright Convention Must Be Repealed' [2003] 40 Houston L Rev 763, 769.

prevalent and seemingly evocative metaphor. In the context of the global copyright relationship between the rich industrialized countries of the North and the poor user countries of the South, the claim of the copyright regime being 'balanced' and 'balanceable' does not work in the practical sense, in the unequal global circumstances.

This book began with a reflection on the concept of knowledge as a global public good and the impediments to its creation and dissemination. The attributes of non-rivalrousness and non-excludability of knowledge goods make them public goods. It has long been a contentious question in developing countries where to draw the line between knowledge that is a public good and knowledge that is subject to private property rights. When private interests take priority over public interests, the proliferation of monopolistic rights acts as a roadblock for public concerns, including education and research. However, as demonstrated in Chapter 1, the Statute of Anne, the world's first copyright legislation, aimed to walk along utilitarian lines to encourage social concerns based on public interests. The Statute of Anne crafted a fine balance between authors' incentives and the means to encourage the dissemination of knowledge and learning. One of the key features of the copyright law was a limited time of protection for those who produced the knowledge goods. It also had a limitation on the enjoyment of ownership rights. The primary purpose of the early copyright legislation was to foster learning and to advance the progress of science and art. However, the objectives of the international copyright regime were different. The purpose of international protection was to safeguard the creative output of one country in another country. The first international convention was the Berne Convention, which dealt with the minimum requirements of protection to copyright owners and was based on the principle of national treatment. But it did not address the special needs of the developing and less developed countries, as the social and economic realities of developing countries were not taken into account at the time of negotiations. The limitations and exceptions contained in the Convention failed to meet the urgent needs of the developing countries, such as bulk access to learning materials at reasonable prices and translated into their regional languages. To address the special needs of the developing countries, the Berne Appendix provided some provisions for compulsory licensing for translation and reproduction of copyrighted works. However, due to the complexities of the provision and administrative burdens, the Berne Appendix provisions have largely remained unused. Moreover, TRIPS also did not prove itself as a success for the development of the developing countries, hence the Development Agenda emerged as a result of the dissatisfaction on the part of the developing countries. The organizations in favour of the Development Agenda did not aim to displace WIPO but to have some fundamental reforms made with a 'more balanced and realistic view of the social benefits and costs of intellectual property rights as a tool, but not the only tool, for supporting creativity and intellectual activity'.[5]

The discussion in Chapter 2 delves deep into the historical evolution of early bilateralism and multilateralism in copyright law. The legal and historical analysis of both general and specific exceptions for education has been conducted. The works are accessible for use only when the lengthy term of protection comes to an end. To access the knowledge goods during the protection period, the user would need some limitations or exceptions for the said purpose. But the Berne/TRIPS Framework has not recognized even a single limitation or exception for education; it recognizes only the limitations that are 'relevant to education', such as making a quotation, illustration for teaching, or personal use. Though these exceptions can be used for education-related purposes, they do not provide access to knowledge goods for the fulfilment of global educational goals. These limitations act as mere vehicles to promote the limited dissemination of knowledge. Moreover, the exceptions to make quotations and illustrations for teaching purposes and the works that are not protected, such as news of the day, do not seem to be capable of providing adequate access to educational material. Also, the use of work for making quotations and for illustration is subject to the requirement of 'fair practice', which is a question to be determined by courts in each case. There exists no limitation or exception that allows reproduction and distribution of the works for the educational purposes of students. The uncompensated limitations are also allowed as long as the amount of use is small. The Berne Appendix can be invoked for a series of compulsory licences in respect of translation and reproduction of works protected

[5] 'Geneva Declaration on Future of World Intellectual Property Organization' (30 September 2004) <www.opensocietyfoundations.org/newsroom/declaration-future-wipo> accessed 13 October 2025.

under the Convention that may be invoked under certain limited conditions by developing countries, particularly for educational and developmental purposes.

Apart from these specific exceptions, the three-step test, formulated as a concise and generalized copyright rule, enables countries to adopt limitations for education. The three-step test's usefulness lies in providing strict guidelines to countries, which cannot be derogated from. Pragmatically, the test does not help in facilitating effective and adequate access to educational materials because it involves considerations such as the economic competitiveness of the use and the question of proportionality of the use to the actual work. Hence, the limitations and exceptions at the international level remain much less than are required to improve the countries' efforts to enhance the degree of knowledge goods. As the minimum rights are derived by consensus at the international level, there is no such set of minimum limitations and exceptions. Limitations and exceptions continue to be a domain of domestic discretion. The limitations and exceptions that are clearly crafted by the Berne Convention fail to address the most pressing needs of the developing countries, such as bulk access to knowledge goods at reasonable prices and translations into their countries' local languages. The limitations and exceptions in the Berne Convention are so malleable that it would require domestic institutional capacity to convert these provisions into reality, which is generally a lacking factor in many developing and least developed countries. The international copyright framework must ensure that domestic institutions receive appropriate returns through the international limitations or exceptions to secure the gains produced through the creation and diffusion of knowledge goods. For development in a true sense, when countries fail to adopt limitations or exceptions, the international copyright framework must fill the gap by supplying them to those countries.

Chapter 3 discusses how the global copyright regime is based upon a 'top-down approach' that largely benefits the interests of the developed world. The discussion shows that the access-related needs of developing countries are more acute than those of developed countries. The readers in poor countries are compelled to pay more for the same book than those in rich countries. The affordability of books needs a vision in terms of a country's GDP per capita. Reiterating Lea Shaver's '4A' approach towards access to knowledge, learning resources must be available, accessible, acceptable, and adaptable. In other words, access has to be understood as the need for bulk access to printed learning resources in regional languages at affordable prices. Chapter 3 discusses the flexibilities that international copyright law offers to developing countries to fulfil their educational goals. Before the Stockholm Protocol of 1967, the Berne Convention did not have any provision for access to translations and reprints of printed books. The 1967 Stockholm Revision of the Berne Convention was an attempt to trade off the interests of developed and developing economies by providing some concessions to the developing countries. However, the Protocol was not accepted by the developed countries, as they were unwilling to facilitate access to developing countries at the expense of their own publishing market. After the Stockholm Protocol, the Berne Appendix was adopted as a special mechanism to facilitate access to copyrighted works by developing countries. Unfortunately, the Appendix also failed to serve its purpose of enabling access to copyrighted materials in all languages because of the complicated and burdensome requirements imposed by it.

Chapter 4 discusses the access to knowledge problems in India and its relation to copyright law. After presenting India's key demographics, three major barriers to accessing learning materials are discussed in detail, namely, exorbitant book prices, language barriers, and digital barriers. The prohibitive prices of books have paved the way to an illegal way of reproducing books, that is, piracy. Like in other developing countries, pirate publishing is growing as a full-fledged business in the Indian market. Low-priced books, no doubt, fulfil the textual need of students, but in an illegal way that contravenes copyright law. There is a plethora of digitized books available online; however, they remain inaccessible to the underprivileged class due to issues related to connectivity, capacity, and technical infrastructure. Apart from the digital incapabilities to foster learning through e-books, language has also been a vital barrier in countries with linguistic diversity. Furthermore, readers in multilingual countries, such as India, face an acute shortage of books in their local language. Most of the books are available only in English and Hindi, while there are more than 19,500 languages spoken in India. This creates a linguistic barrier in accessing books, due to which readers have to confront difficulties in comprehending the text. Chapter 4 further reflects upon the state governments' efforts in establishing public libraries. This chapter also shows the historical evolution of the Copyright Act 1957. It covers an interesting discussion that took place among members of the Joint Committee of the Houses on the Copyright Bill regarding the term of copyright protection, criminal sanctions for copyright infringement, and translation rights. As discussed in Chapter 4, various substantial amendments have been made to the copyright legislation in India, specifically regarding the compulsory licensing provisions. These provisions are, in particular, significant for the access objectives as they allow for an application for compulsory licensing for translation and reproduction of works for the purposes of teaching, scholarship, or research. The 2012 amendment has been a radical transformation for the purposes of education. Moreover, this chapter looks at how Indian copyright law has addressed the education and research-related exceptions and limitations. After discussing the exceptions and limitations, the chapter covers a detailed analysis of the most significant decision given by the High Court of Delhi in *Rameshwari Photocopy Services*. This decision contextualizes the tensions between copyright law and access to learning materials. The interpretation of fair dealing in this case is crucial for developing countries in order to facilitate access and, hence, participation in the global knowledge economy.

In the international human rights instruments, there is no use of the phrase 'right to access learning materials'; hence, Chapter 5 views the concept of access to knowledge (A2K) as a 'part' of the international human rights regime. It has been argued that the right to access print books need not be introduced as a 'new' human right. Rather, the right to access can be viewed as an implicit specification of the human rights given in the Universal Declaration of Human Rights (UDHR). While reflecting on the minimalist versus expansive approach to human rights, Chapter 5 presents reasons that suggest converting access needs into a right may not be a good idea. Furthermore, this chapter discusses the intriguing conflict between copyright and access as part of human rights. The external and internal conflicts between the two regimes have been pinpointed. There are several points of conflict between the two regimes as outlined in the UDHR and International Covenant on Economic, Social and Cultural Rights (ICESCR). The TRIPS Agreement also contains various points of intersection between human rights and copyright. The chapter goes on to discuss how international documents like the UDHR,

ICESCR, and the TRIPS Agreement attempt to balance the interests of the creator with those of society. The need to apply the proportionality principle when balancing access needs with copyright law is emphasized. Copyright need not be conferred upon the creator in a manner that is grossly disproportionate to what is required by that protection. In this context, apart from the legislature, the judiciary has an instrumental role in balancing copyright with user rights.

Under the existing copyright regime, we have few options as courses of action to improve access to knowledge. The TRIPS Agreement resulted from negotiations between developed and developing countries. In the agreement, there is 'ample wiggle room'[6] to implement the agreement in the interest of the developing countries. While the less developed countries must adhere to the international minimum standards of the agreement, they should adopt a development-oriented approach with regard to these standards that are open to interpretation. Hence, the less developed countries are free to choose a favourable approach that suits the needs of their own economic and local conditions. The manner in which treaties are interpreted impacts the rights of developing countries. In the TRIPS Agreement, the Preamble acts as a guiding source for the interpretation of its provisions, many of which contain constructive ambiguities and leave room for interpretation. Such provisions can be interpreted in light of the language used in the Preamble, to promote the developmental objectives and public interest needs of developing countries. For example, the phrase 'promoting the public interest in sectors of vital importance to their socio-economic and technological development' in Article 8 of the agreement gives substantial discretion to the member states, as the areas of vital importance differ from nation to nation. It enables developing countries to pursue their own policy objectives in line with their development priorities.

From a development perspective, it is essential to interpret the limitations and exceptions to copyright in a manner that enables developing member states to bridge the existing knowledge gap. Among exceptions, fair use provisions are significant for the purposes of education and private use. To improve access to copyrighted works and achieve the goals of

[6] J.H. Reichman, 'From Free Riders to Fair Followers: Global Competition under the TRIPS Agreement' [1996] 29 NY University J Int'l L & Politics 11, 28.

education, developing countries should be allowed to maintain or adopt broad exemptions for educational, research, and library uses in their national copyright laws. It is important to note that a country may tailor the limitations and exceptions as per its local needs; however, final responsibility lies with the national courts, who have to interpret the provisions keeping in mind the country's policy objectives.

One of the biggest lacunae in the international copyright system is the absence of an explicit provision on the right to access copyrighted material. In light of the special needs of less developed countries, commentators have proposed establishing an international fair use doctrine within the international copyright system. Some have stressed the need to articulate specific limitations and exceptions for educational purposes. However, such proposals are not sufficient to meet the special educational needs of developing countries, though the public interest objectives given in the TRIPS Agreement are primarily construed to include public interest in accessing the knowledge. This interpretation, however, remains IP-centric and views users' access rights as an exception to it. Proposing explicit user access rights, Dreyfuss stated that 'user access did not need specific delineation when it was the background rule; only the exceptionalism of IP rights required express definition. But if the new background is proprietary control, then the exceptionalism of user rights now needs to be embedded into positive law.'[7] This rights rhetoric is based on the rationale that access rights are not exclusive rights that can be transferred, but are simply beyond the owner's control. The concept of a user's access right has already been delineated by Canadian courts.[8] The Canadian court's rhetoric of rights speaks of achieving a proper balance between protection and access. The Supreme Court of Canada has adopted a concept of treating copyright defences, such as fair use and fair dealing, as user rights. This rhetoric balances the rights of owners with the rights of users, and this approach finds the concept of balancing the rights of owners with exceptions to be illogical and biased. Yet, the courts in all countries, in particular in the less developed countries, cannot be

[7] Rochelle Cooper Dreyfuss, 'TRIPS—Round II: Should Users Strike Back?' [2004] 71 University of Chicago L Rev 21, 27.

[8] Referring to *CCH Canadian Ltd. v Law Society of Upper Canada* [2004] 1 SCR 339; *Théberge v Galerie d'Art du Petit Champlain Inc* [2002] SCC 34.

assumed to have such an expansive approach towards users' access rights. Summing up that the current copyright regime lacks any concrete provisions that favour access to knowledge in developing countries, there is a call for codification of some significant principles and overall objectives that serve as a basis for balancing copyright protection and access to knowledge.

ANNEXURE A

Total Notifications under the Berne Appendix (Status on 22 August 2025)

S. No.	Member State	Notification No.	Notification Date	Article Availed
1	Jordan	281,232	27 April 2004	II[*] & III[†]
2	India	280,110	20 June 1984	II & III
3	Bangladesh	269,234	1 June 2004	II & III
4	Kuwait	271	27 Nov 2015	II & III
5	Cuba	270,238	28 June 2004	II & III
6	United Arab Emirates	266,236	15 July 2025	II & III
7	Vietnam	241,265	26 July 2004	II & III
8	Thailand	167,239,264	2 June 1995	II
9	Yemen	254,263	14 April 2008	II & III
10	Algeria	256,262,194	30 March 1998	II & III
11	Sri Lanka	248	27 Sept 2005	II & III
12	Syrian Arab	245	03 Nov 2004	II & III
13	Sudan	240	26 July 2004	II & III
14	Mongolia	190,237	12 Dec 1997	II & III
15	Philippines	235,179	18 March 1997	II & III
16	Oman	233	6 May 2004	II & III
17	Egypt	128	14 March 1990	II &III
18	Mexico	109, 79	3 June 1976	II & III
19	Niger	91	17 March 1978	II & III
20	Lesotho	124	28 June 1989	II &III
21	Suriname	83	23 Nov 1976	II & III
22	Tanzania	156	25 April 1994	II &III
23	Tunisia	74	16 May 1975	II &III
24	Samoa	250	21 April 2006	II
25	Singapore	198	21 Sept 1998	II &III
26	Uzbekistan	244	19 Jan 2005	II & III

S. No.	Member State	Notification No.	Notification Date	Article Availed
27	Korea	224	28 Jan 2003	II & III
28	Liberia	122	8 Dec 1988	II & III
29	Cambodia	287	9 Dec 2021	II & III
30	Vietnam	290	16 Oct 2024	II & III
31	Saudi Arabia	292	6 Feb 2025	II & III
32	Republic of Maldives	294	22 Aug 2025	II & III

* Article II: Limitation on the Right of Translation
† Article III: Limitation on the Right of Reproduction
Source: Author's compilation from the WIPO website: https://www.wipo.int/wipolex/en/treaties/ShowResults?search_what=N&treaty_id=15> accessed 22 August 2025.

Index

For the benefit of digital users, indexed terms that span two pages (e.g., 52–53) may, on occasion, appear on only one of those pages.